GOD AND MORA]

C000085332

God and Moral Obligation

C. STEPHEN EVANS

OXFORD
UNIVERSITY PRESS

OXFORD
UNIVERSITY PRESS

Great Clarendon Street, Oxford, OX2 6DP,
United Kingdom

Oxford University Press is a department of the University of Oxford.
It furthers the University's objective of excellence in research, scholarship,
and education by publishing worldwide. Oxford is a registered trade mark of
Oxford University Press in the UK and in certain other countries

Published in the United States of America by Oxford University Press
198 Madison Avenue, New York, NY 10016, United States of America

British Library Cataloguing in Publication Data

Data available

ISBN 978-0-19-969668-0 (Hbk)
ISBN 978-0-19-871537-5 (Pbk)

Preface and Acknowledgements

It is common to refer to our moral obligations collectively as constituting the moral law. Is this simply a way of speaking or does this language capture a deep truth? Many morally earnest people would affirm that there is indeed something about our moral obligations that gives them the status of law. But what kind of law? Must there be a law-giver? If so, who is that law-giver?

A traditional answer is that morality is grounded in God. Modern and contemporary philosophers have tended to find this view simplistic and naïve. In this book I defend the claim that there is truth and wisdom in this traditional view, and that the philosophers who have dismissed the claim have been much too hasty. Our moral obligations either are identical to divine commands or are grounded in such commands. However, I argue that God communicates his requirements in many ways, including through conscience, and this makes it possible for people who do not believe in God nonetheless to have an awareness of their moral obligations.

In defending what is usually called a "divine command" account of moral obligations I rely on the work of several contemporary philosophers, particularly Robert Adams, Philip Quinn, and John Hare. I have tried to write in a clear and straightforward style, avoiding needless technicalities, because the issues are ones that many thoughtful people who are not professional philosophers will find interesting and important. I have tried not only to present arguments for the view that moral obligations should be understood as divine requirements, but also to present and respond to the most common objections made to such a view. I have also tried to show the strengths of the view that moral obligations are divine commands by comparing it with other popular views about the foundations of morality, and showing that when such views give no significant role to God they weaken or undermine their accounts. I have also tried to include a plausible account of how God communicates his requirements to his human creatures.

It is not merely secular thinkers who have tended to dismiss the idea that moral obligations are God's laws and therefore require

God as a ground. Many religious people have thought that a "divine command" account of moral obligation is a rival to some other popular approaches, particularly "natural law ethics" and "virtue ethics." An important part of this work is an argument that it is a mistake to think of these approaches as rivals. A religiously grounded ethic needs all three types of accounts to do full justice to all of morality.

This book is primarily a work in the foundations of morality, or metaethics, and not philosophy of religion or theology. However, I hope it is clear that the conclusions reached have profound implications for those fields. In particular, if moral obligations are divine requirements, then humans who are aware of moral duties have a kind of direct awareness of God, and those who do not realize that moral obligations are God's requirements may nonetheless be brought to see this through reflection on the nature of moral duties. A divine command account of moral obligations also explains why many theologians have held that every sin is a sin against God, even if most sins are also sins against our human neighbors.

I owe a large debt to many people for helping make this book a reality. My students in my graduate seminar on the Foundations of Morality read and discussed several chapters. Greg Mellema and Dan Baras read through the whole manuscript and gave me many excellent criticisms and suggestions. A number of others read parts of the book in draft form. Robert Roberts provided some penetrating suggestions dealing with Chapter 3. Mark Nelson provided a host of stimulating comments and criticisms of Chapter 5. Terence Cuneo gave me some excellent advice about Chapter 6, and gave me invaluable help in understanding Thomas Reid's approach to morality. I also owe a big debt to Ryan West, who put together the Bibliography and helped me avoid numerous mistakes. I must also thank Mark Mitchell, who prepared the Index, and Karl Aho, who made some important last-minute corrections. I deeply appreciate the generous help all these people provided.

I also want to thank Robert Adams and Mark Murphy. Neither read this beforehand, but Adams' work provided the major inspiration for the book. Mark Murphy will doubtless disagree with many of the claims and arguments found in it, but it will be evident throughout how much I have learned from his work. Both are models of how Christian scholars should do philosophy.

Finally, I must say some words about some of those I love. My parents, Charles and Pearline Evans, now deceased, taught me right from wrong, and they taught me how important it is to love God and to love the good. I owe more to my wife Jan Evans than I can ever repay. My life with her has demonstrated to me that moral obligations and joy can walk hand in hand.

C. Stephen Evans

Baylor University, 2012

Contents

1

God and Moral Obligations

Is there a connection between religion and morality? Ivan Karamazov, in Dostoevsky's *The Brothers Karamazov*, famously declares that if God does not exist, then "everything is permitted." Speaking for the opposition, Walter Sinnott-Armstrong has recently argued that the claim that there can be morality without God "should not be controversial" because "there is just plain morality."[1] I shall argue in this book that the truth lies somewhere between these two claims. It is not quite right to say that there would be nothing left of morality if God did not exist. However, Sinnott-Armstrong's view is incorrect as well. Leaving God out of the picture when it comes to morality puts pressure on us to revise our understanding of morality or even lose faith in morality altogether. In particular, the part of morality termed "obligation" threatens to drop out of the picture or be transformed beyond recognition.

Of course the claim that morality depends on God is ambiguous and can be interpreted in a number of different ways. One way it might be understood is as a claim that a person must believe in God to act morally or have a moral character. Religious belief is necessary to be a moral person. This seems implausible, since there seem to be many non-religious people of high moral character, and I have no reason to argue otherwise.

A second way the claim might be understood is as an epistemological claim: God is the basis of our knowledge of morality. If there is a God, this second claim will doubtless be true in some sense, because if humans are created by God, all of their knowledge must be derived from cognitive capacities God has given them. (And if theism is false, the claim will just as obviously be false.) However, assuming the truth

---

[1] Walter Sinnott-Armstrong, *Morality ~~Without God?~~* (New York: Oxford University Press, 2009), p. xi.

of theism, this epistemological claim is relatively uninteresting. A more interesting epistemological claim would be to assert that moral knowledge (or justified belief) depends on religious knowledge (or justified belief). One might suppose, for example, that a person must believe in God in order rationally to believe that there are objective moral obligations. I shall reject this claim, and also reject the view that moral knowledge must be derived from a special revelation from God. Though I reject these claims, I do acknowledge that belief in morality without a religious foundation can be problematic, and I certainly wish to affirm that special revelation is an important source of moral knowledge.

For my purposes, the relevant interpretation of the "morality depends on God" claim is *ontological*. I am interested in the claim that some features of morality, particularly features of moral obligations, exist because of God. God is the ground of moral obligations and a crucial part of the explanation of such obligations.

MORAL OBLIGATIONS: A FIRST LOOK

What is a moral obligation? In a sense this whole book is intended to answer that question, and, as we shall see, there are a large variety of possible answers. Nevertheless, some kind of preliminary view is necessary in order to get started. First, to what do obligations pertain? Most commonly, it is actions (or act-types) that are regarded as morally obligatory, though it is not necessary to limit our obligations to actions. We might have obligations to do what we can to bring about certain ends. In this case we fulfill our obligations through actions but the obligation might not be to perform any specific action. It is also perfectly intelligible to believe we have moral obligations to develop or acquire virtues or character traits. I believe, for example, that humans have obligations to have (or acquire) such traits as mercifulness, compassion, generosity, and courage. However, even in this case, the story about how one goes about acquiring (or maintaining) such qualities will very likely include actions and choices about actions, since most accounts of the virtues stress the role that practice plays if they are to be developed and/or retained.

So let us say that obligations apply primarily, though not exclusively, to actions. Moral philosophers disagree about whether some moral obligations are "absolute" and hold unconditionally or whether all obligations are "*prima facie*," liable to being overridden in special circumstances, but it is not hard to give examples of acts that most people would consider to be morally obligatory in at least the *prima facie* sense: refraining from killing an innocent person, telling the truth, refraining from stealing another person's possessions, keeping a promise.

The concept of an obligation is one of a "deontic" family of concepts, which include "being forbidden," and "being permitted," as well as "being obligatory." Given one of these concepts the others can be defined as well. An act that is forbidden is one that it is obligatory to refrain from doing. An act that is obligatory is one that it is forbidden to refrain from doing. And a permissible act is simply one that is not forbidden. (This obviously assumes that what is obligatory is also permissible. One might also conceive of what is permissible as "merely permissible," meaning that it is neither obligatory nor forbidden.) It is difficult to define any one member of the family by itself. There are of course terms that are roughly synonymous in English. An act that is forbidden is one that "must not" be done; an act that is obligatory is one that "must" be done. An act that is permissible is one that "may" be done, and so on. However, it is not likely that anyone who fails to grasp the concepts of being obligatory and forbidden will understand the relevant senses of "must" and "may."

It is helpful here to remember that terms in the obligation family also have a use outside of morality. We humans recognize legal obligations of various kinds, familial obligations, and obligations of etiquette, as well as more specialized forms of obligation that we incur when we participate in specific forms of social interchange. (For example, the obligation an umpire in baseball has to call balls and strikes consistently with the rules that define the strike zone.) Many of these obligations coincide or at least overlap with moral obligations, but this is by no means always the case. Imagine, for example, a racist society with unjust laws that require citizens to practice invidious forms of racial discrimination. In such a situation, a person's legal obligations might conflict with the individual's moral obligations. Moral obligations seem to be a particular species of obligation, as different from legal obligations, for example, as legal obligations are from obligations of etiquette.

I shall defend the claim that each type of obligation embodies a particular kind of social institution and is part of a particular system of social interaction. In the chapters that follow I shall repeatedly appeal to the analogies between moral obligations and the other forms of obligation, particularly legal obligations, in order better to understand moral obligations. For now it is enough to notice that all forms of obligation involve notions of what people "may" do, or "must" do, or "must not" do, though the thrust of these "modal" terms will reflect the specific social institutions these forms of obligation are linked to.

THE TASK OF METAETHICS

Virtually all human persons recognize the importance moral obligations play in human life. Even those who are skeptics about the reality or validity of such obligations acknowledge that most people do believe that morality is important, and even moral skeptics admit that human societies would likely be fundamentally different if people generally ceased to believe that they were subject to moral obligations. Despite this consensus about the importance of morality, there is little agreement as to the nature of moral obligations. Are there facts about what are our moral obligations? If there are such facts, how do they arise? How can they be explained? If there are no such facts, then how should we understand obligations? Answering such questions is the task of that branch of philosophy called metaethics, usually defined as the attempt to understand the foundations of ethics, carried out at least partly by reflection on the meanings of ethical terms.

Actually, metaethics covers far more than this, because ethics itself deals with far more than questions about moral obligations. For example, ethical or moral philosophy (I shall use "ethics" and "morality" interchangeably) also asks questions about the good. What is goodness? Are there different forms of goodness? What is good for humans? These questions are connected to many others. Since many think the good for humans is, or at least includes, happiness, how should happiness for humans be understood and how can it be achieved? Moral philosophers also ask about justice and about the implications of morality for social institutions. Questions about specific forms of human excellence also arise. Are there forms of excellence ("virtues") a human life should strive to actualize, such as wisdom, compassion, and courage? If so, what do these qualities consist in, and how can they be achieved? For all these first-order ethical questions, sometimes called questions of "normative ethics," there are corresponding metaethical questions about the foundations or origins of whatever ethical truths (or claims, or prescriptions, or expressions) there may be.

This book will focus mainly on metaethical questions that arise in connection with moral obligations. However, it will not be possible or even desirable to answer those questions in isolation from other metaethical questions, or from various first-order questions in ethics, since obligations themselves are related in complex way to goods and virtues of various kinds. Because of the complexity of ethics, I believe we should resist reductive theories that try to explain the whole of ethics in terms of one fundamental principle or concept, but this recognition is fully compatible with the need to understand the various ways the different parts of ethics are connected.

ALTERNATIVE ACCOUNTS OF MORAL OBLIGATIONS

There are a variety of ways of categorizing the different possible ways one might understand moral obligations. One important divide is the distinction between cognitive and non-cognitive theories. Cognitive theories, which come in many varieties, see moral obligations as facts or realities, the sorts of things that people can have true or mistaken beliefs about, and hence are sometimes described as forms of "moral realism." To claim that "Jim is morally obligated to report the income he received from the lecture" is to affirm something that could be true or false, and thus can be an object of knowledge. Non-cognitive theories such as emotivism and prescriptivism, in contrast, deny that moral utterances express propositions with objective truth values. Emotivism, for example, sees propositions about moral obligations that appear to express facts as disguised expressions of emotions. "Jim is morally obligated to report the income he received from the lecture" does not express a proposition that could be true or false, but rather is an expression of the approving emotion possessed by the person who utters the sentence. (Or, perhaps the sentence expresses a positive emotional response to Jim that would be present if Jim did report the income.) Obviously the accounts given of exactly what attitudes or emotions moral statements express can vary greatly and can be much more sophisticated than these fairly crude examples, but the general thrust of the view is clear enough.

A prescriptivist account differs from an emotivist account in viewing moral utterances as attempts to prescribe how others should behave. On such a view a moral utterance expresses not just an emotion (though it could do this as well) but a conviction of the speaker about how people should act. I shall call all views of this general type expressivist accounts of morality. Expressivist views are by definition non-cognitivist; they imply that moral claims are neither true nor false.[2]

There are many problems with expressivist views, but the most serious issue concerns the implications of such views for normative ethical claims. Suppose that a claim that a certain act is obligatory is just an expression of the speaker's emotions and/or a conviction of the speaker about how people should behave. To say "you must answer honestly" is just to say something like "I strongly approve of your answering honestly" or "I will that you and everyone should answer honestly." In such a case what authority does the moral claim have? The fact that some individual (or even most people) would approve or disapprove of some act would not appear to have the kind of weight or significance we think attaches to morality. One can well imagine someone who accepts expressivism replying to someone who has given a moral injunction as follows: "Why should I care that you disapprove of my action or about what you think about how I should behave?" As one might expect, there are moves the expressivist can make to try to salvage some kind of authoritativeness for moral expressions, but a central problem of metaethics has here come clearly into view: What is the source of the authority of morality, and in particular the authority of moral obligations?

Cognitivists also need to explain the authoritativeness of moral obligations, if they believe, as most objectivists about morality do, that it indeed has authority. Suppose that there are objective moral facts. How exactly do such facts gain authority over us? The existence of such obligations can seem puzzling. If moral obligations are objective in this way, then people can be right or wrong in their beliefs about

---

[2] This definition is stipulative. Terence Hogan and Mark Timmons have a view they call "Cognitivist Expressivism," in which they say that moral assertions can be beliefs, but beliefs of a distinctive kind, in that they are not primarily to be understood as representing moral facts. A view of this sort just will not count as expressivist in my sense. See Terry Horgan and Mark Timmons, "Nondescriptivist Cognitivism: Framework for a New Metaethic," *Philosophical Papers* 29 (2000), pp. 121–53.

their obligations. Similarly, feelings of obligation can be appropriate or inappropriate; I might feel obligated to do what I am not in fact obligated to do, or fail to feel obligated to do what I should do. Many find the existence of such things as moral obligations that are distinct from our feelings and beliefs odd or strange. How do they arise? How do we account for such obligations?

Explaining objective moral obligations turns out to be difficult indeed. There are a large variety of proposed answers but many of them are mutually exclusive, and none are without difficulties. The difficulties are great enough that some moral philosophers simply conclude that there are no such obligations. J. L. Mackie, for example, developed a classic "error theory" account of moral obligations.[3] Mackie concedes that our ordinary moral language is committed to objective moral obligations, affirming that "objectivism about values" is something that has "a firm basis in ordinary thought, and even in the meanings of moral terms."[4] Most people believe there are such things as objective moral obligations; Mackie just thinks that such beliefs are false. One of his primary arguments for what he calls "moral subjectivism" is the fact that it is very difficult to give a good explanation of how there could be moral obligations.[5] At least if one assumes a naturalistic universe, the existence of such obligations would be "queer" (in the sense of being odd and inexplicable), and in such a situation Mackie thinks it more reasonable just to give up belief in objective moral obligations altogether.

Not surprisingly, Mackie's claims here, along with just about every other view in the neighborhood, turn out to be controversial. Some of his fellow naturalists, such as the "Cornell realists," vehemently deny that moral obligations do not fit into a naturalistic world.[6] There is therefore a kind of three-party dispute about moral obligations. Most theistic moral philosophers, as well as the majority of ordinary religious believers (at least in the case of the Abrahamic faiths) affirm the existence of objective moral obligations, and also think that such obligations in some way depend on God, though there is quite a bit of disagreement among religious thinkers as to just how God helps to

---

[3] J. L. Mackie, *Ethics: Inventing Right and Wrong* (London: Penguin Books, 1977).
[4] Mackie, p. 31.
[5] Mackie, pp. 38–42.
[6] See, for example, Richard Boyd, "How to Be a Moral Realist," in Geoffrey Sayre-McCord (ed.), *Essays on Moral Realism* (Ithaca, NY: Cornell University Press, 1988), pp. 181–228.

make sense of morality. Making sense of how God could be the basis of moral obligations is the primary task of this book. I shall try to show that *divine authority* has an important role to play in making sense of the deontological dimension of ethics.

Many naturalists agree with religious thinkers that there are objective moral obligations, but hold that God is not necessary to make sense of such obligations; moral obligations can be given a naturalistic explanation. Other naturalists agree with Mackie (and Nietzsche) that objective moral obligations do not make sense in a naturalistic universe. This three-party argument means that theistic moral philosophers who think morality does require God must fight a "two-front war." They must defend the reality of objective moral obligations against moral skeptics, while at the same time trying to show that such obligations are difficult to explain without God. However, the same three-party situation makes possible some unusual alliances for theists, since it allows them to make common cause with some naturalists in defending objective moral obligations, and common cause with other naturalists in defending the claim that such obligations are hard to make sense of in a naturalistic universe. At the very least the fact that some of the arguments for these claims are defended by naturalists helps alleviate the suspicion that the theistic arguments beg the question by assuming a theistic worldview at the outset.

Of course, as is usually the case in philosophy, matters are not as simple as this three-party argument model might suggest. There are theists who agree with some of the claims of the naturalists who defend moral objectivity. There are also "ethical non-naturalists" who agree with theists that ethical truths cannot be explained naturalistically, but don't necessarily think God plays an essential role in ethics. In addition, a place in the narrative must be found for "constructivists," a strand in contemporary ethics inspired by Kant. Constructivists do not fit neatly into the "three-party argument schema," since they think (with moral objectivists) that moral obligations have a kind of authoritativeness and objectivity, but reject (with moral subjectivists) the view that moral obligations are constituted by objective facts. I shall give a fuller treatment of constructivism, as well as a fuller account of expressivism and some other metaethical views, in Chapter 5. At this point I need to say more about why one might think that divine authority and divine commands have an important role to play in making sense of moral obligations. To make sense of such a claim I need to say more about the special character of such obligations.

THE UNIQUE CHARACTER OF MORAL OBLIGATION: THE ANSCOMBE INTUITION

To be morally obligated to perform an action is to have a powerful reason to perform that action, a reason many would describe as a decisive or overriding one. It is thus understandable that many attempts to explain moral obligations take the form of trying to show that we have a powerful reason to perform whatever action the obligation covers. Kant's attempt to ground morality in practical reason is perhaps the paradigm case of this strategy, but consequentialist moral philosophies, such as utilitarianism, can be seen as a variation of this move as well.[7] If we think an obligation is simply something one has a good reason to do, and also assume that people have good reasons to seek maximal good results, then to show that some action A that some person is considering will achieve better results than any alternative action might seem to be a demonstration that the person has a moral duty to perform A.

However, although it is certainly true that a moral obligation gives an individual a reason for acting in a certain way, it does not follow that an explanation of a reason for action is *eo ipso* an explanation of a moral obligation. People frequently have reasons to perform actions, even powerful and decisive reasons, which they have no moral obligation to do. Suppose I am offered $5,000 to give a lecture this afternoon. The lecture is one I have given before and will require little work for me. I have the time to give the lecture and no pressing responsibilities that would conflict. In this situation I would have very powerful reasons indeed to accept the invitation, but it does not follow that I am morally obligated to do so. If I decide to spend the afternoon meditating, or reading a novel, or playing golf, instead of giving the lecture, some might judge me unwise or frivolous, but few people would say that I have thereby done something immoral. To have a moral obligation to perform an act is to have a reason of a

---

[7] Of course Kantianism and utilitarianism can be interpreted as first-order normative ethical theories, rather than metaethical theories. However, it is not that easy to disentangle what is normative and what is metanormative in thinkers such as Kant and Mill, and reading the distinction back into their work can be anachronistic. The move I want to highlight in both is an attempt to understand obligatory actions as actions one has a reason to perform. In this chapter I try to show that there are features of moral obligations that resist this reduction. This is not so much metaethics as providing some of the data which metaethics should account for.

special type to perform the act, and an explanation of moral obligations must illuminate this special character that obligations possess. An analogy with legal obligations may make this point clearer. To have a legal obligation to perform an act is surely to have a reason to perform that act, but no one would think that merely having a reason to perform the act is thereby to have a legal obligation to perform the act. Most of the autobahn highways in Germany have no speed limits. Since I am not experienced at driving an automobile at high speeds, I have very good reasons not to drive my car in excess of 100 miles per hour (or 150 kilometers per hour) when driving on an autobahn in Germany. However, I have no legal obligation to drive slower than 100 miles per hour when on the autobahn. Obviously, the fact that I have a decisive reason to drive slower than 100 miles per hour would still not constitute a legal obligation. There are situations in which I would have a decisive reason to violate my legal obligations. Obvious examples would include the racist laws passed by Nazi Germany, or the segregationist laws in the pre-civil rights era American south. Or, to stick with my highway speed thought experiment, imagine that Porsche, in an attempt to sell more high-powered sports cars, has bribed the German legislature to pass a law that cars on the autobahn must drive faster than 100 miles per hour.

Another way of making this point is to remind ourselves that there are different types of "ought-statements." If I am driving on the autobahn, I ought not to drive in excess of 100 miles per hour, but this "ought" is not a legal obligation. In a similar way, to go back to my earlier example, there may be a sense in which I ought to accept the invitation to give the lecture and thereby earn $5,000, but this "ought" is not an expression of a moral duty.

The special character of the moral "ought" is a major theme in one of the most influential articles in ethics published in the twentieth century, G. E. M. Anscombe's "Modern Moral Philosophy."[8] Anscombe begins with a striking observation about the differences between Aristotle and modern moral philosophy:

> Anyone who has read Aristotle's *Ethics* and has read modern moral philosophy must have been struck by the great contrasts between them.

---

[8] Reprinted in *The Collected Philosophical Papers of G. E. M. Anscombe, Volume 3: Ethics, Religion, and Politics* (Oxford: Basil Blackwell, 1981), pp. 26–42. Originally published in *Philosophy* 33 (January, 1958), 124.

The concepts which are prominent among the moderns seem to be lacking or at any rate buried or far in the background, in Aristotle. Most noticeably, the term "moral" itself, which we have by direct inheritance from Aristotle, just doesn't seem to fit, in its modern sense, into an account of Aristotelian ethics.[9]

When Aristotle uses terms like "should" or "ought," they relate to what is good or bad in the sense in which one can explain what is good and bad for something in terms of what is needed for that thing. In that sense one can say that a machine "needs oil, or should or ought to be oiled, in that running without oil is bad for it, or it runs badly without oil."[10] When Aristotle says that a person ought not to act unjustly, he was thinking in a roughly analogous way: justice is a virtue needed for human flourishing and being unjust is therefore harmful to a person.[11]

However, Anscombe maintains, in modern moral philosophy, terms like "should" and "ought" have a special moral sense "in which they imply some absolute verdict (like one of guilty/not guilty on a man)."[12] Our ordinary senses of "ought" and "should" and "must" take on a new sense, one they did not have in Aristotle, in which a person is thought to be "obliged" or "bound" or "required" to do something.[13] Anscombe thinks that the explanation for this change lies in history: "Between Aristotle and us came Christianity, with its *law* conception of ethics. For Christianity derived its ethical notions from the Torah."[14] For Anscombe, the link between divine law and moral obligations is not merely historical, however, and the loss of belief in God carries with it a cost: "Naturally, it is not possible to have such a [law] conception unless you believe in God as a law-giver; like Jews, Stoics, and Christians. But if such a conception is dominant for many centuries, and then is given up, it is a natural result that the concept of 'obligation', of being bound or required as by a law, should remain though they had lost their root."[15]

Anscombe follows up these claims with some advice for her philosophical contemporaries: They ought if possible to drop the concept of moral obligation altogether, and do moral philosophy in the way that Aristotle did, focusing on virtues and vices.[16] To a significant degree,

---

[9] Anscombe, p. 26.   [10] Anscombe, p. 29.
[11] Anscombe, p. 41.   [12] Anscombe, p. 29.
[13] Anscombe, pp. 29–30.   [14] Anscombe, p. 30.   [15] Anscombe, p. 30.
[16] Anscombe gives this advice with one important qualification. She says that until an adequate moral psychology is developed, it will not be possible to make much progress on an understanding of virtuous actions and the virtues in general.

this advice has borne fruit; in the last half century we have seen a significant revival of virtue ethics. One might have thought that Anscombe would have made a case for the revival of a divine law ethic. However, she makes no such appeal, since in the overwhelmingly secular context of contemporary philosophy, she did not see that as a realistic possibility. However, in ways that might well have been surprising to Anscombe, in the time since "Modern Moral Philosophy" was published there has also been a significant increase in ethical views that do make the notion of divine law central to ethics.[17]

I do not cite Anscombe here to settle any important issues. Both her historical claim that our modern conception of morality is fundamentally indebted to the Judeo-Christian tradition and the substantive claim that thinking of moral duties as law-like in character requires an actual law-giver can be disputed. I find the former claim exceedingly plausible myself, and much of this book will be devoted to a defense of the latter, but such issues cannot be decided by appeal to authority. Rather, my purpose in discussing Anscombe's well-known article is to further motivate what I shall call the "Anscombe intuition." This intuition can be initially expressed as follows: Moral obligations as experienced have a unique character, and attempts to explain moral obligations must illuminate that special character. To show that we are morally obligated to perform some action it is not enough to show that we have a strong or even decisive reason to perform that action. If citing a reason to perform an act is to illuminate why the act is obligatory, the reason must be such that it accounts for the special nature of obligation.

What is that special nature? There are, I think, several features that stand out in Anscombe's reflections on moral obligation. The first is that a judgment about a moral obligation is a kind of "verdict on my action," analogous to the verdict given in a criminal trial of guilty or not-guilty.[18] Although moral obligations may differ in degree of

---

[17] Most notably Robert Adams, *Finite and Infinite Goods* (New York: Oxford University Press, 1999), and Philip Quinn, *Divine Commands and Moral Requirements* (Oxford: Oxford University Press, 1978). Quinn and Adams have several important articles as well. Besides their work, other significant recent defenses of a divine command theory include John Hare, *God's Call: Moral Realism, God's Commands, and Human Autonomy* (Grand Rapids, MI: Wm. B. Eerdmans, 2001), and C. Stephen Evans, *Kierkegaard's Ethic of Love: Divine Commands and Moral Obligations* (Oxford: Oxford University Press, 2004).

[18] Anscombe, p. 33.

weight or seriousness, there is nevertheless a way in which they are binary: either I am obligated to perform an act or I am not obligated to perform an act.

To be sure this binary character does not hold in the case of specific acts that fulfill what Kant called "imperfect duties." I may have a duty to be generous to the poor, but this does not mean that I have a duty to help every poor person I might come in contact with. So the binary character of a duty is clearest in the case of so-called "perfect duties," which often take the form of prohibitions. If I have a duty not to lie, then I ought not to lie on this particular occasion. Moreover, there is still a sense in which the binary character of duty is reflected even in imperfect duties. For even in these cases, the qualities I am enjoined to manifest exclude their opposites. If I am called to be generous and compassionate, I must not be miserly and hard-hearted. Rather, it ought to be a settled matter which of these qualities I should seek to acquire and exercise.

A second important feature of moral obligation follows from this. Once an individual has recognized that he or she has a moral obligation, then (with some exceptions to be explained below) further deliberation about the action is unnecessary. (Again, this is clearest in the case of perfect duties.) I may say to myself: "I don't need to consider this any further; this is something I know I must not do." The act is one that I am *obliged* not to do; it is *forbidden*. This is quite different from a situation in which one is considering the goodness or badness of the consequences of actions, since goodness or badness in such contexts is always considered with respect to degrees, and further reflection about what the consequences of the act might be or how they should be evaluated would always seem to be in order.[19] A moral obligation therefore is something that has the function of bringing reflection to closure.

Of course reflection is often appropriate when dealing with obligations as well; a person may always reflect on the nature of the obligation itself or about whether he or she is really obligated. Reflection about how an obligation should be fulfilled or exactly what the

---

[19] One might think that obligations come in degrees as well, but this is mistaken. Obligations can differ in weight or seriousness. An obligation to save innocent life is more weighty than an obligation to meet someone for lunch. But there is still an important sense in which the obligations are binary; they either hold or they do not hold.

obligation amounts to is often in order. Those who believe that there are *prima facie* obligations that can come into conflict may have to reflect on which obligation takes precedence over the other. Despite such exceptions (and possibly others) it is generally the case that a person who recognizes an obligation concerning an action has recognized something that bears directly and immediately on that action. A person may have many reasons for performing or not performing an action, but moral obligations are reasons that trump other kinds of reasons (or at least ought to do so), and this means they can help bring reflection to a close and make action possible.

A third feature of moral obligations is that they involve accountability or responsibility. Someone who has failed to do what he or she was morally obligated to do is someone who is deserving of blame; in some cases the blameworthiness is such that the person might even deserve punishment. Moral obligations here, as in so many other respects, are analogous to other forms of obligation. The person who breaks the law intentionally and knowingly is subject to legal sanctions. The person who intentionally is rude and violates some obligation of etiquette is deserving of social disdain.

A final feature of moral obligations is one that distinguishes them from other types of obligations: moral obligations hold for persons simply as persons. They are not obligations that hold simply for Athenians by virtue of being citizens of Athens, or obligations that hold for Texans by virtue of being residents of Texas. There are of course obligations that hold because of special relationships people have to each other, and some of those are moral in character. However, the obligations towards others rooted in special relations are not moral in character *automatically*, even though some of my moral obligations stem from special relations. The obligations that stem from special relations overlap extensively with moral obligations, but the various forms of obligation must be distinguished. Since familial and political obligations in some cases actually *conflict* with moral obligations, it is not the case that they are moral obligations simply by virtue of being family obligations or political obligations. A person who is subject to moral obligations has a standard by which other kinds of obligations should be judged, and only those that pass this test count as moral. Thus a person does not have moral obligations simply because the person belongs to a family or a state, even though a person does have moral obligations to the family and the state, and this means that one's moral identity is more fundamental and encompassing than one's identity as a member of a family or nation. Having moral obligations is a status that one acquires by virtue of being human; it is not a status reserved for those from good families or who are citizens of particular nations. It is this feature of moral obligations that seems most lacking in Aristotle's ethics. Aristotle has much to say about the obligations of citizenship and friendship, but little to say about what obligations apply to human beings simply as human beings.

As I have already said, this account of what I would call the phenomenology of moral obligations leaves many substantive questions unresolved. Indeed, someone might agree that I have accurately described the way people usually think about moral obligations, but still hold to an error theory, which affirms that there are no such things. Nevertheless, if we want to give an account of moral obligations, it is important to reflect on their special character. Even error theorists need a clear understanding of what they are rejecting, as J. L. Mackie makes clear. In the remainder of this book, unless I make it clear that I am making an exception, when I speak of moral obligations I am speaking of them as having the features highlighted here: they involve a kind of verdict on an action, they make it possible to bring reflection on action to closure and make a decision about the action by providing a decisive reason for action, they are the kinds of things people are rightly held responsible for doing or omitting, and they hold for human persons just as human persons.[20]

The unique character of moral obligations is generally recognized but hard to explain. Ronald Dworkin provides a clear example of what I mean by this. Dworkin distinguishes between happiness and what he calls "living well," a concept that he clearly understands as involving a moral dimension, and claims that we are *responsible* to do the latter: "We have a responsibility to live well and believe that living well means creating a life that is not simply pleasurable but good in that critical way."[21] The fact that we are responsible for living life a certain way looks like an obligation, but Dworkin seems baffled when he tries to account for this fact. It would be natural to think that the

---

[20] This list of features is not exhaustive. I shall return to this ground in Chapter 2 and there I add two senses in which moral obligations possess a kind of universality.

[21] Ronald Dworkin, "What Is a Good Life?" *New York Review of Books* (LVIII, 2; February 10, 2011), p. 42 (article is pp. 41–3). For a fuller discussion, see Dworkin, *Justice for Hedgehogs* (Cambridge, MA: Harvard University Press, 2011).

fact we are responsible implies we are responsible to someone, but Dworkin cannot fathom who that might be:

> You might ask, responsibility to whom? It is misleading to answer: responsibility to ourselves. People to whom responsibilities are owed can normally release those who are responsible, but we cannot release ourselves from our responsibility to live well. We must instead acknowledge an idea that I believe we almost all accept in the way we live but that is rarely explicitly formulated or acknowledged. We are charged to live well by the bare fact of our existence as self-conscious creatures with lives to lead.[22]

Dworkin's reply seems only to deepen the mystery of moral obligation; what he offers seems more like elegant testimony to a perceived conviction that we are indeed subject to an obligation to live a moral life than an explanation of why we have such an obligation. I think Dworkin shares the Anscombe intuition as to the distinctive character of moral obligations, but has no way of accounting for such obligations. I shall say more below about the situation of people such as Dworkin.

We could summarize the Anscombe intuition in the following way: Moral obligations have a law-like character, one which many modern moral philosophies have failed to do justice to. The most important question Anscombe's article raises is the substantive one I have already alluded to: Does this law-like character require an actual law-giver?

SOCRATES COMPARED WITH ARISTOTLE

One might think that Anscombe's views would imply that belief in moral obligations (in the sense explained above) could only develop as a result of belief in the kind of law-giver God accepted by Christians, Jews, and Muslims. If one means by this that the concept of a moral law must be derived from a revealed, positive divine law, of the sort contained in the Bible or the Qur'an, Anscombe herself denies that this is the case, citing the Stoics, who maintained that "whatever was involved in conformity to human virtues was required by divine law."[23] So perhaps Anscombe did not mean to hold that Christianity (or something like Christianity) was necessary, either historically or

---

[22] Dworkin, "What Is a Good Life?", p. 42.   [23] Anscombe, p. 30.

conceptually, in order to have a belief in moral obligations as law-like realities. But what does her claim amount to? Or, more importantly, what claim in this neighborhood is actually defensible?

Suppose it is true that Aristotle lacked the concept of moral obligation. It does not follow from this that he could not have had the concept. In fact, I think a good case can be made that Socrates, the teacher of Aristotle's teacher, did indeed have the concept of moral obligation, at least if we assume, as many scholars do, that the portrayal of Socrates given in Plato's *Apology* is historically accurate. As part of his defense at his trial, Socrates recounts an episode from earlier in his life, in which he and four others were ordered by the existing Athenian rulers to go and get Leon of Salamis to be executed. It is clear that Socrates regards this action as morally evil, since he says the purpose of the government in issuing the order was "to implicate as many people as possible in their wickedness."[24] Socrates recounts that he refused to obey the government order, even though he knew that he likely would be put to death for his refusal, because "it mattered all the world to me that I should do nothing wrong or wicked."[25]

Some reflection on this episode, and on other passages in the *Apology*, will show that Socrates does have a concept of "wrongness" that is quite closely linked to the concept of moral obligation. First, note that Socrates does not seem to consider the consequences of his actions at all. His refusal to participate does not save Leon of Salamis, since the four others ordered to fetch him all obeyed the government. The only likely difference Socrates' refusal made was to make his own death highly likely, something that would have occurred if the government had not fallen before it could act against him. Socrates seems to think of the act he has refused to do as one on which a verdict has been rendered, one that makes the act forbidden and makes further reflection unnecessary, since it would simply be unthinkable to do such a thing.

Furthermore, it is clear that this prohibition is one that has overriding importance for Socrates. As he says elsewhere in the *Apology*, a person who is "worth anything" is someone who "has only one thing to consider in performing any action—that is, whether he is acting

---

[24] *Socrates' Defense (Apology)*, in *Plato: The Collected Dialogues*, ed. Edith Hamilton and Huntington Cairns (Princeton, NJ: Princeton University Press, 1961), p. 18. Hereafter referred to simply as *Apology*.

[25] *Apology*, p. 18.

rightly or wrongly, like a good man or a bad one."[26] The importance of moral goodness for Socrates is shown, among other ways, by his request that after his death his fellow Athenians "plague" Socrates' sons, as Socrates has plagued the Athenians, if his sons are ever found to be "putting money or anything else before goodness."[27]

Nor can any good reader of the *Apology* miss the strong sense of personal responsibility that pulses through the dialogue in Socrates' every statement. Early in the dialogue Socrates expresses this sense of being bound to do what he must do: "Where a man has once taken up his stand, either because it seems best to him or in obedience to his orders, there I believe he is bound to remain and face the danger."[28] Socrates clearly sees himself as someone who is "under orders." He not only wants to do what is right and avoid what is evil; he feels he *must* live in that way, and that he would be blameworthy if he did not. Socrates sees his whole life as a kind of "posting" or "assignment," comparing his calling to the philosophical life to a soldier who has been ordered to a post.[29]

It is also clear that Socrates' concern with living in accordance with morality is one that he sees as applying to humans as humans, rather than merely to Athenians or Greeks. Though Socrates acknowledges he has special duties to his fellow Athenians, he claims that his mission of inspiring others to be morally good by testing and examining them is a mission that extends to all kinds of persons: "I shall do this to everyone that I meet, young or old, foreigner or fellow citizen . . . "[30] Despite the fact that doing what is morally right has led to a sentence of death, Socrates never wavers in his conviction that the moral life is the best life for any human being to live. He even goes so far as to maintain that he does not believe that "the law of God permits a better man to be harmed by a worse," and, even more strongly, that "nothing can harm a good man either in life or after death."[31]

I conclude that Socrates did indeed possess a concept of moral obligation that is strikingly similar to that concept Anscombe says was lacking in Aristotle and that she says we owe to Christianity. Obviously Socrates did not get it from Christianity. Nevertheless, it seems that Anscombe is right to this extent: Socrates does think, as do Christians, that our moral duties are linked to a God or gods to whom we are responsible. Unlike Aristotle's God, whose function in ethics only seems to be to serve as a model of what an exemplary life

---

[26] *Apology*, p. 14.   [27] *Apology*, p. 26.   [28] *Apology*, p. 15.
[29] *Apology*, p. 15.   [30] *Apology*, p. 16.   [31] *Apology*, pp. 16 and 25.

of contemplation might be like,[32] Socrates seems to believe in a God (or gods) who is concerned about humans and how they live.[33] Furthermore, the God Socrates believes in is a God who ought to be *obeyed* because he has authority.[34]

If Socrates' view of the important role God plays in humans' moral lives were not otherwise clear, it becomes undeniable when Socrates discusses the "divine sign" that he claims to have had. This divine sign, which Socrates says began in early childhood, is a "sort of voice" that comes to Socrates when he is considering some action and which he says "dissuades me from what I am proposing to do."[35] It is clear that Socrates sees this divine voice as one that forbids him to perform actions; he relies on these commands to such an extent that he actually argues that the fact that his voice did not oppose him when he made his defense at the trial is evidence that he was doing what is right in making that defense, even though it led to his condemnation.[36]

DO WE NEED A LAW-GIVER TO HAVE LAW-LIKE MORAL OBLIGATIONS?

It is clear then that it is not necessary to be an adherent of Judaism or Christianity in order to have a robust belief in moral obligations.

---

[32] One might think God has some other roles to play in ethics for Aristotle, but providing a model for emulation certainly seems the most important. For a good discussion of the role God plays in Aristotle's ethics, see John Hare, *God and Morality: A Philosophical History* (Malden, MA: Wiley-Blackwell, 2009), pp. 7–72, and also pp. 251–60.

[33] It is, I believe, unclear whether the Socrates of the *Apology* is a polytheist, a henotheist, a monotheist, or perhaps someone who is moving in the direction of monotheism. At times in the *Apology*, Socrates refers to "god" in the singular and other times "gods" in the plural. Interestingly, it seems to me that when he is addressing his interlocutors (his accusers or the jury), he tends to use the plural, perhaps reflecting the polytheism of Athenian religion. However, when he speaks about his own convictions, he more often speaks of "the god" in the singular. Of course this could simply be a reference to one particular God, and does not imply a commitment to monotheism. In what follows in the text I will speak of "God" when discussing Socrates' views for the sake of simplicity, but I do not thereby wish to commit to the claim that the historical Socrates was a monotheist.

[34] See, for example, *Apology*, p. 15, where Socrates says that we must obey "God and other superiors" and that obedience to God takes precedence over obedience to human beings.

[35] *Apology*, p. 17.   [36] *Apology*, pp. 24–5.

Socrates as well as the Stoics cited by Anscombe show that this is so. Nevertheless, one might argue that a transcendent law-giver, a divine being who has genuine authority, is necessary to have genuine moral obligations.

It is crucial to distinguish ontological and epistemological versions of this claim. The claim that God is in fact the basis of moral obligations must be distinguished from the claim that one cannot believe in moral obligations without belief in God. Ontologically, this book is a sustained argument that God does provide the best explanation for why there are moral obligations. The argument for this will consist in part of an attempt to show how God helps explain such obligations, and in part in attempts to show that alternative explanations fail or at least face daunting problems.

One might think that this argument, if successful, will also support an epistemological dependence between God and moral obligations. One might think that if it can be shown that God provides a plausible explanation of moral obligations, and if no alternative explanation is available, this would provide those who do not believe in God with a reason to doubt the reality of moral obligations. This seems to be the view of Anscombe herself, who urges her secular colleagues to simply drop belief in moral obligations if they can, since they cannot make rational sense of them.[37]

If this is indeed Anscombe's view, I disagree, at least in part. It is true that a person who cannot explain or make sense of moral obligations ontologically has some reason to doubt their reality. But it also is the case that people can sometimes have good reasons to believe in the reality of something they cannot explain or make sense of. A clear (if somewhat clichéd) example is the following: Imagine a person who is ignorant of chemistry and comes from a tropical climate. Assume that this person has never seen snow or ice, and is for the first time shown ice by a visitor. The fact that the person cannot explain or make sense of the transition from liquid to frozen water is not a very good reason to doubt the reality of the ice that he

---

[37] Actually, I think Anscombe has a more complex reason than this for her advice. She thinks her secular colleagues would be better off dropping the concept of moral obligation, not just because they cannot make sense of it, but because in their attempts to make sense of it they transform the concept in ways that are morally corrupting. For example, she argues that contemporary moral philosophy must seriously inquire as to whether it might be morally right judicially to punish a person known to be innocent. See Anscombe, pp. 34–41.

perceives. I believe that a person who is aware of moral obligations but who cannot explain them may be in a similar situation.

Anscombe thinks that contemporary moral philosophers who try to make sense of moral obligations without divine commands have an unintelligible concept of "obligation," one which possesses merely "psychological" or "mesmeric" force.[38] However, I do not think this is necessarily the case. Suppose, for example, that moral obligations are the kinds of things one might *experience*, as in "I became aware that I was obligated to tell the truth to her." If so, a person might well be reasonable to believe in the reality of such obligations, even if the individual cannot explain them. Indeed, the person might be reasonable to continue to believe in moral obligations even if the person has a very unclear or confused understanding of what an obligation is.

Nor is it necessarily the case that a person who does not believe in God could have no concept of a moral obligation at all. Here we need to remember that moral obligations are a species of obligation, and that there are other kinds. A person who is aware of moral obligations might well think of them as "law-like" in the following sense: moral obligations are *like* legal obligations in that they help us render verdicts on actions, give us powerful reasons to act, and so on. The analogy between moral obligations and other forms of obligations might be sufficient to give an individual some idea of what a moral obligation is, even if that person cannot explain how such obligations come about.

If we suppose, as I shall argue to be the case, that moral obligations depend on God ontologically, it does not follow that belief in God is necessary to believe in moral obligations. Of course, from a psychological perspective it is obvious that someone might believe both atheism and in the reality of moral obligations simply by being irrational. However, I believe that both truth and charity demand more than this; I want to say that someone might well be reasonable to believe in moral obligations without belief in God.

If I am right in my claims about the dependence of moral obligations on God, and the necessity to relate these obligations to God in order to understand them properly, it will follow that failure to believe in God will normally put some pressure on a belief in moral obligations. Even Kant, who thought that morality was something

---

[38] Anscombe, p. 32.

reason required, said that a person who is an atheist will be tempted to think that the moral obligations are merely "empty figments of the brain."[39] However, Kant thought, and I agree, that this is a temptation that should be resisted. A naturalist who is aware of moral obligations may well have a keen sense of a lack of fit between that person's beliefs about morality and the person's general worldview. They may indeed recognize what Mackie calls the "queerness" of morality in their world. My own view is that this tension in their worldview is best alleviated by doubting naturalism and considering the possibility that there is a divine law-giver. However, I can well imagine that there are people who take themselves to have very strong reasons to reject theism. My own advice to such people would be as follows: "Do not give up your belief in morality, even if it does not make sense to you." I think that such people are not only likely to be morally better off, but perhaps also more likely eventually to see the problems with naturalism.

THE ROAD TO BE TRAVELED

I shall argue then that moral obligations understood in the Anscombian way do indeed require a divine law-giver, a being who possesses moral authority. Paradoxical as it may seem, however, I deny that a person who does not believe in God ought to give up belief in such moral obligations, since I believe that obligations are in some cases experienced realities which a person may reasonably continue to believe in, even if the person has no adequate explanation for the reality.

To make the case for the dependence of moral obligations on God a large number of topics must be treated. I need to show how God does account for moral obligations, as well as argue that secular substitutes for God are not satisfactory. I shall try to show the advantages of basing moral obligations on divine authority, and respond to the main objections that are commonly urged against giving God's laws an important role in ethics. A key part of this task will be arguing that God does indeed possess the required kind of authority.

However, many other issues must be discussed as well. These include the relations between moral obligations and other parts of morality, including the good and what is generally called "natural law theory." It is also important to treat the relation between moral obligations and human virtues, because the full significance of moral obligations does not become clear until we see the role they are intended to play in personal transformation. Although moral obligations are extremely important, their importance may be linked to ends beyond themselves.

To some degree the complex relationships between these issues means that all of this should be treated simultaneously. For example, in explaining a divine command account of moral obligation, it would be helpful to have in mind the relation between such a theory and natural law ethics as well as virtue ethics. Obviously, however, everything cannot be said at once. What I propose to do is tackle the issues in what seems a logical order, while giving previews about other issues to be discussed later. This will result in some unavoidable repetition, but it will also allow some important ideas to be emphasized through such repetition.

Here is the order I shall follow. In Chapter 2 I will give an account of a divine command view of moral obligations, and try to exhibit its strengths. This account will also touch on the question as to how God's commands could be made known to humans. I will also give a brief treatment of the place such an ethic may have in a pluralistic society such as is found in North America and most European countries, and offer an argument that a divine account of obligations is not "sectarian" in any objectionable sense.

A fuller account of a divine command account will require a look at the relation between it and what are sometimes viewed as alternative religious metaethical views, namely natural law theory and virtue ethics, a task that Chapter 3 will undertake. I will try to show that these three kinds of theories are not necessarily rivals, but can be understood as providing complementary answers to different questions, with all three kinds of views having important roles to play in ethics.

Chapter 4 will consider a number of objections to a divine command view of obligations, some ancient and some contemporary, and try to show that the alleged problems can be resolved. Chapter 5 will review some influential secular metaethical views of moral obligations. I shall argue that some of these views are fully compatible with a divine command account of moral obligations. I will then highlight weaknesses in those accounts that are genuine rivals to a divine command view, and show how divine authority can remedy those weaknesses.

In the concluding chapter I shall raise the question of moral skepticism: even if it is true that a divine command account would provide the best explanation of the existence of moral obligations, perhaps such obligations do not exist. I shall admit that such a moral skepticism cannot be proven to be wrong, but nevertheless argue that we have powerful reasons to reject such a view. I shall then revisit the question as to how divine commands can be known and defend the claim that humans have a natural capacity to know about morality. I shall finish with some reflections on the value of God-given moral principles of obligations, arguing that such principles are not burdensome limitations on human autonomy but a gift for which we should be grateful. We need to recover the vision of the moral law as a gift intended for human flourishing, a view that is clearly articulated in the attitude of the Jewish people towards the Torah.

2

What Is a Divine Command Theory of Moral Obligation?

How could God provide a foundation for moral obligations?[1] There are a variety of different kinds of answers to this question, but one of the most attractive and straightforward is to understand moral obligations as divine requirements. There are a variety of things that might aptly be described as divine requirements: divine commands and divine laws, among others. For some purposes it may be important to distinguish these.[2] I shall initially define divine requirements for humans, however described, simply as God's will for humans insofar as that will has been communicated to them. For simplicity of exposition, and because it is the language most often used in the tradition, I shall speak most often of God's expressed requirements as divine commands. Much of what I will say could, with some modifications, be translated into these other idioms, and I want "divine commands" here to be understood in an expansive way, i.e. as equivalent to communicated divine requirements. (I shall maintain that expressions of God's will that are not in the form of imperatives can function like commands.) Thus I shall pursue the question of how God might provide a foundation for moral obligations by exploring the viability of what is generally called a divine command account of

---

[1] Some paragraphs from the early part of this chapter are taken, with modifications, from "Moral Arguments for Theism and Divine Command Accounts of Moral Obligation," in Colin Ruloff (ed.), *Reason and Christian Belief: New Essays in Philosophical Theology* (Notre Dame, IN: University of Notre Dame Press, forthcoming).

[2] One might think that "divine expectations" should be part of this group, but I have been persuaded by Gregory Mellema that moral expectations should be distinguished from moral requirements, and thus that divine expectations differ in important ways from divine commands. See his *The Expectations of Morality* (Amsterdam: Rodopi, 2004), especially pp. 103–13.

moral obligations. (For the sake of brevity I will sometimes refer to such a view as a DCT, short for "divine command theory.")

There are also many different types of views that could properly be described as divine command theories of moral obligation, but the kind of view I find most attractive is the type defended by Robert Adams.[3] Adams sees moral obligations as identical to the commands of a good and loving God, or the commands of God understood as essentially good and loving. Alternatives to this view might hold that moral obligations, rather than being identical to divine commands, are caused to exist by divine commands, or that such obligations supervene on divine commands. I will give some attention to these alternative views in Chapter 4, but I shall begin with the simpler view that the relation between divine commands and moral obligations is one of identity.

It is important to recognize that this account is only an account of moral *obligations* and thus should not be confused with a general "voluntarist" view of ethics, in which all ethical truths are grounded in the divine will. As I will explain later, the kind of DCT I want to defend not only is consistent with but actually presupposes that there are ethical truths that do not depend on the divine will.[4] Adams himself rests his account of moral obligation on a Platonic theory of the good. Other divine command theorists, such as John Hare, while not rejecting Platonic views altogether, presuppose a more Aristotelian view of the good.[5] Some theory of the good must be presupposed, however, since an important part of what makes God's commands binding is that God is himself essentially good and thus his commands are directed to the good.

Part of the motivation for a DCT is the Anscombe intuition defended in Chapter 1, which implies that there is something distinctive about *obligations*. To say that I have a moral obligation to ๑ is not simply to say that I have a reason to ๑, or even to say that I have a decisive reason to ๑. Rather, an obligation is a distinctive kind of reason, with several important features. It is the kind of reason that

---

[3] Adams, *Finite and Infinite Goods*, pp. 231–76. In my *Kierkegaard's Ethic of Love* I argue that Kierkegaard holds a view similar to Adams and defend the plausibility of the view against secular rivals.

[4] This does not necessarily mean that no explanation of these ethical truths, such as truths about the good, can be given, but just that the explanation will not come from God's commands.

[5] See John Hare, *Why Bother Being Good? The Place of God in the Moral Life* (Downers Grove, IL: InterVarsity Press, 2002), pp. 134–53.

can bring closure to deliberation, since even to deliberate about whether I should do what I am morally obligated to do is usually a sign of moral weakness. To say that I have a moral obligation to ↄ is to say that I must ↄ, and it is to say that there is someone who has the right to expect me to ↄ, and who may rightly be disappointed in me and blame me if I fail to ↄ. For me to be subject to a moral obligation is to be liable to a kind of claim that someone has on me, a claim that has a binary, verdict-like character; it either holds or it does not hold. We saw in Chapter 1 that although moral obligations are aimed at the good, they are not reducible to the good. An act might be good to do, even the best act a person could possibly do in some situation, without necessarily being a moral obligation.

Adams accommodates this insight by defending a social theory of obligations, which is an attempt to explain moral obligations by situating them in relation to obligations in general, which come in several varieties, including legal obligations, social obligations, and family obligations.[6] How do these special kinds of claims we call obligations come into existence? The particular obligations that fall into these categories overlap partially (though by no means completely) with moral obligations and with each other. On a social theory of obligations these distinctive kinds of claims that persons can make on other persons are all the result of the particular social institutions and relations in which persons participate. Being a parent, for example, is a social role that is partly constituted by the obligations one takes on by becoming a parent. Hence, it is not accidental but essential that children have the right to certain things from their parents, and that parents have obligations to provide those things.

It is easy to see that someone who accepts this kind of social theory of obligation must reject a voluntarist view about normative claims in general. Someone who accepts a social theory of obligation is committed to the claim that there are social institutions that directly give rise to normative claims. There are normative truths about parenting that arise from the institution of parenting, and do not depend on the volitions of particular individuals. Someone who understands what it is to be a parent also understands that certain things are required of parents. The same thing will be true of the social relation of creature to creator. It will be true with respect to this relation, as in others, that

---

[6] See Adams, *Finite and Infinite Goods*, pp. 231–48.

someone who has graciously been given a great good should be grateful to the benefactor, and that someone who has acted in a loving way is deserving of being loved in return, and these truths are independent of any commands God has given. In Chapter 3 I shall appeal to this point in order to argue that a DCT should not be understood as an alternative to a natural law view of ethics. On the contrary, a DCT presupposes views that can legitimately be described as natural law views.

If God exists and is a genuine person, then the relation between creature and creator is a genuine social relation, and like other such relations, carries with it distinctive obligations. On the theistic conception of God, God is essentially good and loving; he has created human persons and given them every good they have, including their very existence. He has also given them the potential for the greatest possible good, an eternal life characterized by friendship with God and others who are friends of God and therefore love the good. A proper social relation with God is one that requires humans to recognize the enormous debt of gratitude they owe to God, as well as the value of an on-going relation to God. Most religious believers have seen this relation to God as one in which God rightly has authority over them. This authority might be explained in various ways, as stemming from God's ownership rights as creator, or as grounded in the gratitude owed to God for God's good gifts, or as grounded in the goods which a relation to God makes possible.[7] However God's authority is explained, most theistic religious believers have thought that God has a rightful claim on humans such that they have good reasons to obey his commands. The claim that God possesses moral authority in this way is certainly one that has been challenged, and making sense of the claim will require both argument and development. Nevertheless, one can see why most religious believers, and even many non-believers, have thought that if there is a God, such a being would have authority.

On Adams' view, the obligations that arise from this particular relation turn out to be identical to our moral obligations. The claim is not that "moral obligation" and "divine command" have the same meaning, for clearly they do not. Rather, the claim is that the two expressions refer to the same reality. The primary reason for thinking this is the case is simply that viewing moral obligations as divine commands makes more sense of these obligations than any alternative account.

---

[7] I discuss the grounds of God's authority on pp. 64–8.

STRENGTHS OF A DIVINE COMMAND THEORY OF
MORAL OBLIGATIONS

I shall briefly describe a number of ways in which seeing moral obligations as divine commands helps make sense of this kind of obligation.[8] I will first list some *desiderata* for a good candidate to be the foundation of moral obligation.[9] The characteristics I list are taken partly from Adams' account, and partly from the features I discussed in Chapter 1 when I described Anscombe's view of moral obligations. Obviously, this account is philosophically controversial, and some may be skeptical about one or more of the features I here identify. However, I believe that most people who believe in morality at all will agree that these are genuine features of morality as they experience it.

One important feature of moral obligations is that they are objective, in the sense that they are the kind of thing that people can be mistaken about. The mistakes can be of various kinds. Sometimes I am obligated to do something, but fail to realize I have the obligation. Sometimes people with "overactive consciences" believe they are obligated to do things that they have no obligation to do. And sometimes people correctly see that they have an obligation in a certain situation but are mistaken about the content of that obligation. So an adequate account of moral obligation should be able to explain how people can have true and false beliefs about their moral obligations.

A second important feature of moral obligations is that they provide compelling reasons of a distinctive kind for actions, of the kind already discussed in Chapter 1. A simple case of obligation will suffice to illustrate the point. Imagine that I have borrowed money from a friend. I now have the money to repay the friend and am obligated to do so. If I am morally obligated to perform an action, then not only do I have a reason to perform that action, the reason is (at least normally) an overriding one. It will not do to say that I don't need to repay the money because I don't want to, or because I can think of other things to do with the money. If I have a good reason for defaulting on my

---

[8] The argument that follows is similar in form to the one Adams himself gives for his view. See *Finite and Infinite Goods*, pp. 252–8.

[9] The following paragraphs are taken, with significant modifications, from C. Stephen Evans and Robert C. Roberts, "Ethics," in *The Oxford Companion of Kierkegaard*, ed. George Pattison and John Lippitt (Oxford: Oxford University Press, 2012).

obligation (say, my children will starve to death if I pay back the money), then the overriding reason must itself be a moral one. An account of moral obligation should help us understand the overriding, serious character of a moral reason for performing an action.

A third feature is closely related to the second. An account of moral obligation should not only explain why we have reasons to perform our moral duty; it should also explain why we should be motivated to do so. It is a striking fact about humans that they do not always do what they have reasons to do; hence being motivated to act morally and having a good reason to act morally are not the same things. An account of moral obligations should help us understand why we should (and do) care about our obligations, why moral reasons should (and often do) move us to action. This is particularly important, since moral subjectivists, such as emotivists and prescriptivists, often argue that moral theories that are realist and objectivist cannot account for the motivating power of morality.

Finally, an adequate account of moral obligation should help us understand the universality of morality. I do not mean by this that there cannot be moral obligations that are in some way unique and tailored to the individual. However, I think that morality is universal in at least two ways. First, all humans are subject to the claims of morality. No one is so "special" that he or she gets a free pass and can ignore those claims. Second, some of our moral obligations extend at least to all human persons. (Some in fact certainly extend further than this, incorporating animals.) If some racist person believes that the world would be a better place if the population were reduced, and proposes to achieve this end by killing people who are members of another race, I have an obligation to oppose this and do what I can reasonably do (taking into account other obligations I have) to stop such evil, even if I do not know the people he proposes to eliminate or have any relation to them except that they are fellow humans. So part of what we want explained is why all humans are subject to moral obligations, and why we have some moral obligations that bear on how we relate to all people, including people we don't even know, and people who cannot benefit us in any way.

The strengths of a DCT are readily apparent when judged by these criteria. First, moral obligations can be objective in relation to human beliefs and emotions, since there will be a fact of the matter about whether God has given some particular command, as well as about the content of the command. We can thus see why people can be both correct and mistaken in their moral beliefs, and why their moral feelings can be both appropriate and inappropriate.

Second, we can understand why moral reasons are overriding in character. If God has created humans such that their final goal is to enjoy a relationship with himself, then establishing and maintaining such a relation is supremely important to humans. If moral obligations are constitutive of this relation, much as other kinds of obligations are constitutive of other kinds of social relations, then those obligations take on an overriding importance if they make possible a relationship that has overriding importance.

For the same reasons, we can explain the motivating power of moral obligations. It makes perfectly good sense that I should want to satisfy the requirements of a being to whom I owe an unlimited debt of gratitude, and whose love for me is such that he intends me to enjoy an eternal happiness in communion with himself and others who love him.[10] This does not imply that all humans necessarily want to do what is morally right; the evidence that they do not is, sadly, all too compelling. A good account of moral obligations should explain why they are motivating, why most of the time most of us care about being moral, and why all of us should care about being moral, but it should not imply that people are always motivated to do what is morally right.

Hence a good account of moral obligations should allow for the possibility that people sometimes do not care about morality, or care enough, and a DCT satisfies this requirement as well. To begin, some people fail to realize that moral obligations are divine commands, and so miss the motivating power that comes from recognizing moral obligations as divine requirements. But even people who do realize moral obligations are divine requirements may not always be moved to do what is morally right. For some people do not care or care enough about God or a God-relationship, even if it is the case that such a relationship is the greatest good a human can have.

My argument that a person who understands a moral obligation as a divine command has a motive to keep the command should not be taken to imply that the motivation thus provided is the only motive we have for being moral. It seems possible (and, from the viewpoint of a theistic view

---

[10] It is clear that the DCT I am here explaining is committed to the existence of normative facts that do not depend on God's commands, a theme that will be developed at length in the next chapter. Those facts may also require explanation, but the explanation will not appeal to divine commands.

quite plausible) for God to endow humans with a moral psychology, in which doing what is morally right can lead to a kind of satisfaction, and doing what is morally wrong can lead to negative feelings of guilt and shame. Thus, the claim that a divine command account of moral obligations helps explain how such obligations can be motivating does not mean that God could not supply humans with a variety of motives to be moral. This is important, because, as I have already argued in the first chapter, people who do not believe in God, and thus do not realize that moral obligations are divine commands, can still have reasons to behave morally that are sufficient to motivate moral behavior.

Finally, we can understand why moral obligations are universal, in both senses identified above. All humans are God's creatures and thus all participate in the social relation that grounds moral obligations. All of them are thus subject to God's laws. Further, if God gives human persons some commands that apply to their relation to all humans, then they will have moral obligations towards all humans. Are there reasons to think God would give any such commands? There certainly are, if we assume, as Judaism and Christianity do, that all humans are made in God's image. God's commands must be directed to the good, since God is essentially good and loving. It is certainly good to love and appreciate the good. It thus makes sense that God would command humans to love God himself, who is supremely good, and all human persons who share in the divine image, and thus must also be good in some deep way. Thus the command to love our neighbors as ourselves, common to Judaism and Christianity, understood in such a way that all human persons are our neighbors, is precisely what one would expect from a good and loving God who creates all humans in his image.

DOES GOD HAVE SOME DISCRETION ABOUT WHAT HE COMMANDS?

On the version of a DCT I am developing, God's commands must be directed at the good, and thus the good is in some sense prior to the morally right and constrains what is morally right. But how tight is this constraint? Does God have some discretion about what he commands?

Many of the well-known defenders of a DCT have thought that the answer to this question was affirmative. Duns Scotus, for example, who took the Decalogue to be a summary of God's commands, held that at least some of those commands could have been otherwise.[11] Scotus divided the Decalogue into two sections or "tables," and held that while the commands in the first table are those that God necessarily issues, those in the second table could have been different. Perhaps Scotus thought about things in the following way. Our highest good is to know and love God, and this requires us to honor and worship God. If God commands the good he must therefore necessarily command us to worship God alone. However, if we take a command like the one not to covet or steal our neighbor's possessions, things might have been otherwise. Perhaps God could have commanded us to refrain from having any private property at all, holding all earthly goods in common as did the early members of the Christian church (according to Acts 4:32–5), as an alternative to the command not to take our neighbor's property. Of course someone might object that such a command would not have served the good as well as the actual command not to steal, and this claim might well be true. However, without having a God-like knowledge ourselves, it is difficult to be sure about how well some command might serve the good. It is easy enough to see that the command not to steal does so, but it is harder to know with confidence that no other command would have served the good equally well. Suppose, for example, God had allowed some kinds of property (along with a prohibition against theft) but proscribed owning property of other kinds.

This kind of discretion is even more plausible with respect to commands God could have issued, not as an alternative to his actual commands, but in addition to those commands. For example, arguably God might well have commanded every human, after reaching maturity, to spend some period of time, such as two years, doing some kind of service to their fellow humans. Such a period of altruistic service might well serve the good, not only by providing practical help to people, but by developing maturity and cementing a concern for others in the people doing the service.

---

[11] See "The Decalogue and the Law of Nature," in *Duns Scotus on the Will and Morality*, selected and translated with an introduction by Allan B. Wolter, OFM (Washington: Catholic University of American Press, 1986), pp. 268–87. This section is a translation of Scotus, *Ordinatio* III, suppl. Dist. 37, according to Wolter. Wolter also provides a useful summary and discussion of this section of Scotus on pp. 60–4 of the same volume.

We can see then why proponents of a DCT, such as Scotus, or, more recently Robert Adams and John Hare,[12] have defended the view that God has some discretion with respect to what he commands, and thus that some of our moral duties could have been otherwise. However, it is important to recognize that even these thinkers have not claimed that God's discretion is unlimited. Some of what God commands he commands necessarily, and thus at least some of our moral duties have some kind of necessity as well.

Proponents of a DCT may well of course disagree about how extensive is the range of God's discretion. Some might think that God's discretion is very broad indeed, while others might think it exceedingly small. As a limiting case on the small end of this spectrum, we could imagine someone who thinks God has no discretion at all. Such a view could be considered a weak or minimal form of a DCT.

Or perhaps we do not have to imagine such a case. On some interpretations, this is precisely the view of Thomas Aquinas.[13] On this reading of Aquinas, given the truths about the good, once God has decided to create a world in which the created objects, including humans, have the natures they have, then his commands for that world are determined. Of course God could have given humans different commands on such a view, but in order for him to do so, he would have to create different natures for some things, thereby changing what is good for them.

THE MODAL STATUS THESIS AND THE DISCRETION THESIS

Reflecting on this issue is important, because it allows us to distinguish two different elements in a DCT. Even a thinker who thinks God's commands could not be different might still hold that those

---

[12] See Adams, *Finite and Infinite Goods*, pp. 255–6, and Hare, *God's Call*, pp. 66–75.

[13] John Finnis seems to suggest such a view in *Natural Law and Natural Rights* (Oxford: Oxford University Press, 1980), pp. 54–5. As is often the case, this reading of Aquinas is not without challenge. Jean Porter has argued that Aquinas does believe God has some discretion with respect to what he commands, because she believes that nature underdetermines the moral law. See her *Nature as Reason: A Thomistic Theory of the Natural Law* (Grand Rapids, MI: Eerdmans, 2005), p. 126.

commands give a new moral quality to the acts that are commanded. I want to distinguish the claim that God has some discretion in what he commands from the claim that God's commands provide a necessary condition for an act to have the kind of moral status that make the act morally obligatory or morally prohibited. I shall call the claim that God has some choice about what he commands the "discretion thesis," while I shall call the claim that an act that God commands acquires a particular moral status in part by virtue of his commands the "modal status thesis."[14] Much of the attention in the discussions of DCTs has been given to the discretion thesis. I want to claim, however, that it is only the modal status thesis that is essential to a DCT. Someone who holds to the modal status thesis without the discretion thesis still should be considered as holding to a type of DCT, even if it is a minimal and non-standard form of the view. The discretion thesis, though significant, is not essential to a DCT. What is essential is doing justice to the Anscombe intuition, by providing an explanation of the special status of moral obligations. The question about how extensive God's discretion is with respect to moral obligations, and even the question as to whether God has any discretion at all, are less fundamental than the question as to whether God by his commands endows human acts with a special moral character.

  To see that this is so, let us imagine that the discretion thesis is false, and that what God commands is fixed by whatever necessary moral truths there are combined with the moral truths that hold because of the character of the creaturely natures God has actualized in creating the universe. On such a view, if God commands us not to steal, then it is good not to steal, so good that no other command on God's part is possible. Even apart from God's command, stealing would then be bad and humans would have good reasons not to steal. Even in this case, however, God's commands could still accomplish something important. The command not to steal raises the stakes, so to speak. For if I steal something and God has commanded me not to steal, I not only do something that is bad, I do something that harms my relation to God. I disappoint God, fail to fulfill his expectations for me, and make it impossible for me to relate properly

<hr>

[14] I introduced this distinction and the terminology in *Natural Signs and Knowledge of God* (Oxford: Oxford University Press, 2010), pp. 137–8, and also employ it in "Moral Arguments for Theism and Divine Command Theories of Moral Obligation," in *Reason and Christian Belief*, ed. Ruloff.

to God. The features that we found to characterize obligations can be accounted for: for example, the fact that God commands an act to be done explains the binary, "verdict-like" character the act possesses, why it is that I may rightly be blamed for failing to do the act, and why I should be motivated to do the act.

To be sure, even apart from God's command the act would have a moral character. I might well have strong, even overriding reasons to avoid performing the act, and someone observing me might well judge me foolish and unwise to engage in stealing. There is even a clear sense in which stealing would be bad, in that I would by stealing be going against the good and thereby showing a lack of commitment to the good. However, none of this changes the fact that God's command introduces a new character to the situation that the act alone without the command would not possess.

Focusing on the fundamental character of the modal status thesis actually helps us see why the discretion thesis might be important as well. Suppose there is a case where two possible acts are at least approximately equally good or equally bad. Without a divine command in such a case it would appear that the acts have the same moral quality. For example, let us imagine a parent is deciding whether to have a baby boy circumcised. Suppose for the sake of argument that the health benefits and other benefits of being circumcised and uncircumcised are roughly equal. There are, let us suppose, some benefits to circumcision, but those benefits have to be balanced against the pain and expense of the procedure, and perhaps some other benefits that accrue to not being circumcised. It would then appear that the choice about circumcision is one that is morally indifferent. However, if God were to command parents to have their male children circumcised the situation would be totally changed. For now a choice not to have one's son circumcised is, for the parent who understands God's requirements, a sign that the parent does not care very much about pleasing God. One's devotion to God would be shown most clearly in a situation where God has given a command, but, apart from this command, there would be little or no reason to go one way rather than another.

Someone might well wonder why God would give commands in such cases, but a plausible answer is not difficult to find. Divine commands in such cases would offer a special test of one's devotion to God. In the more normal case where God's commands are aligned with what is good, then one has two kinds of reasons to perform the act. One may be motivated by the intrinsic goodness of the act or by the desire to fulfill God's requirements. However, in a case where there are equally good possibilities God might command, it is the command itself that must be motivating.

HOW ARE GOD'S COMMANDS PROMULGATED?

It is generally accepted that laws must be promulgated to be authoritative. This is clear in the case of legal obligations. A law that was passed in secret and never revealed to anyone would hardly be binding on the citizens of a state. It is true that it is often said that ignorance of a law is not a valid excuse for not obeying the law, but this principle surely assumes that the law in question is a matter of public record and that the individual who should obey the law could have known about it.

Something similar must hold for moral laws as well. One can see this by comparing a DCT to a divine will account of moral obligations. Suppose one says that moral obligations are established by God's will alone, rather than God's commands. A morally right act is one that conforms to God's will and a morally wrong act is one that does not so conform. The difficulty with such a view is that it seems to make morality impossible unless God's will is somehow expressed in such a way that it can be known. If God's will constitutes our moral obligations, and God's will is a closely guarded secret, then the best humans could do would be to guess about their moral obligations. As Robert Adams notes, someone who plays a game with you in which they expect you to behave in a certain way, and views you negatively if you do not, is not playing a very nice game if the person fails to communicate those expectations to you.[15] We would regard such a person as manipulative or even sadistic.

So if God's will is to be the basis of morality, that will must be one that can be known. But such an expression of God's will is simply what might be called an expression of God's requirements.[16] One

---

[15] See Adams, *Finite and Infinite Goods*, p. 261.

[16] Here it might be thought that one could speak of God's expectations instead of God's requirements. However, God might expect someone to behave in a certain way, or prefer someone to act in a certain way, without requiring this. So requirements and expectations are not identical. One might think of God's expectations as God's desires

form these requirements often take will be explicit commands. However, in cases where the person whose requirements are at issue has the right kind of claim on the individual subject to the requirement, it does not seem necessary for what is willed to be expressed as an explicit command. We can see this in the common expression, "Your wish is my command." In other words, what we have been calling commands do not necessarily have to take the form of grammatical imperatives. If my relation to someone is of such a nature that it is vital for me to please that person, then a mere expression of a desire on the part of that person may have the effect of a command. To be relevant to morality, God's will must be expressed in some way, but any expression of God's will would be significantly like a divine command for a human being who is subject to God's authority and for whom a God-relation is the highest good. In what follows when I speak of "divine commands" I will use the term "command" in an extended sense to refer to what God wills humans to do insofar as his will has been communicated to humans.

So how might God communicate his requirements to humans? Some might think that God's commands would have to be communicated through a special revelation, for example in the Hebrew Bible, or the Qur'an, or the Christian Bible. There are good reasons one might think this would be the case. Indeed, later in the book I will respond to an objection that is rooted in the view that if God does not communicate his commands in this way, their authority is undermined.[17] However, a proposal that God's commands must be promulgated solely through special revelation has one decisive disadvantage. If God's commands can only be known through a special revelation, then humans who have no access to that revelation can have no access to God's commands. If God's commands are identical to moral obligations, then those humans have no way of knowing what their moral obligations are. However, it is hard to see how an unknowable moral obligation could be an obligation at all. Unknowable moral obligations would, from an existential point of view, not be much different from non-existent moral obligations; neither would provide me with moral guidance. Certainly, those who have no way of knowing about their

---

that do not amount to a decisive preference. Gregory Mellema has given a clear and rigorous treatment of the notion of moral expectations in *The Expectations of Morality*.

[17] See Chapter 4, pp. 110–17.

moral obligations should not be blamed or held responsible for failing to live up to those obligations.

It certainly seems possible that God might provide a special revelation, or even multiple special revelations, and thereby provide knowledge of his requirements. I believe that the knowledge provided by such a revelation would have some epistemic priority over other ways of coming to know God's requirements, such that if there is a conflict, the teachings of a recognized special revelation, properly interpreted and understood, should generally be regarded, by those who accept that revelation as genuine, as trumping claims made on other grounds. (This claim requires an "all other things being equal" proviso, since one's confidence that one has interpreted a special revelation properly might be low in some cases, and thus it is conceivable that what is known by special revelation would not always take precedence over what is known in other ways.) So I do want to give special revelation an important role as a means whereby God might promulgate his commands. However, anyone who wants to advocate a plausible version of a DCT must deny that God's commands are promulgated exclusively through a special revelation. At least this is the case if we think that morality is a fundamental element of human existence, not something possessed only by those who have access to an historically contingent revelation that is limited by time and geography.

What are the means, other than a special revelation, by which God might communicate his commands? Richard Mouw lists the following methods as possibilities: natural law, the *magisterium* of an ecclesiastical body, specific commands God might communicate to individuals in some way, "examining our natural inclinations," and listening to our conscience.[18] Most of these means are somewhat unclear and stand in need of some elucidation. How, for example, might God communicate specific commands to individuals? A variety of methods are conceivable: God might speak through a "voice" (either audible or an inaudible "inner voice"), a dream, or simply by giving the individual an irresistible conviction that some particular course of action is God's will for that individual.

However, though such an individual revelation is conceivable as one means whereby someone could come to know God's command, this is unlikely to be the normal or usual way in which people come to

[18] Richard Mouw, *The God Who Commands* (Notre Dame, IN: University of Notre Dame Press, 1990), p. 8.

know their moral duties. Young children usually come to know their moral duties from other humans, and it is not uncommon even for adults to be taught their moral obligations by others. So one way humans could come to know God's requirements is simply to be taught by other humans what those requirements are. (This could take two forms: (1) teaching God's requirements to others, understood as God's requirements. (2) Teaching what are in fact God's requirements to others (i.e. our moral obligations) without recognizing that they are in reality God's requirements.)

However, it does not seem plausible to say that teaching by other humans could be the only means of learning about God's requirements. After all, those who teach others may have been taught themselves, but it would seem that at some point someone must have learned their duties in some other way. If moral obligations are divine commands, there is no reason to deny that the content of those commands, once known, could be passed down from generation to generation, whether recognized as God's commands or not, but it does not appear that this would be the only way God's commands could be known.

In addition to special revelation and learning from others, what ways of learning about God's commands might there be? Robert Adams endorses all the ways that Mouw mentions, and adds to them the important addition that "some theists might well suppose that God's commands are promulgated largely, though not exclusively, through human social requirements."[19] This claim calls to mind the Hegelian view that our highest ethical requirements, which Hegel calls *Sittlichkeit*, are embedded in the traditions and customs of a people in whose history "Spirit" has come to full development. "Ethical life" for Hegel is to be found in the "laws and institutions" that constitute "duties binding on the will of the individual."[20] I am sympathetic to some aspects of this idea. Specifically, I agree with Adams that one should not think of God's requirements as consisting of a "separate system" that is parallel to but higher than human systems of social requirements.[21] As I have already said, social relationships per se generate obligations of all types, and there is every reason to think that legal obligations, family obligations, and other types of obligations will overlap extensively with

---

[19] Adams, *Finite and Infinite Goods*, p. 264.
[20] *Hegel's Philosophy of Right*, trans. T. M. Knox (Oxford: Oxford University Press, 1967), p. 106.
[21] Adams, *Finite and Infinite Goods*, p. 264.

moral obligations. (It is easy to see that the degree of overlap might differ significantly from one society to another.) Moreover, as I have already endorsed the view that much of our understanding of moral obligations is learned from others, there is every reason to agree that people often become aware of their actual moral obligations by being taught about humanly required obligations. At least this will be so to the degree that there is significant overlap between those human obligations and their actual moral obligations.

However, I have significant doubts about whether merely being part of a human system of obligations gives us a decisive reason to think that an obligation is one that is imposed by God, though it certainly might give us a *prima facie* reason to think this is the case. As I noted above, people might often come to know what are in fact their actual moral obligations by being taught what their societies require of them. However, it is important for a DCT (and indeed for any viable account of moral obligations) that it preserve the distinction between genuine moral obligations and systems of obligations grounded in such human institutions as the family and the state, however much these two types of obligation may overlap. The reason for this is that it is vital that we allow for the possibility of a moral critique of humanly grounded systems of obligation, which would obviously be impossible or at least very difficult if morality is simply identified with these human systems. The fact that an action is required or prohibited by the state or familial customs then is at most a *prima facie* reason for thinking that such an act is a moral duty.

Of the various possibilities Mouw and Adams discuss, I believe that listening to the dictates of conscience is worthy of special attention. The term "conscience" has been used in a variety of ways in the history of western philosophy. I shall use it to denote a faculty whereby humans can immediately discern the rightness or wrongness of particular acts or of general principles about how one should act (perhaps by way of discerning the right-making or wrong-making character of some general feature of the act or act-type). This definition leaves many things open. One might, for example, think that conscience operates only with respect to particular acts, or only with respect to more general principles. An advocate of conscience might think the faculty is highly reliable (even infallible) or think (as I do) that it is highly fallible. The definition is consistent with a variety of views as to how humans have or acquire these abilities. Conscience in my sense is closely connected to what many philosophers have called "ethical intuitionism."[22] Though intuitionism is much disputed, it is worth noting that even many philosophers who reject intuitionism and the view that humans have a moral faculty as such still rely on ethical intuitions themselves or at least regard them as having some epistemic weight.

The claim that humans have a faculty that could be variously designated as a "moral sense" or "conscience," though certainly controversial, has a long philosophical history. Many medieval philosophers discussed "conscience" and "synderesis" (often distinguished) as powers to arrive at moral judgments. In the modern period, Anthony Ashley Cooper, the Earl of Shaftesbury, gave an influential defense of a "moral sense," and exercised a strong influence on such thinkers as Francis Hutcheson. Hutcheson influenced Thomas Reid, who defended what Terence Cuneo has termed an "agency-centered" intuitionist view of ethics.[23] Reid in turn had an influence on H. A. Prichard and thereby on such twentieth-century intuitionists as G. E. Moore and W. D. Ross.

To take conscience as one way in which God might make known his commands to humans is to regard such a faculty as one God intended humans to have so that they could have some knowledge of their moral obligations. Though this is fully compatible with various naturalistic causal stories about how humans might have acquired such a faculty, this view requires that conscience be in some way part of human nature, an expression of what might be termed God's design plan for humans.

Such a view by no means implies that human moral judgments are completely independent of social and cultural influences; one can easily imagine various moral traditions that might enhance or distort the functions of conscience. Even if humans have a natural capacity for discerning their moral obligations, this capacity very likely will require education and cultural development to be actualized. Moral intuitions here can be compared to mathematical insights, which are

---

[22] For a clear discussion of ethical intuitionism and defense of the claim that this plays a role in our moral knowledge, see Robert Audi, *Moral Knowledge and Ethical Character* (Oxford: Oxford University Press, 1997), pp. 32–58. Also see Robert Audi, *The Good in the Right: A Theory of Intuition and Intrinsic Value* (Princeton, NJ: Princeton University Press, 2005), which contains an invaluable history of intuitionism as well as a valuable constructive theory. More recently Audi has responded to objections in "Intuition, Inference, and Rational Disagreement in Ethics," *Ethical Theory and Moral Practice* 11 (2008), pp. 475–92.

[23] Terence Cuneo, "Reid's Ethics," *The Stanford Encyclopedia of Philosophy* (Spring 2011 Edition), ed. Edward N. Zalta <http://plato.stanford.edu/archives/spr2011/entries/reid-ethics/>.

arguably grounded in a natural human capacity, but which clearly require some nurture and education to be actualized. The fact that our moral capacities require education and cultural development in turn implies that the way the capacity functions will be influenced, perhaps heavily, by such factors.

The effect of cultural traditions can certainly be seen in the differences in moral beliefs and practices found in various cultures. However, it is also undeniable that there are profound areas of consensus between various moral cultures, even those that developed in relative independence of each other, which might well be attributed to some common human faculty. The vast majority of human cultures have recognized duties to be truthful, to keep one's word, to practice hospitality, and many others.[24]

The notion of conscience is by no means limited to western philosophy or even western culture. Kwame Gyekye claims that something very much like the notion of conscience plays a central role in the ethical thinking and practices of traditional African cultures. He gives as an example of this "the Akan notion of *tiboa*: conscience, moral sense—a sense of right and wrong."[25] Gyekye makes it clear that this African notion of *tiboa* gives rise to judgments about obligations that satisfy what I have called the Anscombe intuition about moral duties. For example, it is *tiboa* that gives rise to "self-sanctioning" in morality by inducing a sense of guilt in those who fail to follow its dictates. Nor is this concept present only in Akan culture, according to Gyekye, since the Rwandan people also have a word for conscience, "*kamera*," that refers to something that is "internally felt" and "situated in the heart."[26]

The view that humans have some kind of native capacity to make moral judgments has been given new impetus by recent developments

---

[24] An impressive list of the agreements of this sort can be found in C. S. Lewis, *The Abolition of Man* (New York: MacMillan Publishing Co., 1947), pp. 95–121. Lewis called these agreed-on moral practices "the Tao." James Rachels argues that at least three moral values are universal or nearly so in human cultures: taking care of the young, truth-telling, and a prohibition against murder. See his "The Challenge of Cultural Relativism," Chapter 2 in his *The Elements of Moral Philosophy*, 2nd edn. (New York: McGraw-Hill, 1993), pp. 15–29.

[25] Kwame Gyekye, "African Ethics," *The Stanford Encyclopedia of Philosophy* (Summer 2011 Edition), ed. Edward N. Zalta <http://plato.stanford.edu/archives/sum2011/entries/african-ethics/>.

[26] Gyekye cites J. J. Maquet, "The Kingdom in Ruanda," in Daryll Forde (ed.), *African Worlds: Studies in the Cosmological Ideas and Social Values of African Peoples* (Oxford: Oxford University Press, 1954), p. 183, for this claim about Rwandan people.

in evolutionary psychology. In contrast to the behaviorism that dominated psychology in the middle of the twentieth century, recent psychology has been increasingly drawn to the idea that humans have "modular specific" cognitive capacities developed under the pressure of evolutionary adaptation. On such a view, moral beliefs and even religious beliefs themselves may be things that human beings are "hard-wired" to acquire in the right circumstances.[27] In light of this scientific theorizing, one can at least say that the idea that humans have a natural capacity for moral judgments is not far-fetched or implausible.[28]

The claim that God promulgates his requirements for humans through conscience and other natural means and does not rely solely on special revelation means that a divine command theory of moral obligation is not one that is overtly "sectarian" in the sense that it would require a link between moral commitments and religious commitments, either of a particular nature or even a general belief in God. I have already argued that one does not have to believe in God to have a rational belief that there are moral obligations.[29] If God reveals his commands to humans through conscience and other natural means, this means that his role in morality may be somewhat "hidden" or at least not perfectly transparent to many humans.

---

[27] For an example of this kind of theorizing about morality, see Leda Cosmides and John Tooby, "Can a General Deontic Logic Capture the Facts of Human Moral Reasoning? How the Mind Interprets Social Exchange Rules and Detects Cheaters," in Walter Sinnott-Armstrong (ed.), *Moral Psychology, Volume 1: The Evolution of Morality—Adaptations and Innateness* (Cambridge, MA: MIT Press, 2008), pp. 53–119. For applications to belief in God itself, see Scott Atran, *In Gods We Trust: The Evolutionary Landscape of Religion* (Evolution and Cognition) (Oxford: Oxford University Press, 2002).

[28] Sharon Street, in "A Darwinian Dilemma for Realist Theories of Value" (*Philosophical Studies* 127, pp. 109–66), argues that evolutionary theory presents a problem for any realist account of ethics, and a DCT is of course a realist theory. However, David Enoch has argued that Street actually provides the basis for an account of how the capacity to grasp moral truths construed realistically might have evolved. See Enoch, *Taking Morality Seriously: A Defense of Robust Realism* (Oxford: Oxford University Press, 2011), especially pp. 163–77. Enoch's argument interprets the evolutionary process in a way that presupposes a naturalistic metaphysic; at least it does not presume a theistic view. So a good case can be made that evolution is compatible with realism even if theism is false. However, if God exists and created the world through an evolutionary process, then the evolutionary process must be one that is suited to achieving God's ends, including (very plausibly) the end of helping humans know their moral duties. This issue comes up again in Chapter 6.

[29] See Chapter 1, pp. 20–2.

However, I argue later that this is not surprising, because God has good reasons to do that.[30]

It is crucial to be clear on just what kind of relationship I am claiming holds between God and moral obligation. If God promulgates his commands through general revelation and in a way that allows for some lack of transparency in the source of the commands, this underscores the fact that the dependence of morality on God is ontological in nature; people can know about morality without knowing that morality depends upon God. Unless we are clear on this issue, any claims about whether morality is or is not dependent upon God will be confused. Such confusion can be seen in Kwame Gyekye's claim that "the values and principles of African morality are not founded on religion."[31] The reason Gyekye gives for this view is that he believes that traditional African religion is a "non-revealed religion," since "it does not seem that anyone in any African community has ever claimed to have received a revelation from the Supreme Being intended either for the people of the community or for all humanity." However, even if Gyekye is right about the character of traditional African religion, it does not follow that traditional African morality is, as he says, "an autonomous moral system" that "does not derive from religion." Gyekye may be right that traditional African morality is not dependent on the revelation claims of any particular religion, but it does not follow from this that moral obligations are not ontologically derived from God, or even that Africans do not believe that moral obligations derive from God. For it is perfectly possible to believe that moral obligations come from God but are communicated by God through such means as conscience.

A RELIGIOUSLY GROUNDED MORALITY IN A PLURALISTIC SOCIETY?

Gyekye's comment about morality and religion in the context of African societies raises questions about the relation of morality to

---

[30] I discuss why God might be partially hidden in Chapter 4, pp. 114–17. For a fuller discussion of the issue, see my *Natural Signs and Knowledge of God*, pp. 12–17 and 154–69. Of course I am not the only one to make such an argument. For discussions of why God might be partially hidden, see Daniel Howard-Snyder and Paul K. Moser (eds), *Divine Hiddenness: New Essays* (Cambridge: Cambridge University Press, 2002).

[31] Gyekye, "African Ethics."

religion in the kind of democratic, pluralistic society that has become increasingly pervasive in North America and Western Europe. Is the idea of a religiously grounded morality simply a non-starter in such a society?

Certainly there are some who would say that there is no place for a religiously grounded morality in a pluralistic society. Richard Rorty, for example, famously argued at one time that religion is a "conversation-stopper" that should play no significant role in "the public square."[32] A host of thinkers have followed John Rawls in holding that, at least with respect to fundamental political issues, the citizens of a liberal, democratic state must appeal to "public reasons" to justify their positions, and reasons that are rooted in religious commitments are seen as falling outside the sphere of public reasons.[33]

What exactly is a public reason? Jeffrey Stout helpfully summarizes Rawls' view, as Rawls developed it in the original edition of *Political Liberalism*, as the claim that "our reasoning in the public forum should appeal strictly to ideals and principles that no reasonable person could reasonably reject."[34] If one combines this principle with the widely accepted claim that people who hold widely different religious beliefs or no religious beliefs at all can be reasonable, it looks as if no appeal to religious beliefs can justify the moral principles that ground our political positions. Does this mean that a religiously grounded morality is not viable in a pluralistic, democratic society?

One might try to evade the problem for a religiously grounded morality by noting that Rawls' restriction does not hold for morality in general but only for those moral principles that are being employed in political decision-making. This seems to allow for the legitimacy of a morality based on religion at least with respect to "private" matters that concern only the relations of individuals. However, I shall not advance this kind of argument, for I do not believe that the distinction

---

[32] See Richard Rorty, *Philosophy and Social Hope* (New York: Penguin, 1999), pp. 168–74. Rorty subsequently softened his position so as to admit that individual citizens in a democratic society can legitimately appeal to their religious reasons to justify positions. See his "Religion in the Public Square: A Reconsideration," *The Journal of Religious Ethics* 31:1 (2003), pp. 141–9.

[33] See John Rawls, *Political Liberalism* (New York: Columbia University Press, 1993). Rawls softens this position somewhat in later editions of this work, but still maintains a somewhat restrictive view of the role of religion in the public square.

[34] Jeffrey Stout, *Democracy and Tradition* (Princeton, NJ: Princeton University Press, 2004), p. 65.

between what is "public" and what is "private" is either clear or sharp, and in any case a morality that has no implications for such matters as social justice would be a truncated ethic that would hardly be worth defending.

The first point to be made in response to a view like that of Rawls is that it is self-undermining. The principle that we must only appeal to ideals and principles that no reasonable person can reject is a principle that many reasonable people reject.[35] It follows that anyone who accepts the principle should reject it. However, the principle Rawls advances is not only self-refuting, but impossibly restrictive, since, given the extent of moral disagreement in contemporary societies, it seems dubious that there are *any* substantive action-guiding ideals and principles that no reasonable person could reject.

What kinds of reasons can legitimately play a role when citizens in a democratic, pluralistic society seek to justify the principles that ground both individual actions and political policies? In such a society, it is easy to understand why appeals to religious beliefs should sometimes, perhaps frequently, be avoided. For an argument to persuade others, the argument must appeal to premises that those others accept or can be brought to accept, or at the very least to considerations that others will find appealing. If I believe that abortion is a great moral evil, and wish to discourage or even prohibit it, it is not likely that I will succeed if my main argument is that abortion is condemned by some ecclesiastical authority, if that authority is not accepted by the majority of citizens. I must look for common ground if I want to be successful, and that will often push me away from appeals to religious beliefs that are not widely shared.

However, as Jeffrey Stout helpfully points out, the fact that I must look for arguments that have the potential to persuade others does not entail that I must give the *same* arguments for all others.[36] It seems quite possible that the reasons that might appeal to one individual will be different from those that might appeal to others. In a democratic society, I have an obligation to give reasons to others and to listen to the reasons of others, but it must not be forgotten that

---

[35] For example, it is rejected by Jeffrey Stout in *Democracy and Tradition*, pp. 67–77. Nicholas Wolterstorff argues strongly against this principle in "Why We Should Reject What Liberalism Tells Us about Speaking and Acting for Religious Reasons," in Paul J. Weithman (ed.), *Religion and Contemporary Liberalism* (Notre Dame, IN: University of Notre Dame Press, 1997), pp. 162–81.

[36] Stout, p. 73.

these others are particular human beings, not the phantom group of "all reasonable people."

When we attend to the actual practice of giving and receiving reasons, it is clear that a divine command view of morality places no unacceptable sectarian restrictions on morality. First of all, as I argued earlier in this chapter, it is part and parcel of the theory that the normative principles of morality can be recognized as valid by people who hold a variety of religious beliefs, or no religious beliefs at all. If God's commands are promulgated through conscience and other forms of general revelation, then a DCT rejects the claim that one must be religious to be moral, and it rejects the claim that one must be religious to have reasonable moral beliefs.

A DCT does claim that the correct metaethical explanation of moral obligations is that they are divine commands. However, even this claim is not sectarian. It is a strictly philosophical claim, defended through reason as is the case for other metaethical theories. Of course it is true that a DCT is unlikely, in the current philosophical milieu, to win universal or even general acceptance, but that is equally true of every other metaethical theory on offer, whether that theory be secular or religious in character. In any case it hardly seems reasonable to refuse to consider the reasons given for a theory on the grounds that those who have not considered those reasons (or even some of those who have considered those reasons) will not believe the theory. Such a restriction on a religiously inspired account of morality would indeed be a philosophical "conversation-stopper."

DOES MORALITY REQUIRE FOUNDATIONS?

In the previous section I made common cause with Jeffrey Stout, who stalwartly defends the view that religious believers may use and appeal to their religious beliefs in the public arena. However, one might think that Stout also poses a challenge for my project, for Stout argues that morality can be justified through an appeal to a type of pragmatism that makes any appeal to "metaphysics" unnecessary.[37] Stout seems to think that it is permissible for religious believers to

---

[37]   See Stout, Chapter 11, "Ethics Without Metaphysics," pp. 246–69.

think of their moral obligations as divine commands, but he clearly thinks that it is possible to make good sense of morality without a religious foundation, and indeed without any kind of foundation whatsoever beyond the social practices of actual human societies.

Stout's account of morality closely follows his interpretation of contemporary Hegelian philosopher Robert Brandom, who gives Hegel's ethical philosophy a pragmatic reading.[38] Hegel's ethics gives a distinctive role to what Hegel calls *Sittlichkeit*, which is embodied in "the laws and customs" of modern societies. *Sittlichkeit* for Hegel embodies in a concrete way the demand of reason, which has been actualizing itself in human history. Brandom, without embracing Hegel's metaphysics of "Absolute Spirit," also sees ethics as an attempt to make explicit the norms that are embedded in the social practices of contemporary societies. Stout similarly sees our ethical norms as "creatures of discursive social practices," in that they are the product of our attempts to reflect on the norms that are already implicit in our practices.

In one sense I believe that Stout is correct. I believe that humans, both as individuals and societies, have some moral knowledge, and this moral knowledge is embedded in our beliefs and practices. I have already repeatedly argued that humans can reasonably believe and even know at least some of their moral obligations, regardless of whether they have any adequate explanation of the source of those obligations. If this is the case, then it certainly is plausible that reflection on our moral practices will sometimes, perhaps frequently in some societies, give us insight into our moral obligations. Robert Adams, who is, as we have seen, the foremost defender of a DCT, goes so far as to say that *Sittlichkeit* might be one of the ways in which God makes knowledge of his commands possible. (Although I have already expressed some skepticism about this aspect of Adams' view.)

However, to say that we can gain knowledge of morality by reflection on social practices does not mean that those social practices can adequately *ground* morality. What is lacking is an account of the *authority* of the norms that are embedded in our social practices. Hegel provides such an account by a metaphysics in which human

---

[38] See Robert Brandom, *Making It Explicit: Reasoning, Representing, and Discursive Commitment* (Cambridge, MA: Harvard University Press, 1994). Stout discusses Brandom at many places in *Democracy and Tradition*, perhaps most significantly in Chapter 12, "Ethics as a Social Practice," pp. 270–86.

societies are interpreted as expressions of God or Spirit. It was in fact exactly this metaphysics which inspired Kierkegaard's protest on behalf of the individual against Hegel. Kierkegaard insisted that an authentic individual such as Socrates could be justified in rejecting the norms and practices of his society. To say otherwise is to make of society itself a god.

Stout, however, clearly wants to distance himself from anything like Hegel's metaphysics. Just as clearly, Stout wants to avoid any deification of existing social norms. He wants to affirm that in some sense moral norms are "objective," which means that everyone in our society could be mistaken about those norms.[39] The crucial question is whether this objectivity requires that moral obligations have some kind of reality, or at least be rooted in reality in some way. Stout claims that no "realist" account of moral truth is necessary.[40] He gives an analysis of different ways we use the term "truth," distinguishing, among others, the "equivalence use," and the "cautionary use." The equivalence use is seen in expressions like "'One ought to keep one's promises' is true if and only if one ought to keep one's promises." This use focuses our attention on the fact that truth of a proposition is determined by the subject matter, what a proposition is about, rather than what the speaker thinks or says. The cautionary use is reflected in statements such as "P is our best moral theory but it might not be true," which points to what we might call the transcendent character of moral truth.

These characteristics of moral truth are precisely those that moral realists have sought to safeguard against various forms of expressivism and subjectivism, which are seen by realists as undermining the objectivity and transcendence of morality. So far as I can see, Stout gives no account of how moral truths can have these characteristics. He rejects any attempt to give morality a "metaphysical" foundation (and here the term "metaphysics" seems to be functioning mainly as a pejorative term of abuse). However, he provides no plausible account of his own as to how moral truths can possess the objectivity and transcendence he sees it as having.

I think it is clear that the fact that various norms are implicit in our social practices gives one no decisive reason to think that those norms are the correct norms, since Stout himself admits that a society could

---

[39] Stout, p. 204.   [40] Stout, pp. 248–56.

be deeply mistaken about things. Even if the fact that I find certain norms embedded in the social practices of my culture gives me a *prima facie* reason to think they are genuine norms, this would hardly be an *explanation* of the authority of those norms. Nicholas Wolterstorff makes this point very clearly:

> From the fact that I require of you that you perform some action, it does not follow that you are obligated to perform that action; conversely, from the fact that I do not require it of you it does not follow that you are not obligated to perform it. Likewise, from the fact that I hold you to account by appealing to some norm, it does not follow that you are obligated to do what I hold you to account for doing by appealing to that norm.[41]

Replacing the "I" in this example with "lots of people" or even "practically everyone in my society" does not appreciably change the situation. It is not that Stout gives a false explanation of the objectivity and authority of moral norms; he gives no explanation whatsoever.

Wolterstorff speculates that Stout thinks he has given an account of the objectivity of moral norms because Stout affirms the objectivity of "excellence" as a kind of value. Perhaps Stout thinks that we have an obligation to produce the greatest amount of excellence we can. Since excellence is objective, there will be an objective truth about how we can best achieve excellence.

Even if we set aside the serious worry, one that I will ignore, that Stout gives no convincing account as to how excellence could be objective, this does not solve the problem of the objectivity of moral obligations. Making value objective only gives us objective obligations if our obligations can be reduced to achieving the greatest possible amount of value, in something like a consequentialist way. However, this is a highly dubious view. There are many possible outcomes I could achieve that would be valuable that I have no obligation to achieve. Such a "maximizing" view of excellence seems very unlikely to do justice to the Anscombe intuition, since it is not easy to see how it could account for some features of moral obligation; for example, it does not explain why moral obligations are binary, overriding, and help bring reflection to closure.

I conclude that Stout provides no significant argument against the project of explaining moral obligations by showing they are divine

[41] Nicholas Wolterstorff, "Jeffrey Stout on Democracy and its Contemporary Christian Critics," *Journal of Religious Ethics* 33:4 (2005), p. 640 (article is pp. 633–47).

commands. Perhaps indeed he does not even wish to provide such an objection. Towards the end of the chapter on "Ethics without Metaphysics" he tells us that "Its [pragmatism's] quarrel is not with the God of Amos and Dorothy Day, or even with the God of Barthian theology, but with the God of Descartes, and with the God of analytic metaphysics."[42] If there is a God, Stout admits, then what has value will indeed be dependent on God. (Presumably God's existence might make a difference not just to value but to obligations as well.) But this is just an admission that moral truths depend on the nature of reality: If there is a God, excellence will depend on God; if there is no God it will not. The cheap shots at Descartes and "analytic metaphysics" have no real bite here. For Descartes was attempting to describe the God of Amos, whether he did so successfully or not. And contemporary analytic metaphysics is simply the attempt to reflect on what is real, and it often proceeds by critical reflection on our (linguistic) social practices.

Jeffrey Stout is right to insist that non-religious people may reasonably believe in moral obligations. And he is right to claim that it is reasonable to think that moral obligations are embedded in some of our social practices. There are of course non-theistic metaethics, attempts to explain how moral obligations hold that do not presuppose God, and I shall discuss some of these views in Chapter 5, and argue that those that are incompatible with a DCT have some striking weaknesses. However, the fact that these alternative metaethical views have been offered at least shows that there is a recognized need to give *some* account of why there should be moral obligations. So far as I can see, Stout offers no explanation at all. Neither has he provided any reason why a divine command theorist should not put forward the claim that moral obligations in fact depend on God, and defend that claim with arguments.

---

[42] Stout, p. 268.

3

The Relation of Divine Command Theory to Natural Law and Virtue Ethics

A divine command theory of moral obligations is thought by many to be a rival to two other types of moral theories often defended by religious thinkers: natural law theory and virtue ethics. In this chapter I want to argue that this way of thinking about the relation of a DCT to natural law theory and virtue ethics is mistaken. There is no necessary opposition between these three types of ethical theory. They can be seen as offering complementary answers to different questions, rather than rival answers to the same questions.

It is true that there are versions of all three types of theory that create a relation of opposition between them. However, I will try to show that such opposition is unnecessary, and in fact is generally the result of an attempt to extend the theory in an unnatural way to cover issues it is not well-suited to cover. Often ethical theorists look for a simple, comprehensive theory, rooted in one basic concept or principle, which will provide a basis for the whole of ethics. When a divine command theory, a natural law theory, or a virtue theory is used in this way, it can become an imperialistic, reductive theory that tries to make the others unnecessary.

One might take as an example what is often called "theological voluntarism," understood as the view that God's commands (or his will) determine *all* moral truths, including truths about the good. If God willed rape or murder or torture to be good, they would be good. Theological voluntarism in this case extends the concept of God's will from an explanation of obligations, which I argue is reasonable, to cover issues it is not well-suited to cover. It is easy to see that such an extended divine command view is incompatible with the kind of natural law theory I will discuss in this chapter. In a similar manner, it is possible to take a natural law theory and try to make it explain all the facts about moral obligations, or to take a virtue theory and try to use it to explain all the moral facts about the good and even about obligations. These are not just logical possibilities, but actual positions that are defended. However, I will try to show that the concerns that motivate natural law theories and virtue theories do not require such extensions. I do not claim that a natural law theory (or a virtue theory) cannot contradict a divine command theory of obligation; certainly many natural law theorists do see their views as ruling out such a divine command theory. What I want to show is that the central insights of a natural law theory or a virtue theory do not require this.

I claim instead that a divine command theory, a natural law theory, and a virtue theory not only can be consistently held, but can have a natural complementary relationship. In particular, the kind of divine command theory I developed in Chapter 2 has a natural affinity both to a natural law theory and to a virtue ethic. To put things as simply as possible, the DCT I defend, rather than being a rival to a natural law theory, actually presupposes some theory of the good, and a natural law theory admirably satisfies this need. Further, the DCT I defend sees the purpose of God's commands to be a vision of transformed persons that requires a theory of the virtues to be completed. One might say that a DCT rests *on* a natural law theory (or something similar that can play the role that a natural law theory plays) and points *towards* a virtue theory.

NATURAL LAW THEORY IN GENERAL

As Mark Murphy claims in his helpful *Stanford Encyclopedia of Philosophy* article on the subject, the term "natural law theory" has been applied to theories of ethics, politics, and civil law, as well as theories of religious morality.[1] Even when we limit the focus, as

---

[1] See Mark Murphy, "The Natural Law Tradition in Ethics," *The Stanford Encyclopedia of Philosophy* (Spring 2011 Edition), ed. Edward N. Zalta (ed.) <http://plato.stanford.edu/archives/spr2011/entries/natural-law-ethics>. Much of what follows is heavily influenced by this article of Murphy as well as his book, *Natural Law and Practical Rationality* (Cambridge: Cambridge University Press, 2001).

Murphy himself does, to theories of ethics, there is a tremendous diversity of views that have been described as natural law theories. For example, most natural law theorists have been theists, but there are secular natural law thinkers such as Philippa Foot.[2] Given the fact that the pre-eminent natural law thinkers, such as Thomas Aquinas, have been theists, should we count such secular theories as natural law theories? Certainly, as Aquinas develops the view, it is incompatible with atheism, since Aquinas thinks of the natural law as constituting part of God's providential governance of the universe.[3] Hence, as Murphy affirms, what we might call the paradigm cases of natural law theory are theistic. However, there are clearly theories that possess some or even many of the features of Aquinas' view that leave out this metaphysical underpinning. Should we say (as Murphy does) that such theories are natural law theories but "nonparadigmatic ones," or should we say that they are not natural law theories at all? Murphy's conclusion seems right: "There is of course no clear answer to the question of when a view ceases to be a natural law theory, though a nonparadigmatic one, and becomes no natural law theory at all."[4]

For my purposes this semantic question is not very important, since I am chiefly interested in the question of the place of divine authority in a religiously grounded ethic. I shall therefore be looking mainly at natural law theories that include a place for God. However, the fact that the question of a non-theistic natural law ethic can be raised at all does suggest a concern over whether God plays an essential role in ethics for a natural law theory. For it is sometimes alleged, both by proponents and critics of natural law theory, that such a view essentially makes ethics autonomous. Famously, the Dutch natural law jurist Hugo Grotius, in the Prolegomena to his treatise "On the Law of War and Peace," published in 1625, seems to suggest that much of ethics would be the same whether God exists or not: "What we have been saying would have a degree of validity even if we should concede that which cannot be conceded without the utmost wickedness, that there is no God, or that the affairs of men are of no concern to him."[5] That there is some basis for this suspicion

---

[2] Philippa Foot, *Natural Goodness* (Oxford: Oxford University Press, 2001).
[3] ST Ia, IIaa, 91, 2.   [4] Murphy, "Natural Law Ethics," p. 7.
[5] Hugo Grotius, *De jure belli et pacis*, Prolegomena, §§ 6, 9, 11, trans. Francis W. Kelsey et al., 2 vols (Oxford: Oxford University Press, 1925), 2:11, 13. Quoted in Francis Oakley, *Natural Law, Laws of Nature, Natural Rights: Continuity and Discontinuity in the History of Ideas* (New York: Continuum, 2005), p. 64.

that a natural law ethic does not depend in a fundamental way on God can be seen from Mark Murphy's own *Natural Law and Practical Rationality*. Although Murphy is himself a theist, in this book he develops an account of practical rationality, including an account of morality, in which God plays almost no role. The index to this volume does not even include an entry for "God." The only significant role played by God in this version of natural law theory is that "religion" is included among the catalogue of basic goods that give humans reasons for action.[6]

MURPHY'S SURPRISING PIVOT

To be fair, Murphy does make a vigorous attempt to show the role God might play in explaining morality in a later work, *God and Moral Law: On The Theistic Explanation of Morality*.[7] Before looking in depth at natural law ethics with Murphy himself as a prime exhibit, I shall take a slight digression to comment on this later book. I feel the need to do so because the situation is odd in several ways. In *God and Moral Law* Murphy, known as a natural law thinker, presents a *critique* of natural law theory. Divine command theory is usually regarded as a rival to natural law theory (though not so by me), yet I, as a proponent of a DCT, find myself in the strange situation of *defending* a natural law theory against a philosopher generally regarded as one of its ablest champions. In the "Acknowledgements" to *God and Moral Law* Murphy confesses to doubts about whether his own earlier work in natural law ethics gives God too small a role in morality, and he describes this book as an attempt to remedy this problem.[8] I take this remark as a further confirmation that God plays no important role in Murphy's *Natural Law and Practical Rationality*. *God and Moral Law* provides a very different take on the matter, but after this section I shall limit my consideration to the earlier work, and I shall try here to explain why.

---

[6] Murphy, *Natural Law and Practical Rationality*, pp. 131–3.
[7] Mark Murphy, *God and Moral Law: On the Theistic Explanation of Morality* (Oxford: Oxford University Press, 2011).
[8] Murphy, *God and Moral Law*, p. vi.

God and Moral Law provides a very interesting and original account as to how God could be part of the explanation of morality, by arguing that God's relation to morality should be conceived as a form of "concurrentism," analogous to the role God plays in sustaining the laws of nature on some accounts.[9] This proposal deserves close consideration, but it is an approach that differs significantly from the one I defend in this work.

I have several worries about the views Murphy develops here, but spelling those out would require virtually another book, so I will here just mention my reservations. One concerns the fact that Murphy tries to show how God is important in explaining the *whole* of morality and not just moral obligations. The project of seeing how God might relate to other aspects of morality is certainly important, but I think that Murphy's approach does not do full justice to the distinctive characteristics of moral obligations. It is difficult to compare his account of how God explains morality and the account I am giving, since the accounts are designed to explain different things. A second worry concerns Murphy's requirement that God explain morality "immediately."[10] Murphy claims that if God is not the immediate ground of morality, then we will have a problem of "divided loyalties," in which finite goods can become rivals of God.[11] Finite goods can become rivals of God; that is the essence of idolatry, and perhaps they need some independence from God for this to be possible. However, recognizing a finite good as good is not itself idolatry, and I suspect that this requirement that God explain morality *immediately* is too strong, because is not consistent with God using various *means* to establish morality. If this requirement is too strong, then Murphy's criticisms of both natural law theory and what he terms theological voluntarism fail. However, I admit that all of this deserves more discussion than I can here give matters. Pursuing these issues here will not advance my project.

The approach Murphy takes in *God and Moral Law* is one which *assumes* the truth of theism and then asks in what way God can explain morality. As he affirms, the book gives a central place to God as *explanans*, without completely ignoring the *explanadum* (the moral facts which need to be explained). However, as Murphy admits, an explanation of morality which is driven by God as an *explanans* in

---

[9] Murphy, *God and Moral Law*, pp. 148–80.
[10] See Murphy, *God and Moral Law*, pp. 61–3.
[11] Murphy, *God and Moral Law*, pp. 95–9.

this way will be devoid of apologetic value.[12] No one will be pushed to believe in God as the foundation of morality by such an argument who did not already believe in God. In this work, by contrast I want to argue that someone who reasonably accepts the existence of morality might be brought to see the reasonableness of believing in God as the explanation of a part of morality, namely moral obligations. My purpose in the first part of this chapter is to show how this project can incorporate what has traditionally been called a natural law approach to ethics. I shall focus therefore on Murphy's earlier *Natural Law and Practical Rationality*.

My own view is that the suspicion (which Murphy supports in *God and Moral Law)* that natural law theories make God unimportant for morality is unwarranted. I think that Murphy's claim that a natural law ethic is not consistent with God's playing a foundational role in ethics fails because it depends on the too-strong requirement that God be the immediate ground of morality.[13] My reason for thinking that God can play an important role in natural law ethics stems from the fact that a natural law theory of rationality requires *some* metaphysical underpinning, and a theistic metaphysic seems to do the job better than any other. Even without bringing God's commands into the picture, the role God plays in giving the natural world a structure in which things have natures that determine what is good for them is important. It may be possible to develop a natural law ethic without God as part of the story, but when God is part of the picture the story seems far more complete and satisfying. Nevertheless, I agree with Murphy that to give a satisfying account of morality as a whole (and specifically of obligations), we need God to play a more central role than simply as the creator of natural kinds that determine the good.[14] In other words, a natural law ethic that sees God as playing a greater role in ethics than simply being the one who determines what is actually good by his decisions about what to create will be a less adequate view than a natural law ethic that sees God as having other roles to play in ethics as well.

[12] Murphy, *God and Moral Law*, p. 5.
[13] Murphy, *God and Moral Law*, pp. 95–9.
[14] In *God and Moral Law* Murphy argues at one point that attempts to explain moral obligations as simply reasonable responses to "value" all fail, but he does not seem to see how God's expressed requirements could help remedy this problem. See p. 98.

NATURAL LAW THEORY AS PRACTICAL
RATIONALITY

How should we understand a natural law theory? Murphy describes such a theory as essentially an account of "practical rationality," which has two main goals. The first is to show how actions can be "practically intelligible," which means showing that the actions have a point or purpose, such that they are worth performing.[15] The second goal is to help humans make decisions as to which of the many worthwhile actions that could be performed should be performed; it is essentially an account of the rationality of choices with respect to actions.[16] Both of these goals are accomplished by giving an account of what is good. For example, taking Aquinas again as the paradigm natural law theorist, the fundamental principle of the natural law is claimed to be that good is to be done and evil is to be avoided.[17] For Aquinas this is a "first principle," like the principle of non-contradiction for theoretical reason, and as such, is regarded as self-evident and not in need of argument. Natural law theories characteristically then give priority to the good. To understand the point of actions and to know what actions are reasonable we must know what is good.

However, it is obvious that such an abstract first principle by itself does not give us guidance with respect to specific actions. We need to know what is good in particular, concrete circumstances. Natural law theorists characteristically offer an account of goods that are universally and naturally good, and most have done so by offering an Aristotelian-inspired account of the good for humans in terms of what completes or perfects human nature, or that enables human flourishing. To be sure, not all natural law theorists have followed Aristotle in this way. Thomas Hobbes gave an account of the natural law that is grounded in a subjectivist account of the good, premised on the psychological fact that all humans desire to survive and to avoid violent death.[18] Some other natural law theorists have defended a more Platonic account of the good, which sees some things, such as knowledge and beauty, as just good in themselves, apart from any

---

[15] Murphy, *Natural Law and Practical Rationality*, p. 2.
[16] Murphy, *Natural Law and Practical Rationality*, pp. 2–3.
[17] ST Ia IIae 94, 2.
[18] See *Hobbes's Leviathan*, reprinted from the edition of 1651 (Oxford: Oxford University Press, 1909), pp. 94–109.

reference to human nature. However, the vast majority of natural law theorists have explained the good for humans in terms of human nature, and I shall take this as a defining characteristic of a natural law theory.

Of course various accounts of what are the basic goods for humans have been given by natural law theorists, as well as diverse accounts of how those are known by humans. One dispute that has been on-going within natural law theorists concerns the latter issue. Many traditional natural law theories have held that an understanding of what is good for humans presupposes and must be derived from an understanding of human nature, since one cannot grasp what perfects or completes human nature without an understanding of that nature. Murphy calls such a view "derivationism," since it maintains that our knowledge of basic goods is derived from a kind of theoretical knowledge.[19] One major alternative to the derivationist account of the knowledge of basic good is what Murphy calls "inclinationism," the kind of view of basic goods that is offered by contemporary thinker John Finnis. For Finnis, one's grasp of basic goods is something that is immediate and self-evident and something that is internal to the life of practical reason. For example, humans have a natural desire to know things, and Finnis thinks that for a being who has such an inclination it is simply immediately evident that knowledge is good.[20]

My purpose in this book is not to articulate and defend a natural law theory of morality, but to argue for the importance of divine authority and divine commands for moral obligations. Hence it is not necessary for me to resolve the disputes that natural law theorists have among themselves. Perhaps both views are right, and the good can be known in both of these ways. I do find plausible Mark Murphy's defense of what he calls the "real identity thesis," which claims that the insight into the good we have through our inclinations and the knowledge we have about human flourishing through our understanding of human nature represent two alternative ways of grasping the same goods.[21] Regardless of whether our grasp of the basic human goods is immediate or derived, I shall assume that a

---

[19] See Murphy, *Natural Law and Practical Rationality*, pp. 6–17.

[20] See Finnis, *Natural Law and Natural Rights*, pp. 60–9.

[21] Murphy states this thesis on pp. 17–21 of *Natural Law and Practical Rationality* and much of the remainder of the book is a defense of it.

natural law theory is one that holds that those goods are in some way determined by our nature, such that if human nature were fundamentally different, what would be good for humans would be fundamentally different as well.

What are the basic goods for humans, according to natural law theories? There are, as one might expect, some differences in the catalogs offered by various thinkers. However, there is also a substantial amount of overlap and agreement, and at least some of what looks like disagreement may be mainly due to the way the goods are described and individuated.[22] Typical goods include life and health, knowledge, beauty (or aesthetic experience), friendship and other social goods (such as being part of a family and community), fulfilling work and activity (including play), psychological goods such as "inner peace" or self-integration, practical reasonableness (or "excellence in agency"), and, in some cases, religion.

Although it is clear that a natural law account of practical reasonableness prioritizes the good over the right, as does utilitarianism and other forms of consequentialism, a natural law theory differs from most forms of utilitarianism in that it does not assume that rationality demands simply that goodness be maximized.[23] A natural law theorist thinks of practical reason as calling for a reasonable response to what is good, but there are a variety of ways that actions can be reasonable or unreasonable as a response to the good. What reason demands is not simply the maximization of some quality such as pleasure, or even the maximization of some aggregate of goods, but that persons respond appropriately to the actual goods they encounter or could actualize. This means that a natural law theorist, like a Kantian, can argue that there may be some types of actions that are always inappropriate or unreasonable, and thus there may be general rules or principles that rule out some kinds of actions absolutely. If human life is a basic good, then murder, understood as the intentional destruction of innocent human life, may be viewed as intrinsically wrong.

---

[22] For a summary of the catalogs offered by various thinkers, see Murphy, "Natural Law Ethics," p. 11.

[23] In speaking of the priority of the "good over the right" I am speaking of "the good" in a non-moral sense. There is obviously a sense of "good and bad" that is moral in character, and in this sense the fact that an act such as murder is morally forbidden is logically linked to its being morally bad.

HOW A DIVINE COMMAND THEORY CAN REST ON A NATURAL LAW THEORY

In a later section of this chapter I will argue that a natural law theory as developed thus far is not well-suited to give an adequate account of moral obligations. Thus, a natural law account of morality that incorporates a divine command account of obligations is a stronger version of the theory. However, I first want to say something about the ways in which a divine command view of obligations can rest on a natural law theory.

One obvious reason why this is so is the fact that a DCT presupposes some theory of the good. It will be recalled from Chapter 2 that it is only the commands of a God who is essentially good that can create moral obligations. The commands of an all-powerful being who had no concern for the good would fail to create any moral obligations in humans, even if humans were created by this being. Although the goodness of what God commands does not by itself make those acts obligatory, God's goodness puts a constraint on what can be morally obligatory. The good itself cannot be determined by God's commands, since it is the good that motivates and provides the point of those commands. Hence it is clear that a DCT presupposes *some* account of what is good, and a natural law ethic provides exactly that.

Of course this by itself does not show that a DCT *must* employ a natural law account of the good. There are other alternatives. Robert Adams, for example, provides a Platonic account of the good to undergird his divine command account. However, if a natural law theory provides a plausible account of the good, then at least it looks like one form of a DCT will be one that rests on a natural law account. However, I think there are reasons to think that a natural law view of the good is not only one that is consistent with a DCT, but one that is specially well-suited for this purpose.

To see this we need to recall again the social theory of obligations which a DCT rests on. As I explained in Chapter 1, a social theory of obligation attempts to explain the distinctive character of obligations by seeing them as grounded in social institutions and practices. Some of the obligations linked to a particular social role are conventional in nature, and rest on social agreements that are the result of voluntary decisions. For example, perhaps if I join the Rotary Club I will be obligated to attend a meeting of the Club every month. The rules of the Club are established by the members of the Club itself, and I obligate myself to abide by those rules by freely deciding to join the Club, knowing what is thereby expected of me. Even in this case the obligation is not wholly conventional in nature, since the obligation rests partly on the principle that humans ought to honor their agreements. That principle does not seem to be purely conventional in character, but rather one that conventionally grounded obligations presuppose.

Other types of obligations seem even less conventional in nature, for example, the social role of being a parent, which certainly carries with it certain obligations towards one's children. Of course some of what is rightly expected of parents is fixed by social conventions and even by the law, but it seems clear that those social conventions and laws are partly designed to make explicit and clear that parents, by bringing children into the world, thereby incur some responsibility to see that those children are properly cared for, and that truth does not seem to be purely conventional.

Why is this the case? A natural law ethic provides a very plausible answer. According to a natural law ethic, human life is a good, and thus humans who decide to bring new human life into the world are bringing a good into the world. However, humans by nature are unable to take care of themselves while they are infants and small children. Parents who bring children into the world but do nothing to see that those children can grow up and flourish thus take an unreasonable stance towards a basic good. The obligations that parents incur by becoming parents thus hold partly because of certain truths about human nature, truths with normative implications.

Of course the children of good and loving parents who take seriously their parental obligations incur obligations as well. In every human culture children owe their parents (if they have been good parents) at least gratitude and respect. Why is this so? Again, a natural law ethic offers a plausible answer. It seems a very widespread human belief that someone who gives someone else a good gift deserves gratitude. A gift is necessarily something good, something that benefits the recipient. A natural law ethic strongly supports the idea that the good is to be appreciated, and gratitude for a gift is an expression of such appreciation. Once more it seems then that the obligations children have towards their parents hold partly because of the truth of a normative principle such as "It is good to feel and express gratitude towards the giver of a gift."

A divine command theory of moral obligations sees the relationship of creature to creator as a distinctive kind of social relationship which carries with it certain obligations, just as is the case for such purely human social relationships as parent to child. In particular, a DCT requires that God possess legitimate authority, so that his commands (or expressed requirements) establish obligations for his human creatures. But it is clear that some normative principle or principles must be the basis of this authority. For a DCT to be plausible there must be some reasonable answer to the question, "Why should a human being obey the commands of God?"[24]

Once more it seems that a natural law ethic provides a plausible explanation of why the requisite normative principles hold. What is required is some normative principle that implies that humans have good reasons to obey God's commands. There are several (not mutually exclusive) principles that could explain or justify divine authority. One is the principle of gratitude just discussed in connection with the obligations of children to parents. Good and conscientious parents give their children a great deal: time, effort, material resources. Gratitude for such gifts is good, and gratitude appropriately expresses itself in respect and appreciation for the parents. However, God as Creator is the giver of every good that any humans have, including their very existence. It seems plausible then that the debt of gratitude humans owe to God vastly exceeds the gratitude they owe to parents or any human benefactor. In fact, the gratitude owed to God must always be far greater than that owed to any human person or even to all human persons to whom one owes gratitude. Since God is the creator and sustainer of those human benefactors, all the goods given by those human benefactors, including parents, are also gifts of God.

A second possible way that divine authority could be justified is to appeal to the goodness of a relation to God. Aquinas, for example, holds that a relation with God is the highest good possible for a human person. The ultimate happiness of a human person is the knowledge of God that is described as the "beatific vision." Obviously if this is so, humans have very good reasons to do what is necessary to achieve such a relation.

---

[24] Actually, the fact that these normative principles must be in place for God's commands to constitute obligations leads to an objection to a DCT. The objection is that the normative principles that hold antecedent to God's commands themselves generate moral obligations, and thus moral obligations cannot be identical to God's commands nor can all of them be generated by God's commands. I will develop this objection and respond to it in Chapter 4.

Why might this give good reasons for humans to obey God's commands? Well, one always has some reason to satisfy someone one wants to have a good relation with. However, in this case, given some plausible assumptions about God and his commands, those reasons for trying to please God are decisive. Many religious traditions have thought that to know God truly a person must be transformed in some ways; for example, they have held that a person can only know God truly if that person resembles God in some way. If this is true, and if God is supremely loving, a person incapable of love cannot really understand God. If God is supremely good, a person who does not love the good cannot love God. If we ask what the point or purpose of God's commands to humans might be, one very plausible answer is that God through his commands wants to help his human creatures transform their characters so as to make it possible for them to know God truly and relate to God properly. Later in this chapter, I will develop this thought by seeing how a virtue ethic can be viewed as the natural *telos* of divine commands and hence of moral obligations. If the purpose of God's commands is a transformation that enables us to flourish and achieve true happiness, then humans have powerful reasons to obey God. Once more the normative principle invoked seems one that is part of a natural law ethic, since it is rooted in the natures of humans and God.

A third possible normative principle that might justify divine authority is the claim that God, by virtue of his creation of humans and the natural world, has a rightful claim to be the owner of that created world and everything in it, including human beings. Many natural law theorists have held that there is a natural right to property. John Locke, for example, held that even in a state of nature a human person would naturally have a right to use and enjoy objects which the individual has "mixed his labor with."[25] If I find a log in the forest, and I trim the log to make wooden boards, from which I make a table, I am properly the owner of the table. To be sure, in the case of human property, Locke holds that ownership rights are not absolute, since humans must necessarily use pre-existent materials, such as the log, that they do not naturally own.[26] Hence Locke held that my

---

[25] John Locke, *Of Civil Government Second Treatise* (South Bend, IN: Gateway Editions, 1955), p. 22.

[26] In this same passage Locke adds a proviso that one legitimately acquires property when one "mixes his labor" with something so long as "there is enough, and as good left in common for others" (p. 22).

ownership rights in the state of nature are qualified by the need to share natural resources with others. Nevertheless, Locke thinks there is a natural right to own that which one's own labor has brought into existence.

If theism is true, then God has brought into existence the whole of the created order solely through his power. Hence if anything like Locke's principle of natural ownership is true, God has a natural claim to own the whole of the natural world, including humans. Nor is there any need to qualify God's ownership in the way Locke suggests human ownership must be qualified, for there is no pre-existent material God does not own, and there are no potential rival claimants to the property. The owner of property is the one who has the right to decide how that property should be used. If humans are God's property, then God surely has the right to establish rules for how humans should conduct themselves.

There are of course objections that could be raised against all of these normative principles invoked to justify divine authority. For example, one might argue, as Mark Murphy has done, that persons cannot rightly be owned, and that the concept of property can only be properly applied to non-personal objects.[27] One point in support of the objection is that we do not (today) think that biological parents own children that they conceive. One might also cite the claim (one that I certainly accept) that no form of human slavery can be morally justified. If humans are free and responsible moral agents, does this not imply that they cannot be owned like an automobile or a computer?

I do not think these objections hold much weight when carefully examined. It is true that parents do not own their children, but they do have special rights (as well as obligations) towards them. In any case parents do not create their children from nothing, and so there is no true analogy to divine creation. As for slavery, the fact that no human person can morally own another makes sense, since no human, no matter how much he or she contributes to the well-being of another, can be the creator of another person. Human slavery is thus always an unwarranted claim to possess what one has not created. However, the same cannot be said of God. In fact, one reason why human slavery might be wrong is that a human person who claims to own another person is unjustifiably appropriating what belongs to God. To claim,

---

[27] See Mark Murphy, *An Essay on Divine Authority* (Ithaca, NY: Cornell University Press, 2002), pp. 94–104.

as Murphy does, that persons cannot be owned by anyone, even by God, may just beg the question in this case, since the issue in dispute is precisely whether the reasons commonly given as to why persons cannot be owned apply to ownership by God. Someone might argue, for example, that human freedom and autonomy show that humans cannot be rightly owned by anyone, including God. However, it seems possible to think of human freedom and autonomy, not as nullifying God's authority, but as a gracious gift of the God who continues to have a rightful claim on humans.

To see this consider the following thought experiment: imagine two possible worlds. In world A humans enjoy libertarian freedom and in world B they do not. In world B God creates human-like beings who have no freedom and who are causally determined to serve him. If God did this, he would in no way be harming or injuring such creatures. Those creatures would be his property, and he would have every right to do what he wished to do with them. In world A, God chooses not to create automatons, but instead creates humans as free beings, so that they have the privilege of voluntarily sharing in God's work. It is hard to see why the fact that God might give these creatures this gift nullifies the rightful claim he has on them. They are still his creatures. It is just that in world A they are given the privilege of choosing freely whether they will serve their creator, while in world B they are not given this gift.

Nor is it the case that humans are necessarily degraded by being God's creations and being subject to his authority. To be a slave of another human is degrading because no human master is completely selfless and good. Slaves are necessarily used as means to the master's ends. God, however, needs nothing from his human creatures, and his creation is an expression of his love and goodness. He wants nothing but the good of his creatures, and his prescriptions are aimed at their good, not at fulfilling his own needs. Hence, to be God's creature is not to be degraded but to be liberated. God has chosen to make humans free and responsible creatures, who have the dignity of deciding for themselves whether they will live by the rules God has designed for their good. However, the fact that God does not force humans to obey him does nothing to undermine the rightful claim he has to their obedience.

I conclude that a natural law ethic is not a rival ethical view to a DCT, at least from the perspective of a DCT, but a plausible foundation for a divine command account of moral obligations. Some account of the good as well as some account of the basis of rightful authority must be given for a DCT to make sense. I do not claim that it is only a natural law ethic that can do this. Hence, it is not quite right to say that a DCT logically rests on a natural law ethic. However, it does seem right that a natural law ethic is especially well-suited to provide the normative principles needed to make sense of divine authority.

DOES A NATURAL LAW ETHIC NEED DIVINE COMMANDS FOR MORAL OBLIGATIONS?

If my argument in the preceding section is sound, then a divine command theorist does not have to see a natural law ethic as a rival, but rather can happily regard a natural law ethic as providing the basis for a divine command view. But how do things look from the other side, so to speak? Is there room within a natural law ethic for a divine command account of moral obligation? Or is it the case that a natural law ethic by itself provides an adequate account of moral obligations, making any appeal to divine commands unnecessary?

Why might a natural law theorist think that a DCT is unnecessary? I believe one reason is a failure to appreciate the distinction between the discretion thesis and the modal status thesis discussed in Chapter 2.[28] Even those DCT theorists, such as Scotus, who affirm the discretion thesis, hold that *some* of what God commands is commanded necessarily. It seems quite possible to affirm that this is true for *all* of God's commands, affirming only the modal status thesis and denying the divine discretion thesis.

Many natural law theorists hold that what is morally right is determined by what is good. God may have some choice over what kind of world to create and what natures to give the kinds that populate that world, but once the character of the world is fixed by God's decree, then the good is also fixed, and the morally right in turn is fixed by the good. Although I believe it is plausible to think that God does have some discretion over what he commands, for the sake of argument I will here concede that this is not the case, and that the

[28] See pp. 34–7.

content of the morally right is indeed fixed by the creaturely natures of things. Given the power of the Anscombe intuition about the distinctive character of moral obligations, it still seems plausible that something important is left out by the natural law theorist who does not bring God's commands into the story.

Suppose that God commands us to do what is morally right, and that the content of what he commands is fixed by the good. Given the powerful reasons we have for obeying God, and the authority God possesses, it still seems true that God's commands add an important dimension to the moral character of what he commands. Even if it is true that we would have good reasons to do the actions God commands us to do even if God did not give those commands, it is also true that we acquire powerful new reasons for performing (or not performing) various acts when God issues commands. The truth of the modal status thesis is unaffected by the truth of the discretion thesis. One may hold then that the content of what God commands is determined by the created natures He has chosen to give things, but still hold that what one might call the preceptorial force of the morally right is due to God's commands.

If we reflect on the matter, it seems odd for a theistic natural law theorist to hold that God's commands add no new moral character to what is commanded, given the normative principles that undergird a claim that God has divine authority. This is especially true since those normative principles all seem to be principles that fit well into a natural law ethic. But if it is recognized that a new moral quality is created by God's commands, it seems appropriate to designate those acts that possess that new quality by a distinctive term. The divine command theorist certainly can acknowledge that we may have good reasons to perform those acts that are our moral obligations, even if God had not commanded them. The defender of a DCT just insists that those reasons do not capture everything that is required for an act to be a *moral obligation*.

A good example of the way in which a natural law theory appears to make unnecessary any reference to divine commands to explain moral obligations can be found in John Finnis' important book, *Natural Law and Natural Rights*. At one point Finnis discusses "Aquinas's reason for saying that law is an act of intellect; this reason has nothing to do with the will of a superior needing to be made known, but only with the fact that it is intelligence that grasps ends, and arranges means to ends, and grasps the necessity of those arranged means, and this is the source of obligation."[29] I agree with Finnis that an intellect that grasps ends, and sees what means are necessary for those ends, has a reason for acting in some ways rather than others. For example, there is clearly a sense in which a person ought to seek to preserve her life and do what is necessary for her to flourish, even apart from any commands of God. But we should remember here that not every "ought" is the "ought" of moral obligation. The "ought" that Finnis describes here sounds very much like what Anscombe calls the "Aristotelian ought," one that is grounded in the purpose or function of a thing. However, the moral "ought" has a different character.

The less than satisfactory character of a natural law ethic that leaves out divine commands can be clearly seen, I believe, in the account of moral obligations given by Mark Murphy in *Natural Law and Practical Rationality*. In this book Murphy develops and defends a natural law account of practical rationality. The account he gives is one that is "naturalist, objectivist, cognitivist, welfarist, anti-particularist, and anti-consequentialist."[30] Most of his view and many of his arguments can be endorsed by a defender of a DCT, including especially his arguments that normative claims are cognitive and objective. Murphy gives a powerful argument that the popular subjectivist accounts of the good (preference theories) are unsatisfactory, and gives a plausible account of the basic goods (life, knowledge, aesthetic experience, excellence in play and work, excellence of agency, inner peace, friendship and community, religion, and happiness) that give humans reasons for action. As an account of the good, a divine command theorist may fully support this view of practical rationality.

Trouble arises, however, when Murphy attempts to extend this account to encompass moral obligations. Murphy begins his attempt to explain moral obligations by defining what he terms "the most fundamental practical sense of ought," which is that "A ought to ϕ if and only if A, whose practical reason is functioning without error, decides to ϕ."[31] This sense of "ought" is clearly not the moral ought, since it implies that what an agent ought to do is fundamentally shaped by such subjective factors as what the agent actually decides. So Murphy introduces another type of "ought" judgment, in which

[29] Finnis, *Natural Law and Natural Rights*, pp. 54–5.
[30] Murphy, *Natural Law and Practical Rationality*, p. 5.
[31] Murphy, *Natural Law and Practical Rationality*, p. 221.

what an agent ought to do is independent of the agent's decision: "A morally ought to ϕ if and only if it is not possible that A, whose practical reasoning is functioning without error, decide to ψ, where ψ-ing and ϕ-ing are incompatible."[32] Murphy claims that this sense of ought "is sufficiently close to that presupposed in moral theory to be called the moral 'ought.'"[33]

Now Murphy is correct that he has here defined a sense of "ought" that is, unlike the fundamental practical ought, independent of the agent's decision. However, there are several ways in which the claim that he has thereby captured the ordinary sense of moral obligation seems dubious. The first is that on his view the fact that a person *morally* ought to perform some act does not imply that the person ought to perform the act; nor does the fact that a person *morally* ought not to perform some act imply that the person ought not to perform the act.[34] The reason this is so is that the agent's actual decision must be factored into the second type of ought but not the first. This seems, as Murphy admits, strange, since we would ordinarily say that what I morally ought to do is what I ought to do. One of the features of moral obligation that I discussed in Chapter 1 is the overriding character of the moral "ought," but that character here seems to have eroded if it has not disappeared altogether.

A second problem, however, is even more serious, in my view. The basic strategy of a natural law theorist is to identify the good, and then understand reasonable actions as those which respond appropriately to the good. The problem stems from the fundamental difference between two different kinds of goods, "agent-relative" goods and "agent-neutral" goods. Roughly, an agent-relative good is a good that is good for some particular agent, while an agent-neutral good is one that is good *simpliciter*, without any specification of the particular person the good is good for. Murphy argues that although the fundamental goods humans pursue are agent-relative, those goods can generate agent-neutral *reasons* for action.[35] The fundamental goods are all goods *for* particular agents. However, in a way that Murphy himself admits is mysterious, agents can recognize and value what is good for others, and thus have agent-neutral as well as agent-relative

[32] Murphy, *Natural Law and Practical Rationality*, p. 222.
[33] Murphy, *Natural Law and Practical Rationality*, p. 222.
[34] Murphy, *Natural Law and Practical Rationality*, pp. 223–4.
[35] Murphy, *Natural Law and Practical Rationality*, pp. 174–82.

reasons for action.[36] The fact that something is good for someone else can then make action on my part to advance that good intelligible.

So Murphy can and does reject the claim that all rational action must be egoistically motivated. Of course individuals often care about others with whom they have special relations, such as friends and family, and thus have agent-relative reasons to advance their good. But Murphy wants to hold that altruistic action on behalf of others is intelligible even if such special relations do not hold. Altruistic actions are thus reasonable.

It is, however, one thing to show that altruistic actions are reasonable, and quite another to show that they are morally obligatory. It is surely the case that many of our moral obligations require us to act in altruistic ways. However, Murphy admits that on his view it is fully rational for an agent to be a "quasi-egoist" who chooses to act only on the basis of a life plan, "the ends of which are all agent-relative goods."[37] A principle of impartiality holds only with respect to agent-neutral reasons for action, but there is no requirement that anyone act on the basis of such reasons. Murphy admits that he wishes he "could defend a more stringent principle of impartiality as a requirement of practical reasonableness," but confesses that he cannot do so.[38]

The reasonableness of "quasi-egoism" infects moral obligations as well. Since I can reasonably act "in grossly partial ways," and the moral ought is generated by what it is reasonable for someone to do, one cannot be morally obligated to take into account the good of others if one chooses to act only on the basis of agent-relative goods, except to the extent that the good of others affects my good and the good of those I care about.[39] Once more Murphy admits that he would like to affirm a "less-qualified principle of impartiality," but cannot do so.[40]

A related problem extends to the question of whether humans have obligations to act justly towards others. Murphy affirms that where genuine communities (ones that involve a common pursuit of an end) exist, then justice is a requirement of reason for the members of those communities.[41] However, there is no universal requirement that humans act justly, for two reasons. First, on Murphy's account

---

[36] Murphy, *Natural Law and Practical Rationality*, p. 181.
[37] Murphy, *Natural Law and Practical Rationality*, p. 203.
[38] Murphy, *Natural Law and Practical Rationality*, p. 203.
[39] Murphy, *Natural Law and Practical Rationality*, p. 225.
[40] Murphy, *Natural Law and Practical Rationality*, p. 225.
[41] Murphy, *Natural Law and Practical Rationality*, p. 234.

the requirements of justice hold only within communities, and for any given person, there will be many other persons who do not belong to that individual's community. Second, there is no rational requirement that anyone belong to a community, "or indeed to pursue an agent-neutral end of any sort."[42] The result is that if grave injustice is being done in some other community, it is not a moral concern of mine at all. If genocide is occurring in Rwanda, and I have some power to do something to stop it, I have no moral obligation to do so. The universality of moral obligations, as discussed in Chapter 1, has been undermined. It is not that on Murphy's view a person cannot have good reasons for acting altruistically; it is that it is hard to see why such a person could be obligated to do so.

If, however, we add to the natural law ethic an account of moral obligations as generated by God's commands, things are entirely different. If God commands us to love our neighbors as ourselves, and tells us that all human persons must be considered our neighbors, then we have powerful and overriding reasons to consider the good of others when acting. Nor will such a concern for others destroy or alienate us from a proper concern for our own well-being, since obedience to God is linked tightly to that very well-being.

Of course Murphy's account of moral obligation is only one natural law account. Other natural law thinkers, such as John Finnis, have attempted to develop a natural law theory that does more justice to the requirement that people care about the welfare of others.[43] However, theories such as those of Finnis have their own difficulties; in particular it is not clear how such a strong commitment to agent-neutrality is consistent with a view of the good that is linked to the flourishing of agents.[44] However, I think the problems of Murphy's account are illustrative of the difficulties that stem from any attempt to explain moral obligations in terms of what is reasonable to do to achieve the good. Moral actions do aim at the good, and they are actions that are reasonable to do. However, I believe a natural law ethic that makes no use of divine authority will have difficulty making sense of the special character of moral duties. Nor is there, as far as

---

[42] Murphy, *Natural Law and Practical Rationality*, p. 234.

[43] See Finnis, *Natural Law and Natural Rights*, p. 125, where he claims that there is a natural moral requirement to seek the common good.

[44] See Murphy's critical discussion of Finnis on agent neutrality, *Natural Law and Practical Rationality*, pp. 174–82.

I can see, any good reason why a theistic natural law theorist should neglect this important resource.

DIVINE COMMAND THEORIES OF OBLIGATION AND VIRTUE ETHICS

What about the relation of a DCT to what is today called virtue ethics? I shall here use the term "virtue ethics" in a broad manner to refer to an ethical theory that emphasizes the central role played in ethics by long-term dispositional states of character of moral agents. Some of these states (the virtues) are excellences such as honesty, courage, loyalty, and justice, while others (the vices) are deficiencies such as cowardice, laziness, and dishonesty. John Doris has argued, relying on empirical psychological findings, that we have reasons to be skeptical about the existence of *global* character traits, for human behavior is often strongly shaped by the effects of specific situations and contexts.[45] A Nazi concentration camp guard might exhibit "kindness" at home in the context of the family and "brutality" in the context of the prison camp. This problem requires the virtue theorist to develop a more fine-grained and qualified account of virtues as traits of character, but we can still meaningfully talk of such traits as tendencies or dispositions in characteristic types of contexts. The notion of "virtue ethics" as an ethics of character is therefore somewhat vague. There are many different ways of characterizing such dispositional traits, and lots of different ways such dispositional traits could figure into an ethical theory. In what follows I shall discuss some different types of virtue ethics, though I shall not try to be comprehensive.

If I am correct in arguing that a DCT is consistent with a natural law ethic, then it is easy to show that a DCT must also be consistent with *some* types of virtue ethics. The reason is that the greatest natural law theorist, Thomas Aquinas, was himself also a virtue ethicist. Indeed, Aquinas uses the virtues as the basic framework for his account of the ethical life, and it is arguable that he regards this account of the virtues as the outworking of his account of the natural

---

[45] See John M. Doris, *Lack of Character: Personality and Moral Behavior* (Cambridge: Cambridge University Press, 2002).

law. Aquinas himself sees virtue, not as a rival to the notion of law, but as the proper end of law, and he clearly thinks this is true for all kinds of laws, including laws given to persons to obey: "Consequently it is evident that the proper effect of law is to lead its subjects to their proper virtue: and since virtue is 'that which makes its subject good,' it follows that the proper effect of law is to those to whom it is given, good, either simply or in some particular respect."[46] If A is consistent with B, and A entails C, then B must also be consistent with C. Hence if a natural law ethic is consistent with a DCT, and a natural law ethic logically requires a virtue ethic, then it must be the case that a DCT is also consistent with a virtue ethic.

Nevertheless, there are, as was the case with natural law ethics, certain versions of virtue ethics that clash with a DCT. The main reason this is so is that a DCT is a type of deontological approach to ethics, one that emphasizes moral duties and some virtue ethicists see a deontological ethic as an alternative to a virtue ethic.[47] For example, Rosalind Hursthouse (at least in some of her work) describes a virtue ethics as an alternative to ethical theories that emphasize moral rules or principles (a deontological ethic) and ones that emphasize consequences (a consequentialist ethic).[48] Someone who thinks of a virtue ethic as an alternative to an ethic of duty will reject a DCT, but not necessarily for any reasons specific to a DCT. Rather, a DCT is rejected for the same reason that a Kantian ethic or natural law ethic or even utilitarian ethic will be rejected, for all of these ethical positions agree that moral duties play an important role in ethics.

It is not always clear when a particular thinker sees a virtue ethic as an alternative to an ethic of duty. Theological ethicist Stanley Hauer-was provides a good example, since he is often interpreted as providing a virtue ethic or "narrative ethic," understood as an alternative to an ethic of duty.[49] However, it is not clear that this is the correct way

---

[46] ST I–II.92.1.

[47] For a good example, see Stan Van Hooft, *Understanding Virtue Ethics* (Chesham, UK: Acumen Press, 2006), especially Chapter 1, where Van Hooft contrasts an ethic of duty with a virtue ethic as taking rival positions on a number of key issues in ethics.

[48] See Hursthouse's *On Virtue Ethics* (Oxford: Oxford University Press, 1999), p. 1; Hursthouse, Rosalind, "Virtue Ethics", *The Stanford Encyclopedia of Philosophy* (Summer 2012 Edition) <http://plato.stanford.edu/archives/sum2012/entries/ethics-virtue>.

[49] Some of Hauerwas' most important works in ethics include *The Peaceable Kingdom: A Primer in Christian Ethics* (Notre Dame, IN: University of Notre Dame Press, 1991), and *A Community of Character: Towards a Constructive Christian Social Ethics* (Notre Dame, IN: University of Notre Dame Press, 1991).

to characterize his work. In an essay where Hauerwas gives focused attention to the relation between virtues and obligations, he rejects the idea of a "pure" virtue ethic, which would presumably be an ethic that would either do without the notion of obligation altogether or else show that obligations are derivable from virtues.[50] It is true that throughout Hauerwas' career, he has focused on the importance of agents' character and motives, and that he has been critical of the view that ethics can be done without taking these into account. However, though Hauerwas himself may have wanted to emphasize the importance of the virtues, it does not follow that he wants to reject the idea that obligations have an important role to play in ethics. Indeed, he affirms that they do: "[W]e need neither an 'ethic of obligation' nor an 'ethics of virtue' as if those were discrete alternatives."[51]

So even though Hauerwas himself has focused almost exclusively on issues of character, his target is not the existence of moral obligations, but the claim that an ethic of obligation by itself captures all that is important in the ethical life.[52] The DCT I am here defending makes no such claim to capturing the whole of ethics. As I have already argued in the preceding sections of this chapter, a DCT can rest on and be a natural extension of a natural law ethic. I shall try to show in what follows that a DCT also has a need for an account of the virtues and that many of the characteristic claims of virtue ethics fit beautifully together with a DCT. I see no need therefore for a divine command theorist to polemicize against Hauerwas or other theological ethicists who share his view.

What kind of virtue ethic constitutes a genuine alternative to the kind of DCT I am defending? So far as I can see, such a virtue ethic would either have to deny the importance of moral duties, as prescribing or forbidding types of actions, altogether, or else show that our moral duties can be derived from and explained by virtue theory. The former type of view is one that is linked to some versions of what is often called "moral particularism." Moral particularism emphasizes the idea that moral judgments are a response to the particular features of a situation, rather than being derived from general principles, and it

---

[50] Stanley Hauerwas, "Obligation and Virtue Once More," in *Truthfulness and Tragedy*, with Richard Bondi and David Burrell (Notre Dame, IN: University of Notre Dame Press, 1977), pp. 40–56. For Hauerwas' rejection of the idea of a "pure" virtue ethic, see p. 43.

[51] Hauerwas, "Obligation and Virtue Once More," p. 52.

[52] Hauerwas, "Obligation and Virtue Once More," pp. 40, 42.

comes in different forms. A strong form of moral particularism would be one that claims that there are no true moral duties that are general in form; at best a principle that we regard as expressing our moral duty gives us only "a general guide or rule of thumb."[53] Such principles can act as guides only because they "encapsulate the acquired and revisable wisdom of our ethical traditions."[54] But we can never deduce what we should do in an actual situation from such a general rule. Rather, after taking account of the concrete features of the actual situation, "you have to form your own judgement and this judgement will go beyond what the principle says to you."[55] Particularism in this form seems well suited to a virtue ethic, in that the virtue ethicist can maintain that the correct moral judgments will be those made by virtuous people, people who possess "practical wisdom."

A DCT ethic rejects this strong form of particularism, as a natural law ethic must do as well.[56] Of course the particularist is right to emphasize that a correct moral judgment requires the agent to have a clear awareness of the concrete moral features of the situation. Moral principles have to be applied to situations, and applying a principle is an exercise of judgment, which is not itself always governed by principles. (If applying a principle always required following another principle, we would quickly generate an infinite regress.) To know that I ought not to lie to my teacher about why my essay is late, I need to understand both that lying is wrong and that my telling the teacher that I was ill when I was not constitutes lying. However, it is one thing to maintain that good judgment is required to apply moral principles correctly; quite another to assert that moral judgments do not rely on principles at all. The strong form of particularism seems to clash with our ordinary moral experience, and it therefore does not seem that it is damaging to a DCT to reject it. A DCT holds that sometimes we are aware of our moral duties, and that this awareness gives us a clear understanding of what we ought to do in particular situations.

There are weaker versions of moral particularism that are much more plausible, but I shall argue that they are fully compatible with a DCT ethic. Such weaker versions might include claims such as the following: There are some moral situations in which moral principles do not determine any unique right answer, and there are some moral situations in which it may be unclear how to apply our moral

---

[53] Van Hooft, p. 21.   [54] Van Hooft, p. 21.   [55] Van Hooft, p. 22.
[56] See Murphy, *Natural Law and Practical Rationality*, p. 215.

principles and thus difficult to apply them. Both kinds of situations would imply that there are some particular judgments that cannot simply be deduced from general principles. A DCT theorist can admit this. For example, a DCT theorist could well agree with the claim that sometimes moral principles, even when accompanied by good judgment in their application, do not deliver a unique answer to the question of what is morally right in particular situations. For it may well be that our moral principles simply do not always tell us what to do (or even what is permissible); some situations fall outside the scope of the principles of duty. From the perspective of a DCT this is not surprising, since obligations constitute only a portion of our moral lives. We can well understand why God would not give us commands to regulate every aspect of our lives. Rather, we would expect God would give us commands that bear on aspects of our lives that have a decisive importance for our relation to him and our moral transformation. (I will say more about this later.)

Neither will it be a problem for a DCT if the principles of morality are sometimes hard to interpret and apply. Once again we can understand why God might give commands that have such a feature. An abstract and general command such as the command to love all humans (understood as our "neighbors") is certainly one that will be hard to interpret and apply. However, it may be that the difficulty is inescapable in principles that are truly universal in scope. It may also be that it is good for us to struggle with the difficulties involved in applying such principles, for such struggles may be one of the ways we make moral progress. In any case, it does not seem necessary for a virtue ethicist to commit to the strong version of moral particularism, as is shown by the example of Thomas Aquinas, who held that there are some principles that hold universally, but who also believed that for some particular cases no rules can be formulated that capture what is morally required.[57] However, it is only the strong version of moral particularism that is inconsistent with there being principles or rules that express moral obligations.

The second way that a virtue ethic could come into conflict with a DCT is by claiming that moral obligations can be adequately explained in terms of the virtues, thus making any appeal to God's

---

[57] For the latter claim, see Aquinas' *Commentary on the Nichomachean Ethics* (II, Lectio 2, 259). Mark Murphy discusses this passage in *Natural Law and Practical Rationality*, p. 269.

commands unnecessary. Michael Slote, for example, has defended a virtue ethic that he calls "agent-based," as opposed to being simply "agent-focused," which is the kind of view associated with Aristotelian-type virtue ethics.[58] According to an "agent-based" ethic, it is the fact that a virtuous agent would act in a particular way θ that makes it the case that θ is actually the correct way to behave.

Slote himself actually makes little use of the idea of moral obligations.[59] Instead, he defends an ethic of "caring," and argues that a life that is shaped by "conscientious" attention to moral obligations is morally inferior to a life that is rooted in more immediate forms of caring.[60] I think Slote here underestimates the importance of duty in the moral life, though later in this chapter I will suggest that there is actually something in the neighborhood of Slote's view that is defensible. However, we can imagine a virtue ethicist similar to Slote who thinks moral duties are more important than he does, but who claims that what makes our moral duties to be our duties is the fact that they are perceived as duties by the virtuous person. Indeed, we don't have to imagine merely such a theory. Linda Zagzebski appears to argue that our moral duties are simply those types of acts which a virtuous agent would feel guilt or shame for not doing.[61]

The type of virtue ethic that Slote and Zagzebski defend is one in which the virtuous agent is the "truth-maker" for normative truths. Courage is good because it is a trait displayed by the "exemplar" of virtue.[62] However, this seems to invert the way things actually are. We don't regard courage as a good thing because it is the kind of trait we find in virtuous people. Rather, we believe courage is a good thing, and so when we find someone who is courageous we have a reason to think that this person is virtuous, at least in that respect. The same thing is surely plausible for duties. We don't believe certain acts become duties because they are experienced as duties by those people we regard as virtuous. Rather, we think that one of the characteristics of virtuous people is that they experience their actual duties as duties.

[58] See Michael Slote, *Morals from Motives* (Oxford: Oxford University Press, 2001), pp. 3–37.

[59] Slote's index does not even have an entry for "obligation" or for "duty."

[60] Slote, pp. 51–62.

[61] Linda Zagzebski, *Divine Motivation Theory* (Cambridge: Cambridge University Press, 2004), pp. 145–59.

[62] For Zagzebski's defense of exemplarism, see pp. 51–8.

Another possible version of a virtue ethic could give an account of the relation between moral duties and obligations that is epistemological rather than metaphysical.[63] According to this view, it is not the fact that a virtuous person recognizes a duty that makes it to be a duty. Rather, it is by looking to exemplars that we come to know what our duties are. So far as I can see, there is no need for a proponent of a DCT to deny that virtuous exemplars provide at least one of the ways in which we come to know about our moral duties.

There certainly are versions of virtue ethics that are incompatible with a DCT. However, it seems that these versions are less plausible than their less-extreme counterparts. We can recognize the important and central role of the virtues in the moral life without denying the importance of moral duties, or implausibly attempting to explain such duties as created by virtuous people. In the final sections of this chapter, I shall try to say something about the ways in which a virtue ethic and a DCT can fit together.

CONNECTIONS BETWEEN THE VIRTUES AND MORAL OBLIGATIONS

One could of course argue that a DCT and virtue theory are compatible but simply fulfill different roles in ethics. Giving an account of our moral duties and giving an account of the characteristics of virtuous people are both important but they are answering different questions about different aspects of our ethical lives. To some degree this answer is right. However, there are some interesting and intimate links between these two aspects of ethics that are obscured when we focus on duty and virtue simply as two distinct aspects of morality.

First, we should remember, as I briefly mentioned in Chapter 1, that our moral duties may include duties to cultivate various virtues. For simplicity in exposition I have discussed duties as duties to act or refrain from acting in particular ways, but it is notable that in the Christian tradition, many of God's commands are commands to acquire or cultivate particular virtues. To choose one example from many

---

[63] Mark Murphy calls this a "metaphysical" version of a virtue ethic, and distinguishes it from an epistemological version. See Murphy, *Natural Law and Practical Rationality*, pp. 213–14.

possibilities, in Romans 12:2 Paul give a command to "be transformed by the renewing of your mind." This is clearly not a duty to perform a specific act-type but a duty to seek to become a different type of person. Later in the chapter (verses 12–13) Paul gives some additional commands that spell out this ideal in terms of particular virtues: "Be joyful in hope, patient in affliction, faithful in prayer. Share with God's people who are in need. Practice hospitality." Here injunctions to act in particular ways ("share with God's people") are blended with commands to acquire the virtues necessary to act in those ways, such as hope, patience, generosity, and hospitality.

Indeed, it is arguable that the fundamental commands of God are indeed, at least in part, commands to acquire virtues. Jesus, drawing from the Hebrew Bible, affirms that the two greatest commands are the commands to "love the Lord your God with all your heart and with all your soul and with all your mind" and to "love your neighbor as yourself," and even claims that "all the Law and the Prophets hang on these two commandments" (Matthew 22:37–40). Even though some commentators have followed Kant, who claimed that the love spoken about here must not be an emotion, but rather a "practical love" that consists solely in action, this seems an implausible reading of this text, since Jesus connects the love in question with the innermost being of the person (heart, soul, mind).[64] It seems more plausible to hold that the love in question is an emotion, or perhaps a disposition to have the emotion when appropriate. Writers on the virtues often stress that some of the virtues consist of emotions or dispositions to have emotions of an appropriate kind. To be a compassionate person is just to be a person who feels compassion when confronted by those who are suffering (and in other situations in which the emotion is appropriate), and who expresses that emotion in actions. Love for God and neighbor can certainly be understood as just such an emotion-disposition.[65] St. Paul echoes Jesus at this very point, claiming that all of the commands of God are "summed up" in the command to love the neighbor, and thus "love is the fulfillment of the law" (Romans

---

[64] For Kant's reading of the command, see *Grounding for the Metaphysic of Morals*, trans. James W. Ellington, 3rd edn. of translation (Indianapolis, IN: Hackett Publishing Co., 1993), p. 12.

[65] See my *Kierkegaard's Ethic of Love*, pp. 191–8, for an account of how the love in question can be understood as involving emotions or emotion-dispositions.

13:9–10). So we may conclude that the supreme commands in the Christian tradition are in fact commands to acquire virtues.

The connections between virtue and duty go in the other direction as well. Not only are there duties to acquire virtues, we must recall, as many deontologists have pointed out, that an account of the virtues may be valuable in giving us an understanding of what motivates moral agents to live in accordance with their duties. Kant famously claimed that the moral person must be motivated solely by respect for the moral law itself, but a defender of a DCT does not have to follow Kant in this regard.[66] It may well be that reliably to fulfill our moral duties certain virtues must be present. If morality demands that a person do something that puts that person at great risk, then courage would seem to be necessary for the person consistently to live up to that ideal. It may well be that a person who is obligated to be truthful will be unable to live up to the demands of duty without a love for the truth and a habit of honesty.

If a DCT is right, then fulfilling our moral duties can be at the same time an expression of devotion to God, thus linking the life of duty to such "theological virtues" as hope and faith. Faith supports the life of duty because trust in God and God's goodness will support the belief that living in accordance with God's commands will ultimately advance what is good and what is good for the person who is living in this way. Such faith can lead to hope even when a person's situation is bleak, since God is the one for whom all things are possible.

It is also worth pointing out that a passionate concern and desire to live in accordance with one's duties is itself recognized by most people as one of the virtues. This virtue is often called "conscientiousness" or "dutifulness," but I think that these terms are not altogether apt to describe the virtue I have in mind. Certainly, one characteristic of a virtuous person is a conscientious concern to fulfill the individual's moral obligations. However, this characteristic is sometimes pictured, in a kind of caricature of Kant, as a legalistic concern for rules, where one does what is right but in a joyless manner, gritting one's teeth and doing one's duty for the sake of duty.

---

[66] This reading of Kant is actually an over-simplification. Recently, scholars have begun paying attention to Kant's own account of the virtues. For a balanced discussion of Kant's view of the virtues, see Robert B. Louden, "Kant's Virtue Ethics," *Philosophy* 61:238 (October 1986), pp. 473–89.

However, it is instructive to note that the biblical writers who understood their duties in terms of God's law did not see them in this joyless way. They did not see God's commands as burdensome or onerous. The book of Deuteronomy contains repeated exhortations to obey God's commands or laws, along with assurances that to choose the way of obedience is to choose blessing. The motivational focus is not on law for the sake of law, but fulfilling the law out of love for the law-giver. Deuteronomy 11:1 is typical: "Love the Lord your God and keep his requirements, his decrees, his laws and his commands always." Such exhortations are almost always accompanied by promises of blessing for those who keep God's laws, and it is therefore not surprising that Psalm 119 celebrates the joys and delights of keeping God's law:

> I will always obey your law,
>   for ever and ever.
> I will walk about in freedom
>   for I have sought out your precepts.
> I will speak of your statutes before kings
>   and will not be put to shame,
> For I delight in your commands
>   because I love them.
> I lift up my hands to your commands, which I love,
>   and I meditate on your decrees. (Ps. 119:44–8)

Nor is this joyous embrace of God's commands limited to the Old Testament. Both the Gospels and the Epistles are full of exhortations to keep God's commands, whether given through the Hebrew scriptures, or through the words of Jesus and the apostles, and the writers regularly conjoin these exhortations with promises of blessing and a joyous life. Jesus' words in John 15:10 express this powerfully: "If you obey my commands, you will remain in my love, just as I have obeyed my Father's commands and remain in his love."

THE VIRTUES AS THE *TELOS* OF MORAL DUTY

There are therefore numerous ways in which virtues and duty are connected. However, I think that the deepest link requires us to reflect on the *telos* of duty. We may begin by considering the contrast Kant draws between a being like God and creatures such as ourselves. The notion of duty, according to Kant, presupposes the possibility of a discrepancy between what an agent ideally should do, which of course for Kant means following reason, and what the agent actually does. God, according to Kant, possesses a "holy will," and therefore there is no possibility that God will ever follow any principles that are wrong.[67] Since we humans do not have such a holy will, we experience the principles of morality as duties that constrain our wills. However, God follows those same principles but does so spontaneously with no sense of constraint at all. The notions of duty and obligation simply have no role to play for such a being.

The distinction Kant draws between beings who are subject to temptation and a being with a holy will suggests that moral duties might play a different role in the life of a human person who begins to resemble a person with a holy will, though this is a possibility that Kant himself did not really exploit. Perhaps, for example, a perfected saint would be such a person, someone who lives the moral life without giving much thought (or any thought at all) to duties, because such a saint simply wants to do what is right.

What I want to suggest is the idea that moral duties might have as part of their function the goal of assisting us to become such persons, or at least as moving us in that direction. I think this is plausible if we think of God's commands as aimed at helping us to become "friends of God," people who can enjoy an intimate and personal knowledge of God and relationship with him. The main obstacle to such a relation to God is surely our character. Even Aristotle understood that good friends must share basic values,[68] and it is surely right that we cannot enjoy friendship with God, who is supremely good and loving, if we do not resemble God by loving the good. If Kant is right in his claim that duty plays no role in the life of a being with a holy will, then perhaps it will be the case that humans who are becoming more like God will find that the place of duty in their lives diminishes as well.

Something like this is suggested in Kierkegaard's greatest book on ethics, *Works of Love*. Throughout most of *Works of Love* Kierkegaard strongly defends an ethic of duty, in which our two supreme duties are to love God unconditionally and to love our neighbors as

---

[67] For Kant's discussion of a holy will, see *Grounding for the Metaphysic of Morals*, pp. 23–4.
[68] *Nichomachean Ethics*, trans. W. D. Ross, in Richard McKeon (ed.), *The Basic Works of Aristotle* (New York: Random House, 1941), 1156b.

ourselves.[69] Kierkegaard argues that the common view that genuine love must be spontaneous and free from any sense of obligation is mistaken: "Only when it is a duty to love, only then is love eternally secured against every change, eternally made free in blessed independence, eternally and happily secured against despair."[70] This view that love should be free from duty is one Kierkegaard attributes to a figure we might call the "unspoiled pagan," someone who has not encountered the Jewish–Christian idea that we are subject to God's law. In contemporary Christendom, however, Kierkegaard describes a different type of figure, someone who has learned from Christianity the importance of moral duty, but thinks that the moral law needs no divine law-giver: "God and the world agree in this, that love is the fulfilling of the Law; the difference is that the world understands the Law as something it thinks up by itself..."[71]

Kierkegaard claims that this is impossible. The moral law can be grounded neither in the decisions of individuals nor in any kind of social agreement.[72] Rather, the true foundation of the moral law is the authority of God, to whom we are completely indebted. Modernity is seen by Kierkegaard as a kind of revolt or mutiny against this divine authority: "The abominable era of bond service is past, and so there is the aim of going further—by means of the abomination of abolishing the person's bond service in relation to God, to whom every human being, not by birth but by creation from nothing, belongs as a bond servant..."[73] The result of this mutiny is moral confusion and skepticism: "As a reward for such presumption, all existence will in that way probably come closer and closer to being transformed into doubt or into a vortex."[74]

Interestingly, after having spent most of the book describing love of neighbor as a divinely commanded obligation, in the concluding chapter of *Works of Love*, Kierkegaard sounds a new theme. He begins by quoting the words of the apostle John: "Beloved, let us love one another."[75] Kierkegaard comments that these words "have an

---

[69] For a full exploration of the DCT found in *Works of Love*, see my *Kierkegaard's Ethic of Love*.

[70] Søren Kierkegaard, *Works of Love*, trans. and ed. Howard V. Hong and Edna H. Hong (Princeton, NJ: Princeton University Press, 1995), p. 29. This quote is in boldface in Kierkegaard's original text.

[71] *Works of Love*, p. 128.   [72] *Works of Love*, p. 115.

[73] *Works of Love*, p. 115.   [74] *Works of Love*, p. 115.

[75] *Works of Love*, p. 375. The biblical passage is from I John 4:7.

intermediate tone or mood," and that in them "you do not hear the rigorousness of duty."[76] Rather, Kierkegaard says, putting words into the mouth of the apostle, "The commandment is that you *shall* love, but ah, if you will understand yourself and life, then it seems that it should not need to be commanded, because to love people is the only thing worth living for, and without this love you are not really living."[77]

The suggestion is that a person like John (as Kierkegaard imagines him), who is "perfected in love" ceases to experience the call to love as a duty. It is not so much that the command itself is changed; the change is that "the person who loves becomes more and more intimate with the commandment, becomes at one with the commandment."[78] We may think of the person who is "perfected in love" as someone who has fully acquired love as a virtue; such a person has a firm and reliable disposition to love other humans, whether the neighbor be the "first person one sees" or someone one has never met.[79] Since "love is the fulfilling of the law," perhaps such a person at least begins to resemble Kant's idea of a being who has no need of duties or obligations. If this is correct, then perhaps the purpose of duties is to help us become transformed into the kinds of people who no longer require the notion of duty at all. It is not a matter of "duty for duty's sake," but rather duty for the sake of personal transformation. If something like this is right, then a DCT requires an account of the virtues in order for us to fully understand the point of our duties. We can thus see that there is something right about Michael Slote's claim that there is a type of moral life that is superior to the life of duty, an "ethic of caring" instead of an ethic of duty.[80]

The problem with Slote's view, however, is that most of us are not saints who have become "perfected in love." Kierkegaard himself warns that it is dangerous even to talk as the apostle talks if one has not attained the moral status of the apostle: "That which is truth on the lips of the veteran and perfected apostle could in the mouth of a beginner very easily be a philandering by which he would leave the school of the commandment much too soon . . ."[81] Kierkegaard reminds us that even though the apostle does not use the imperative mood, the words are still the words of an apostle, and thus have divine

---

[76] *Works of Love*, p. 375.   [77] *Works of Love*, p. 375.
[78] *Works of Love*, pp. 375–6.   [79] *Works of Love*, pp. 154–74.
[80] See Slote's discussion of this in *Morals from Motives*, pp. 38–58.
[81] *Works of Love*, p. 376.

authority. The apostle speaks "almost as if it had been forgotten that love is the commandment," but it is still the apostle who speaks. Such words, Kierkegaard affirms, "are not the beginning of the discourse about love but are the completion."

From the point of view of Christian theology, the connection between moral duty and personal transformation may be more complicated than it appears at first glance. Kierkegaard speaks of the moral law as a "school," and he here echoes a traditional Christian view that one important function of the moral law is to be a "schoolmaster." Though the moral law aims at our transformation, it begins by helping us see how much we need to be transformed. It points to a problem of moral guilt and a need for atonement that requires more than a philosophical remedy. So Christians have some additional reasons for thinking that it is dangerous to "leave too soon" the life of moral duty.

Kierkegaard is, I believe, right to emphasize that for most of us the life of duty remains vitally important. We are not good enough that we can simply "love and do what we will." Perhaps we could safely follow this advice (from Augustine) if our love were truly perfected, but few of us would dare to make such a claim.

Nevertheless, it is important to recognize the limits of moral duty as well. In this chapter I have argued that a DCT is far from constituting a complete ethic. It rests on a framework of normative truths, including an account of the good, such as a natural law theory provides, and it needs an account of the virtues as well. These kinds of ethical theories not only answer different questions than does a DCT. They also provide a context which transforms our understanding of moral obligations themselves. Kierkegaard suggests that there is something transitional and provisional about the life of duty, even if the transitional period is the whole of temporal existence. Perhaps there are some who can at least begin to approximate the life of the saint who is perfected in love even short of eternity. For such people the life of duty becomes increasingly less central.

4

Objections to Divine Command Theory

In the last chapter I argued that a DCT does not provide a comprehensive and complete ethical theory. It needs an account of the good as well as an account of the virtues. Nevertheless, though a DCT is not a complete ethical theory in itself, it provides an important part of the story. Moral obligations can be convincingly explained as God's commands. A DCT of the type I am defending is now sufficiently familiar that it has inspired a number of objections. Paradoxically, one might even say that this fact is a tribute to the force of a DCT, since a philosophical theory that does not inspire objections must be one that is uninteresting. No one bothers to refute a theory that does no work. In this chapter I shall try to explain and respond to many of the common objections that are raised against a DCT. Some of these objections can be easily rebutted, since they are either rooted in misunderstanding or perhaps are directed against different forms of a DCT. Others, however, are directed at the specific features of the kind of view I am defending, and thus will require careful critical examination. I shall begin with objections of the former sort.

I realize that for many people it will be a decisive objection to a DCT that such a view commits its holder to belief in the existence of God. Those who are dogmatic atheists, or who are firmly convinced that no reasonable person should believe in God, are unlikely to take seriously the possibility that moral obligations are divine commands. Perhaps some of these people might be open to reconsidering these matters if they could be shown that a DCT is markedly superior to secular rivals; I shall make an effort in this direction in Chapter 5. In this chapter I address those who are not dogmatically convinced of atheism (including theists), but are inclined to think that moral obligations can be given a good explanation that makes no reference to God.

THE *EUTHYPHRO* PROBLEM

Perhaps the most common objection to a DCT is usually called the *Euthyphro* objection, since it is inspired by the Platonic dialogue of that name. Many introduction to ethics textbooks dismiss the idea that God plays any significant role in ethics by appealing to this objection.[1] In the *Euthyphro*, Socrates interrogates the character for whom the dialogue is named, who claims that holiness (or piety in many translations) can be understood as "that which is pleasing to the gods."[2] After some initial sparring and clarification of Euthyphro's thesis, Socrates poses the critical question: "Is what is holy holy because the gods approve it, or do they approve it because it is holy?"[3] The question poses a dilemma. If Euthyphro says that what is holy has that quality simply because the gods approve of it, then the gods' approval appears to be arbitrary; they have no reason to approve of it. On the other hand, if he says that the gods approve of what is holy because it is holy, then holiness must be some quality that is independent of what the gods approve, and which can there-fore serve as the ground of their approval.

The *Euthyphro* does not, on the surface at least, seem to be about morality but holiness or piety. However, many philosophers have thought that a similar dilemma can be raised about moral theories that ground moral qualities in what God commands (or wills or approves of) by asking a question parallel to the one Socrates posed. Suppose that what is morally good is understood to be what God approves of (or commands or wills). Does God approve of what is good because it is good? Or do the things that are good gain that status because God approves of them? If God approves of them because they are good, then goodness must be independent of God's approval. However, if things are good simply because God approves of them, God's approval seems unmotivated. This has two undesirable results. First, it looks as if things like hatred and cruelty would be good if God approved of them, surely an untoward result. Second, it looks as if it will be impossible meaningfully to praise God

---

[1] For a clear example, see the very popular text by Rachels, *The Elements of Moral Philosophy*, pp. 46–50.

[2] *Euthyphro*, trans. Lane Cooper, in *Plato: The Collected Dialogues*, ed. Edith Hamilton and Huntington Cairns (Princeton: Princeton University Press, 1961), p. 174.

[3] *Euthyphro*, p. 178.

as good, since whatever he approves will be good by definition, and so God would be good no matter what he did, so long as he approved of himself and his actions.

I shall be concise in dealing with this problem, since a powerful rebuttal is now common in the literature.[4] The Euthyphro problem does present grave difficulties for a universal voluntaristic ethical theory that tries to base all ethical properties in God's commands or will. Such theories have been developed. William of Ockham, for example, is widely regarded as having developed such a theory of morality.[5] However, the DCT presented in this book, following the work of Robert Adams and others, is radically different from such a view, since God's commands are only regarded as the source of moral *obligations*, and the theory explicitly affirms that some objective theory of the good is necessary as a foundation for this account of the morally right.

Restricting the account to moral obligations allows the defender of a DCT to escape the dilemma implicit in the Euthyphro question. If asked, "Are moral obligations duties because God commands them?" the proponent of a DCT answers yes. However, this does not imply that God's commands are arbitrary. God's commands are aimed at the good and therefore are certainly not arbitrary. Nor is praise of God as good empty of content, since God can rightly be praised (among other things) for the ways in which his commands further the good.

Does this mean that God has no choice about what he commands? In Chapter 2 I distinguished two aspects of a DCT, the modal status thesis and the divine discretion thesis. I there argued that even someone who accepts only the modal status thesis still holds a minimal version of a DCT, since on this view God's commands are necessary for moral obligations to have the character they actually

---

[4] Besides the pioneering work of Philip Quinn and Robert Adams, I would cite the excellent discussion in David Baggett and Jerry L. Walls, *Good God: The Theistic Foundations of Morality* (New York: Oxford University Press, 2011), particularly chapters 2, 6, and 7, and John Milliken, "*Euthyphro*, the Good, and the Right," *Philosophia Christi* 11:1 (2009), pp. 145–55.

[5] For an example of the attribution of such a view to Ockham, see Baggett and Walls, *Good God*, pp. 35–6. Interestingly, they do not actually cite Ockham's own work. For an essay that suggests that the historical Ockham was not the radical voluntarist he is commonly thought to be, see Marilyn Adams, "Ockham on Will, Nature, and Morality," in Paul Spade (ed.), *The Cambridge Companion to Ockham* (Cambridge: Cambridge University Press, 1999), pp. 245–71.

have as moral duties. So even if God has no choice about the content of his commands, the commands would still be important.

However, I think that the divine discretion thesis is plausible as well, since it seems likely that in some cases God has alternatives he could command that are equally conducive of the good, and God will sometimes have reasons to give commands about such matters. If this is so, does this bring back the problem of arbitrariness, at least with respect to this class of God's commands? I think there is no real difficulty here. As I have already argued in Chapter 2, if we ask why God might give a command in such a situation, a plausible answer is that such commands would provide a special test of devotion to God, and perhaps be especially conducive to practices that would nourish such devotion. Since the two possible actions are equal in the goodness they would produce, in such cases love and devotion to God would be the only motivation for the choice of the one act over the other. As to the claim that God's choice of one act over the other would be arbitrary, there is no more reason to think this would be the case than we would have in the case of a creative artist who, faced with two equally good combinations of colors for a particular painting, chooses one of them. The same kinds of reasons the artist might give can be attributed to God. Perhaps the artist simply takes delight in one of them and so chooses it. Perhaps the artist simply views this as a way to express freedom and creativity. Or perhaps the artist simply thinks that such a "Buridan's ass" situation must not lead to inaction, and so chooses one of the options, so that the painting can go forward.[6] If this involves arbitrariness, it does not seem to be an objectionable kind.

I conclude that the Euthyphro problem, however devastating it may be for broadly voluntaristic theistic theories of ethics, is not a problem for a DCT of the type developed here. The proponent of a DCT does not have to accept what Louise Antony calls a "divine independence theory" with respect to moral obligations, but can reject such a view without the implication that the divine commands that constitute moral obligations are arbitrary or unmotivated.[7]

---

[6] In the Middle Ages philosophers discussed a famous problem posed by Buridan, as to how a donkey who was faced with equally inviting bales of hay to his left and right, could choose one rather than starve.

[7] See Louise Antony, "Atheism as Perfect Piety," in Robert K. Garcia and Nathan L. King (eds), *Is Goodness without God Good Enough?* (Lanham, MD: Rowman & Littlefield, 2009), pp. 67–84. See especially p. 71.

THE "HORRIBLE ACTS" OBJECTION

Another common objection to a DCT is that it violates deep moral intuitions about what is morally right. Even if one claims that God's commands determine only our moral obligations and not the good, there may still be a difficulty lurking in the area. For surely there are some acts, such as rape and torture, that are morally wrong, and would be wrong no matter what God commands. God could no more make such acts morally permissible by a command than he could make them good. Louise Antony, for example, argues that if a DCT is correct, then the following would be true: "If God had commanded us to torture innocent children, then it would have been morally right to do so."[8] One can see that this criticism is closely related to the Euthyphro objection since the issue concerns a seeming arbitrariness in what is taken to be morally wrong. Perhaps indeed it is the same objection in a different form.

The standard (and obvious) response to this charge is to point out that the type of DCT I am defending sees God as necessarily good. It is built into the theory that only the commands of a God who is necessarily good and loving could generate moral obligations; the commands of a supernatural evil being could not generate such obligations. It follows from this that God could not possibly give commands to do what is morally horrible because of the intrinsic badness of such acts. (Although, given our fallible understanding of the good, it is conceivable that God might give commands that appeared bad to us, at least initially.) Antony considers this response, but seems not to understand it, alleging that someone who claims this has abandoned a DCT and accepted a divine independence theory. We have, however, seen that this is simply mistaken; even if God's commands are ones he necessarily gives, they still endow what he commands with an important moral quality.

Recently, some critics have argued that this response to the "horrible acts" objection is not adequate. They argue that even if it is conceded (perhaps just for the sake of argument) that God cannot command what is bad, a DCT still has unacceptable consequences. Walter Sinnott-Armstrong, for instance, says that "even if God in fact never would or could command us to rape, the divine command theory still implies the counterfactual that, if God did command us to

---

[8] Antony, "Atheism as Perfect Piety," p. 71.

rape, then we would have a moral obligation to rape. That is absurd."[9] Erik Wielenberg has made a similar argument.[10] Baggett and Walls call this objection the "extended arbitrariness objection" to a DCT.[11]

On standard logical accounts of counterfactuals with impossible antecedents, the necessary falsity of the antecedent renders the conditional true, but vacuously true. On such a reading, the proposition "If God commanded torture of innocent children, it would be morally obligatory to torture innocent children" is true, but it is true for exactly the same reason that "If $2 + 3 = 6$, then circles would have four sides" is true. Wielenberg and Sinnott-Armstrong must believe that counterfactuals involving God commanding horrible acts must be true according to a DCT in some non-trivial way. However, it is claimed, since we can see that these counterfactuals are in fact false (also in some non-trivial sense), this shows that a DCT is unacceptable. Unfortunately, however, the critics provide no logical semantical theory to explain and justify these claims, with their non-standard interpretation of counterfactuals, but seem to rely on intuitions.

I shall grant for the sake of argument that the claim that the proposition "If God commanded torture of innocents, then torture of innocents would be morally obligatory" does seem intuitively to follow from a DCT, and also that the proposition nevertheless seems intuitively false. However, such intuitions hardly settle the issue.

This can be seen by considering some recent work by Alexander Pruss.[12] Pruss (who actually does not support a DCT) argues that an argument exactly parallel to the criticism made against a DCT can be made against any metaethical theory. Consider the following criticism of a Kantian ethical perspective: "If the categorical imperative required us to torture innocents, it would be morally obligatory to torture innocents." If one assumes that the categorical imperative decides what is morally obligatory, then one has reason to think that this proposition is entailed by a Kantian type theory. At least one has the same kind of

[9] Walter Sinnott-Armstrong, "Why Traditional Theism Cannot Provide an Adequate Foundation for Morality," in Garcia and King (eds), *Is Goodness without God Good Enough?* p. 106.

[10] See Erik Wielenberg, *Value and Virtue in a Godless Universe* (Cambridge: Cambridge University Press, 2005), pp. 41–3, 48–9.

[11] See "Appendix A" to Baggett and Walls, *Good God*, pp. 207–16, for their very clear statement of the objection and response. They use the acronym "DCM" instead of "DCT."

[12] Alexander Pruss, "Another Step in Divine Command Dialectics," *Faith and Philosophy* 26:4 (October 2009), pp. 432–9.

reason one has to think that an analogous proposition follows from a divine command theory. However, just as was the case for the proposition entailed by a DCT, this proposition about the categorical imperative's dictates seems false. A similar line of argument could be developed for any metaethical theory. Hence, this criticism of a DCT proves too much; if it is sound it would show the falsity of every metaethical account.

Notice that one cannot respond to Pruss simply by claiming that in the case of the Kantian ethic, it is impossible for the categorical imperative to imply that it is right to torture innocents. For that is exactly what the critic of a DCT has conceded with respect to a divine command theory: that it is impossible for God to command that innocents be tortured. So the two cases are identical in that the relevant conditional propositions have impossible antecedents. Any apparent difference in intuitive force in the cases must stem from the fact that the impossibility of God commanding the torture of innocents is not as *obvious* as the impossibility of deriving such a moral claim from the categorical imperative. But this is at best an epistemic fact about us and implies nothing about what is metaphysically possible or impossible. Perhaps if I understood God and God's nature adequately, the impossibility of God making such a command would be even more intuitively obvious to me than the impossibility of deriving an obligation to torture innocents from the categorical imperative.

Pruss himself speculates that the appeal of this type of objection to a DCT stems from the fact that "we reason poorly about outlandish counterfactuals . . . and *very* poorly about *per impossibile* counterfactuals."[13] I think Pruss is right about this and also right in his speculation that if we are tempted by the claim that such counterfactuals in the case of God are true or false in a more substantial way, this may simply reflect the fact that we do not have a clear grasp of God's essence, and thus fail to understand what is really possible and impossible for God.[14]

THE AUTONOMY OBJECTION

Many critics object that a divine command theory of moral obligations is objectionable because it undermines the autonomy of humans

---

[13] Pruss, pp. 437–8.   [14] Pruss, p. 439.

as moral agents, and they believe that such autonomy is essential to morality. This criticism can be developed in a stronger or weaker form. In the strong form, the charge is that morality, to be recognized as morality at all, must be based on reasons or arguments that humans can recognize for themselves.[15] So, for example, for James Rachels, a DCT does not even qualify as a moral theory, because morality requires moral agents to base their actions on reasons and arguments that they have autonomously recognized. Alternatively, the critic might admit that a DCT is a moral theory, but argue that it is a bad theory, because it infantilizes humans, conceiving of us as childlike creatures incapable of deciding important matters for themselves, needing to be told what to do.[16] These two forms of the autonomy objection raise different issues and therefore I will respond to them separately.

Let me begin with the claim that a DCT does not even count as a moral theory because a genuine moral theory must ground morality in principles and/or arguments that an agent can recognize as true and/or sound for herself. The first point to make is that on the DCT I have developed a person does not have to recognize a moral obligation as a divine command in order to have knowledge or at least justified belief that he or she has the obligation. It is difficult to see how Rachels' argument could apply to individuals who are not aware that their moral obligations are divine commands. Such people recognize their moral obligations, presumably in the same ways as other people, and it is hard to see how the fact that those obligations are really divine commands could undermine their autonomy, since they are ignorant of that fact.

So Rachels' argument must be intended to show that it is coming to *believe* that one's moral obligations are divine commands that undermines autonomy. However, it is not easy to see why this should follow. It is true that a DCT implies that there are objective moral principles (or at least one such principle) that a person ought to follow. However, surely merely accepting a moral theory that implies that there are such principles does not violate autonomy, since many

---

[15] Rachels, *The Elements of Moral Philosophy*, pp. 9–14, 44–50.
[16] For an example of this type of criticism, see Patrick Nowell-Smith, "Morality: Religious and Secular," in Baruch Brody (ed.), *Readings in the Philosophy of Religion* (Englewood Cliffs, NJ: Prentice-Hall, 1974). Nowell-Smith describes a divine command theory as "infantile" and claims that adherents to such a view show a low level of moral development.

moral theories (utilitarianism, for example) also say that there are objective moral principles that an individual should follow. If one supposes that an individual has come to accept a DCT on the basis of a philosophical argument (for example, one that argues that a DCT explains morality better than any competing theory), then it is hard to see how this could undermine the moral agent's autonomy. Rachels' requirement that the individual form moral beliefs on the basis of reason and/or arguments that the individual has considered for herself would seem to be met.

Perhaps Rachels, or someone else impressed by the autonomy objection, might argue that things are different when the objective moral principles come from God. Why might this be so? Possibly the idea is that simply following the dictates of another person would not count as following moral principles at all. The critic might reason as follows: One could imagine my neighbor Fred giving me orders as to how I should live my life. If I believe Fred is a very wise person and understands morality deeply, it might make sense for me to follow his demands. But in that case I am not regarding Fred as having practical authority, but epistemic authority. I follow his lead because he is a moral expert and knows better than I do what morality requires. Even in this case it could be argued that the individual who follows the policy of always doing what Fred says is not living autonomously, since it is arguable that a moral agent ought to seek to understand for herself why she should follow the principles she follows. However, if we assume that I regard Fred as having genuine practical authority, such that Fred actually creates my moral obligations by his commands, then matters are even worse. The fact that Fred tells me to do something gives me no moral reason to do it, unless there are some special circumstances that give Fred some authority over me.

All this seems right in the case of Fred the neighbor. But the case of Fred is very different than the case of God. Even in Fred's case, in some situations Fred's orders might create moral obligations. Suppose, for example, it is wartime, and Fred has been appointed air raid warden, and given authority to order the people in my neighborhood to extinguish their lights during air raids. In that situation Fred's order to extinguish my lights arguably does create a moral obligation to extinguish my lights. Similarly, as I argued in Chapter 3, God must have genuine moral authority in order for God's commands to create moral obligations. However, if I have good reasons to believe that God has this moral authority, and also good reasons to believe he has issued commands, then I would have good reason to follow God's orders. If I have good reasons to believe that all of the moral obligations I have are in fact God's commands, and that part of their moral status as duties stems from that command, then I would have good reason to hold a DCT. All of this is perfectly compatible with autonomy in Rachels' sense.

Let me now consider the second version of the autonomy objection, which does not claim that divine commands are incompatible with the kind of autonomy a moral agent must have, but rather that following divine commands would be a kind of childish version of morality. In effect the criticism in this case is that a God who expected us to live by his commands would be a God who did not really respect us, but regarded us as parents regard young children who are not really capable of making good decisions. Or perhaps the critic thinks the problem lies with the person who accepts a DCT; such a person is content with the moral standpoint of a child and shrinks from adult responsibility.

In responding to this I shall forgo the temptation to argue that adult humans often behave very childishly indeed, especially if they are compared with a being who is morally perfect and omniscient. Instead I shall begin by pointing out that a God who gives humans free will must certainly place some value on that freedom, and thus must respect it. On this assumption, even if God gives us commands, by giving us freedom to obey or disobey his commands he treats us as moral beings who have the opportunity freely to follow his principles. We thus have the dignity of being free participants in God's great plan for the universe, rather than helpless pawns or ignorant slaves.

However, it is easy to see that God does not necessarily infantilize humans by giving them commands as to how they should live. Whether something like that is true would depend on the nature of the commands God gives. Perhaps if God gave humans detailed instructions on a minute by minute basis for every detail of their lives then this criticism would have weight. For in that case human persons would not need to use their rational faculties or develop them in order to know how to live. The task would simply be to listen to God's continuing instructions and follow them.

However, if we assume that God does not give such commands, but rather gives humans commands that are at least somewhat general in nature, this would not follow. Imagine, for example, that God gave humans just one command, "to love their neighbors as they love themselves." Such a command is highly general and abstract, and will require that humans fully engage their rational faculties to understand its implications and apply it. Even if we assume that God gives multiple commands (such as in the Decalogue) those commands still have to be interpreted and applied, and their implications thought through.

God might well decide to give commands of just this nature so as to require humans to develop the capacities he has given them. In a similar way, wise and good parents give their children rules to live by, but as their children grow and become mature, the rules given are few in number and are the kinds of rules that require good judgment to interpret and apply. One might object that eventually good parents want children to be fully independent and this might imply that God should similarly want us to be free of his authority eventually. Perhaps something like this is the case. In Chapter 3 I speculatively suggested that for the perfected saint, the morality of duty may have little or no importance. Most of us, however, are very far from being perfected saints. For creatures like ourselves divine authority remains important.

This seems especially true if we consider that there is an important disanalogy between the parent–child relation and the creator–creature relation. Children eventually become adults and parents hope they will become their equals in intelligence and moral insight. However, humans never become God's equal either in intelligence or moral insight, and there remains a valid sense in which even mature adults rightly think of themselves as inferior to God in both moral knowledge and desires. There is thus good reason to think that even mature adults should welcome God's commands, since those commands come from the one who has the best possible understanding of human life and the good, and who gives the commands to assist us in making progress towards our own ultimate good. The amazing thing is not that God gives us commands, but that, although we are finite, sinful mortals, he accords us the dignity of becoming his co-workers and participants in the divine plan.

THE PRIOR OBLIGATIONS OBJECTION

The third objection I want to consider to a DCT is one that Richard Wainwright calls the Cudworth objection, since it can be found in the writings of Ralph Cudworth, a seventeenth-century English philosopher often described as one of the Cambridge Platonists.[17] It is rooted in a worry that a DCT is too narrow and does not account for all genuine moral obligations. I shall call this objection the "prior obligations objection."

A full-fledged DCT holds that all moral obligations are divine commands.[18] (Or, on some versions, that they stem from divine commands.) The prior obligations objection argues that there must be some moral obligations that are not grounded in divine commands because they hold antecedently to or independently of divine commands. Specifically, the claim is that humans have a moral obligation to obey God. This obligation is not itself grounded in God's commands. Rather, it is precisely because there is a prior obligation to obey God that God's commands can create new obligations. There must therefore be some moral obligations other than those that are created by God's commands.

The defender of a DCT might respond by arguing that these "prior obligations" to obey God are not actual obligations but just hypothetical ones: To say that we have a prior obligation to obey God is just another way of saying that we are obligated to obey God *if* God issues commands, but there is no actual obligation until a command is issued. The conditional proposition itself can be understood as simply spelling out the meaning of the claim that God has moral authority. To say that God has moral authority (as the proponent of a DCT certainly must) is just to say that he has the right to issue commands that ought to be obeyed. There are certainly moral *truths* (such as

---

[17] For a clear discussion of this line of argument, found in Cudworth and many other thinkers, see William Wainwright, *Religion and Morality* (Aldershot, UK: Ashgate Publishing, 2005), pp. 80–3. Cudworth's own argument is found in *A Treatise Concerning True and Immutable Morality* (London: J. and J. Knapton, 1731); reprint edition (New York: Garland, 1976), pp. 20–6. For a contemporary version of the argument, see R. Zachary Manis, "Virtues, Divine Commands, and the Debt of Creation: Towards a Kierkegaardian Christian Ethic," Ph.D. Dissertation, Baylor University, 2006. There is also a forceful statement of this line of criticism in Nicholas Wolterstorff, *Justice: Rights and Wrongs* (Princeton, NJ: Princeton University Press, 2008), pp. 273–84.

[18] Some of the ideas in this chapter, and particularly the content of this section is taken, with modifications, from "Divine Commands as the Basis for Moral Obligations," invited plenary address at a conference on "The Future of Creation Order," organized by the Association for Reformational Philosophy on their 75th anniversary, Free University, Amsterdam, the Netherlands, August 16–19, 2011. A revised version of this paper will be published as part of the conference proceedings and thus may overlap to a degree with some of the material in this chapter.

"God has rightful authority over his human creatures" and "God's commands should be obeyed") that do not stem from divine commands, but a DCT does not deny this. The DCT says only that there is a category of moral truths, truths about actual moral obligations, that are linked to divine commands. There is certainly a sense in which it is true, antecedently to God's actual commands, that humans ought to obey any commands God issues, but the truth of this "ought" statement is not one that a defender of a DCT should find troublesome.

To see the strength of this reply, consider the fact that an analogous "prior obligations" objection could be directed at other metaethical theories of obligation. The Kantian says that our moral obligations are those that can be derived from the categorical imperative. One might object that this cannot be so, since there is at least one obligation not derived from the categorical imperative, namely the obligation to follow the categorical imperative itself. The critic might urge that this obligation must hold prior to any derived from the categorical imperative itself, and thus not all obligations can be derived from the categorical imperative.

Such an objection to a Kantian theory would be wrong-headed. The Kantian could rightly reply that to claim that we have this prior obligation is just to say that the categorical imperative does in fact possess genuine moral authority. But it is hard to see how the claim that the categorical imperative has moral authority could be the basis for an objection to its moral authority. The supporter of a DCT can say something similar about God's authority.

The critic might object that there is nothing hypothetical about the fact that we ought to obey God. It is a standing obligation, not a hypothetical one. However, I argued in Chapter 1 that not all "oughts" are moral "oughts" and thus it is not the case that every true sentence containing the verb "ought" expresses a moral obligation. There are lots of different senses of "ought," and the fact that it is true that a human ought to obey God does not imply that this sentence expresses a moral obligation. One might, for example, consistently claim that it is true that one ought to satisfy one's moral obligations without regarding that truth as itself stating one of our moral obligations. To say that one ought to satisfy one's moral obligations is just to say that those obligations have genuine authority.

If someone does not find these responses compelling, there is one other interesting line of response (not an alternative but a supplementary response) that is open to Jews and Christians who take the Hebrew Bible to be a genuine revelation from God. If we look at the actual commands God gives to his people as recorded in the Bible, we find that one of the more frequently expressed commands is that "God's people should obey all his commands." For example, in a long list of specific commands given in Leviticus 19 we encounter this one: "Keep my decrees" (v. 19). In several chapters of Deuteronomy, Moses repeatedly represents God as commanding the Israelites to "be careful to do what the Lord your God has commanded you" (Deuteronomy 5:32). These repeated commands from God to "keep all my commands" we may find initially puzzling, as we no doubt would if a human legislature were to pass a law requiring citizens of a state to obey all the laws of the state. However, if a DCT is correct, and our moral obligations are identical to divine commands, then by issuing such a command to obey his commands, God would convert the antecedent fact that humans ought to obey his commands into an actual moral duty, in what we might call a "bootstrapping" manner. On this view it is both true independently of God's commands that one ought to obey God, but also true that "one ought to obey God" is in fact a moral obligation, because God has commanded us to keep his commands.

I therefore do not find the prior obligations objection to be a significant problem for a DCT. Note, however, even if one accepted this objection, much of the substance of a DCT would remain. One could still hold that God's commands are sufficient for moral obligations, even if they were not necessary. God could still create obligations for humans by giving commands, even if not all moral obligations arise in this way, and someone who agrees with the prior obligations objection could still hold that the vast majority of our moral obligations are generated from or identical to divine commands. Those who are aware of such obligations have a kind of *de re* awareness of God as authoritative Lord and of ourselves as subject to that authority, even if they do not understand that the obligations they sense are in fact God's requirements for their lives.

THE SUPERVENIENCE OBJECTION

I have, for the sake of simplicity of exposition, usually described a divine command theory of moral obligation as affirming that moral obligations simply are identical to God's commands or requirements for humans. However, as I noted in Chapter 2, divine command theory can also be understood as claiming that God's commands bring about or cause the existence of moral obligations, or as the claim that moral obligations supervene on God's commands (no doubt together with some other facts as well). In this section I shall deal with an objection to the identity version of a DCT, discussing the other two forms in the next section when I deal with a related objection.

A clear version of what I shall call the supervenience objection to the identity version of a DCT can be found in Mark Murphy's *An Essay on Divine Authority*.[19] Murphy describes what I call the identity version of a divine command theory as "reduction DCM" (for divine command metaethics), and he argues as follows: "[R]eduction DCM must be false, for it, in conjunction with a very weak and plausible claim about God's freedom in commanding, entails that the moral does not supervene on the nonmoral."[20] If true, this would be a devastating objection, since supervenience of the moral on the non-moral is an essential part of our concept of the obligatory.

To explain this objection I must first say something about the claim that the moral must supervene on the non-moral. The idea behind this claim is simply that the moral properties of things are fixed by their non-moral properties. Moral properties, such as being obligatory, do not "float free" of their other properties. Thus, it cannot be the case that two actions are exactly alike except that one of the acts is morally obligatory and the other is not obligatory. I agree with Murphy that if a DCT were incompatible with the supervenience of the moral on the non-moral, this would be a problem for a DCT.

Why does Murphy think that supervenience creates a problem for an identity version of a DCT? The problem is created by the plausible claim (one that I have endorsed in Chapter 2) that God has some freedom in giving his commands to humans. Murphy argues that if we agree that God has some freedom about what he commands, then there will be two possible worlds which are exactly alike in their natural features, but in which God gives different commands. If moral obligations are determined by God's commands, then it follows that actions in one of those worlds will be exactly like those in the

---

[19] The objection is found on pp. 82–92.
[20] Murphy, *An Essay on Divine Authority*, p. 83.

other except for being morally obligatory. But this violates the supervenience of the moral on the non-moral.

Now one might think that there will be a relevant difference between the acts in these two worlds, namely that in one world the act is commanded by God and in the other it is not, and that this difference could be the basis for the difference in moral status. However, Murphy correctly points out that if God's commands are *identical* to moral obligations, then the fact that God commands one act and not the other, while a genuine difference between the two actions, will not be a difference in the *non-moral* properties of the two actions but a difference in moral properties, and thus it will not be the case that moral properties supervene on non-moral properties.[21]

There are a couple of possible responses to Murphy at this point that I will eschew. One would be to reject the divine discretion thesis and hold that God's commands are determined by the character of the world God decides to create. In such a case supervenience will be maintained, since God's commands in different possible worlds will always be shaped by differences in the natural properties of those worlds. Although I have argued that such a view would still be a weak form of a divine command theory, since I accept the divine discretion thesis, I will not rely on this reply.

A second possible reply to Murphy would be to claim that the supervenience relation that holds for morality is only a weak supervenience, rather than a strong supervenience. The difference between strong and weak supervenience is a difference in the strength of the modality of the claim that one kind of thing necessarily is fixed by another. Strong supervenience says that the claim that "property x supervenes on property y" is a claim that in any possible world whatever has property y will also have property x. Weak supervenience holds only that it is necessarily the case that anything that has property y in some particular world will also have property x in that world. As Murphy notes, weak supervenience might allow the defender of an identity version of a DCT to preserve divine freedom, since it requires only that God's commands in some particular world are consistent, and this would allow God to give different commands in other possible worlds.[22]

---

[21] Murphy, *An Essay on Divine Authority*, p. 92.
[22] Murphy, *An Essay on Divine Authority*, pp. 88–9.

Murphy has two arguments against weak supervenience as a defense of an identity DCT.[23] I think those arguments are not decisive. However, I shall not contest the issue because I think there is a much stronger reply to his objection, one that is compatible with strong supervenience.

The reply I want to make begins by considering what kinds of properties moral properties are supposed to supervene on.[24] In the discussions of this issue one sometimes finds the claim that moral properties must supervene on non-moral properties, and sometimes one finds the claim that moral properties must supervene on natural properties. Perhaps for a metaphysical naturalist, these terms would designate the same set of properties; the non-moral properties and the natural properties are identical. However, this is not the case for a theist, and obviously theism must be considered as a possibility if one wishes to look at the case for a divine command theory of obligation. Besides the properties an act or substance may have that are purely "natural" (whatever that may mean) there are other properties that are linked to the relation an act or substance may have to God. Let us call those properties "supernatural properties," by which I do not of course mean that they are miraculous, but only that they are properties possessed because what has the properties has a certain kind of relation to God.

The strength of the supervenience intuition lies in the plausibility of the claim that two acts cannot be different only in their moral properties. However, there is no reason why a proponent of a DCT, who holds that God makes a huge difference to morality, should hold that it is only natural properties that may make a difference to the moral status of something. Supernatural properties may possibly make a difference as well. In other words, the non-moral properties will include supernatural as well as natural properties.

If God gives a command to perform or refrain from performing some act, then that act will have a supernatural property ("being commanded by God") that another similar act will not have. However, as Murphy rightly claims, if God's commands simply are identical to moral obligations, then this supernatural property will also be a moral

---

[23] Murphy, *An Essay on Divine Authority*, pp. 88–9.

[24] For a response to Murphy that is entirely different than mine see Michael Almeida, "Supervenience and Property-identical Divine Command Theory," *Religious Studies* 40 (2004), pp. 323–33. Almeida thinks that the claim that two things are metaphysically identical does not preclude a supervenience relation between them. For Murphy's reply see *Religious Studies* 40 (2004), pp. 335–9.

property and will not count as a non-moral property. However, there is no reason to think that the property of "being commanded by God" would be the only supernatural property an act commanded by God will have. The act very plausibly will also have such properties as "being pleasing to God" or "being preferred by God." Even if "being commanded by God" is a moral property, there is no reason to think these other supernatural properties must be moral properties. It is extremely plausible to think that any act that has the property "being commanded by God" would also differ in other supernatural properties, such as "being pleasing to God." Such properties are non-moral properties (albeit supernatural ones) and thus the supervenience principle ("No difference in moral properties without some difference in non-moral properties") is preserved. Nor does it seem plausible to say that the fact that God's commands must correspond to these non-moral properties in some way restricts God's freedom. It surely is no limit on God's freedom to say that God must act to secure ends that please him or that his acts must reflect his preferences.

Murphy might object that such supernatural properties are not the right kind of properties to make a difference in moral properties. For a property to make a difference to the moral status of an act, perhaps the property must be one that is "internal" to an act or person, rather than a relational property. However, it is easy to see that many important moral qualities depend on relationships acts and persons have to other acts and persons, and it is hard to see why relations to God should be excluded from having moral import. At least it is hard to see how this could be maintained without simply begging the important questions that divide a DCT proponent from someone who holds a different view of moral obligations.

Consider, for example, the property of being truly and deeply happy. Hardly anyone would think that this property could not have moral significance; for many moral theories it has very great importance. However, if a relation of friendship with God is necessary to be truly and deeply happy, and if such a relation requires that God be pleased with the one who wishes to be God's friend, then it is hard to see why the property "being pleasing to God" would not be one that could alter the moral status of an act or person.

One might argue that a person's happiness is a natural fact, and that differences of this sort would be differences in natural non-moral properties, and thus I have not shown that a supernatural property can affect moral status. However, I think this reply shows only that differences in supernatural properties may make some difference to the natural properties something possesses, which further strengthens the claim that acts commanded by God do differ in their non-moral properties, natural as well as supernatural. The fact that there are differences in natural properties that *follow* from differences in supernatural properties does not mean God's freedom is limited, because the differences in natural properties in this case are differences that result from God's decision to command an act. Since the differences in natural properties are not independent of that decision, they cannot be seen as limiting that decision, and thus there is no impingement on God's freedom.

The fact that God's decision to command an act will also bring it about (the act has certain properties it would not otherwise have) blocks one other possible objection to the view that a DCT must undermine the supervenience of the moral on the non-moral.[25] Someone might argue that in a "Buridan's ass" situation, in which God is deciding whether to command act A or act B, God might have no preference or desire for either act, but simply chooses arbitrarily, as a human in such a situation might do so as to avoid paralysis. In that case, the critic might argue, there will be no properties such as "God prefers act A" to be part of the non-moral properties on which the moral properties must supervene. However, if God's decision to command A by itself changes other properties of A, then it will still be true that the principle of "no difference in moral properties without a difference in non-moral properties" will be preserved. For act A will now, as a *result* of God's command, have such properties as "being pleasing to God" or "being conducive to a better relation to God." And those properties are surely non-moral properties, and may even be causally linked to such natural properties as "being conducive to the agent's happiness."

THE "MYSTERIOUS RELATIONSHIP" OBJECTION

The preceding objection posed by Murphy is linked to, indeed is really part of, a broader objection to divine command accounts of obligation that might draw on some of Murphy's arguments that God

[25] I thank Blake McAllister for calling this objection to my attention.

does not possess moral authority.[26] Murphy himself does not make this objection in the form I here present it, and I do not assume that he would do so. However, it is a line of argument that might well be attractive to someone who finds plausible Murphy's criticisms of attempts to argue that God possesses moral authority, the foundation to any DCT.

Here is how the argument might go. Exactly what is the relation between God's commands and moral obligations according to a DCT? It seems there are three possible ways one might understand this relation, corresponding to three different versions of a DCT: (1) God's commands are the cause of moral obligations; God brings them into existence by his commands. (2) Moral obligations supervene on God's commands. (3) God's commands are identical to moral obligations. Suppose that these are the only ways God's commands and moral obligations could be related. If none of these views give a plausible account of how God's commands and moral obligations could be related, then no version of a DCT is plausible. Murphy provides arguments against all three views as to how divine commands and moral obligations could be related. If the relation between divine commands and moral obligations is just mysterious and no plausible view of how they fit together can be found, then a DCT is implausible. Murphy's arguments against these three possibilities could be read as an argument that no version of a DCT is viable.

What are the arguments against these various views of the relationship? They are of course different, since the views being criticized are different. I shall in this section focus on Murphy's criticisms of a causal version of a DCT. I shall ignore the supervenience version of the DCT, since Murphy's main argument against it is that a supervenience view is entailed by the causal view, and so will fail if the causal view he criticizes fails. The argument against an identity or reduction version of a DCT was discussed in the previous section of this chapter and rests on the claim that an identity version of a DCT is inconsistent with moral supervenience, combined with some plausible views about divine freedom. Since I have already responded to this argument, essentially the "mysterious relation" objection has already been answered, since if my argument is sound then at least one of the three ways God's commands might be related to moral

---

[26] See Murphy, *An Essay on Divine Authority*, pp. 70–92.

obligations is viable. However, I think it is worth looking at the objection Murphy raises to the causal version of a DCT to see what can be learned about the plausibility of other versions.

Before doing that I would like to argue that we might know *that* moral obligations are grounded in God's commands, even if we did not know exactly *how* the two were related, indeed, even if we found the relation mysterious. To see this consider a parallel worry about legal obligations. Imagine a state where the laws are determined solely by the decisions of a legislative body. In such a state it would seem that legal obligations are tightly linked to those legislative actions. Suppose someone objected in the following way to a "legislative decision" theory of legal obligations: "There are only three ways in which our legal obligations could be linked to the decisions of the legislature. We could say that the legislature causes the existence of those legal obligations, that the existence of those obligations supervenes on the actions of the legislature, or simply that the legal obligations are identical to the laws passed by the legislature. However, there are powerful arguments against all three of these possibilities. Therefore, it is unreasonable to think that legal obligations depend on the legislature."

I suppose the best response to such an argument would be to respond to one or more of the arguments against the three possibilities and give a satisfying account of how legal obligations are related to the actions of the legislature. However, note that it would be reasonable to think that legal obligations are grounded in the acts of the legislature even if we were unable to do this, and unable to say exactly how the legislature's decisions are linked to those legal obligations. We could know *that* our legal obligations were determined by the legislature even if we were unsure as to the ontological status of legal obligations and their relation to legislative acts. Similarly, I would argue that it might well be possible to know that God's commands or decrees generate moral obligations even if we could not decide if the relation between God's commands and our moral obligations should be understood as a causal one or as identity, or in some other way.

I shall now examine Murphy's argument against a causal version of a DCT, one that holds that God's command to ϕ causes it to be the case that humans have an obligation to ϕ. Murphy's objection is essentially that the causal history of how an obligation comes into being plays no normative role in helping us understand why the obligation holds. Suppose, for example, that God commands us to keep promises. If Murphy is right in his claim that the history of how an obligation comes to hold plays no role in explaining its normative status (a view I find dubious), then "the complete *normative* account of why one ought to keep promises would be simply that it is obligatory to keep promises. It would be no more appropriate for one to talk about God's command in one's normative account of why one ought to keep promises than it would be for one to talk about the complete evolutionary history of the pain mechanism in providing a normative account of why one ought not to inflict needless pain."[27]

The problem with a causal version of a DCT, as Murphy sees things, is that such a view does not allow for God's commands to be at least partially *constitutive* of one's reasons for actions. It is true, says Murphy, that if God commands some person A to ϕ, this implies it is obligatory for A to ϕ, and thus A must have a good reason to ϕ. However, it does not follow from this that it is the fact that God commands A to ϕ that itself partly constitutes the reason.[28] And the latter is what is required for divine authority. A bully who threatens to beat me up if I do not follow his orders gives me a reason to follow his orders but does not thereby have moral authority over me.[29] Moral authority thus requires more than causal control over my behavior.

Murphy claims that it may appear that a causal version of a divine command theory is plausible because it is easy to confuse a metaethical version of a DCT with a normative DCT.[30] A normative version of a DCT is the claim that "the state of affairs *its being obligatory to obey God* obtains."[31] However, Murphy insists that on a metaethical view of a DCT, "there is no prior normative state of affairs *its being obligatory to obey God* that obtains," because all such obligations come into existence through God's commands.[32]

It is clear, I think, that Murphy's arguments at this point blend with the "prior obligations" objection discussed earlier in this chapter. The

---

[27] Murphy, *An Essay on Divine Authority*, pp. 74–5.
[28] Murphy, *An Essay on Divine Authority*, p. 73.
[29] See Murphy's discussion of moral authority, *An Essay on Divine Authority*, pp. 8–19. Actually, it is not clear that Murphy's argument here works. It is true that a bully does not have moral authority, but I am skeptical that Murphy has adequately distinguished between bullying and cases of genuine authority, because it seems that the bully's commands do partly *constitute* reasons for me to act as he directs me to act (assuming the other conditions are in place). I thank Mike Cantrell for calling this problem with Murphy to my attention.
[30] Murphy, *An Essay on Divine Authority*, p. 75.
[31] Murphy, *An Essay on Divine Authority*, p. 75.
[32] Murphy, *An Essay on Divine Authority*, p. 75.

response to the problem should be clear as well. Murphy is mistaken to saddle the defender of a metaethical DCT with the view that all normative claims about what humans ought to do come into existence by way of divine commands. As we saw in the previous chapter, a plausible DCT presupposes something like a natural law ethic, which licenses practical oughts of various kinds, at least hypothetically. In order for a DCT to be plausible, it must be the case that it is true that *if* God gives commands, those commands ought to be obeyed. For that is the meaning of the claim that God has authority. A proponent of a causal version of a DCT should say that it is the fact that God has that authority that gives him the causal power to establish moral obligations.

Another way to make this point is to concede that *mere* causal power is not sufficient to be the basis of moral obligations. The exercise of moral authority must be seen as a special kind of causal power, just as the exercise of legal authority on the part of a legislature would be the exercise of a special kind of legal power. It is the proper exercise of this authority that counts as causing an obligation to come into existence. It is only if we distinguish this special kind of causality from mere causality that one can distinguish a genuine authority from a bully. If one wishes to think of a DCT in terms of causality instead of identity, the proper way to do so is to focus on the special kind of causal power possessed by someone who has moral authority.

THE PROMULGATION OBJECTION

If God's commands constitute moral obligations, they must be made known to people in some way, since a command is not merely an inner willing that an act be performed, but requires that what the commander wills be expressed in some way to those who are subject to the authority of the commander. In Chapter 2 I explained and endorsed the view that God makes his commands known in a variety of ways that are forms of general revelation and not merely through special revelation.[33] One can easily see the advantages of such a view. For if God's commands can only be known through special revelation, this

---

[33] See pp. 37–45.

would seem to imply that those, who because of accidents of time or geography have no access to that revelation, would have no way of knowing about their moral obligations, and this would seem to undermine the intuition that morality is a fundamental feature of human existence.

Despite this advantage, this view makes a DCT vulnerable to a particular type of objection, which has recently been developed in somewhat different ways by Wes Morriston and Erik Wielenberg.[34] I shall discuss Wielenberg's version of the problem. Wielenberg admits that "if God did exist, He would be authorized to impose certain moral obligations on human beings."[35] For example, Wielenberg agrees that if God has created us, then we might owe him a debt of gratitude that would make obedience to God's commands obligatory. However, the problem is that for this to happen, the recipients of the commands must know that the commands come from God. Otherwise no obligation is generated.[36]

Wielenberg gives the following kind of analogy to support his point. Suppose I owe my friend Dave a favor, and Dave wants me to repay him by loaning him my car. If Dave asks for the car in that situation, perhaps I ought to loan it to him. However, if Dave were to leave an anonymous note asking for the car, no obligation would be generated. I need to know that the note comes from Dave in order for Dave's request to generate any obligation.[37] Similarly, Wielenberg claims, "if God is to impose moral obligations on humans by way of his divine commands, He must get his intended audience to recognize that the commands are coming from Him."[38] The problem is that this seems impossible, at least in the case of reasonable non-believers in God, for it seems hardly possible for such a person to recognize a command as coming from a being that he does not believe exists.[39]

---

[34] See Wes Morriston, "The Moral Obligations of Reasonable Non-Believers," *International Journal for Philosophy of Religion* 65:1 (2009), pp. 1–10; Wielenberg, *Value and Virtue in a Godless Universe*, pp. 56–64.

[35] Wielenberg, p. 56.

[36] Wielenberg, p. 61.

[37] Wielenberg, pp. 60–3.

[38] Wielenberg, p. 61.

[39] Morriston's argument similarly presupposes the existence of reasonable non-believers, an assumption that could be challenged, and has been by Douglas Henry. See Morriston, p. 2, and Douglas Henry, "Does Reasonable Nonbelief Exist?" *Faith and Philosophy* 18 (2001), 75–92; and also "Reasonable Doubts about Reasonable Nonbelief," *Faith and Philosophy* 25 (2008), 276–89.

A command contained in a special revelation from God that clearly came from God would appear to meet the requirement that the source of the command be evident. However, if one agrees with Mouw and Adams that God's commands can be communicated through such means as reason and conscience this would not appear to be the case.

Actually, I think that one of Wielenberg's premises in this argument is false. It is not true that a person who does not believe in God could not recognize a command as coming from God. For one of the ways God might make his reality known to humans is by communicating commands to them. Of course, if the non-believer successfully recognizes the command as coming from God, he will no longer be a non-believer, but there is no reason why this could not happen. However, I shall not pursue this line of thought, because I think the deeper problem Wielenberg is pointing to lies in the idea that for God to successfully communicate a command to humans, he must, so to speak, communicate the command in such a way that it is obvious that the command comes from God. This in effect means that such a communication of a command would be a special revelation. However, I have argued that God is not limited to special revelation in communicating his commands.

Arguments such as Wielenberg's seem to pose a dilemma for the defender of a DCT. One can hold that God's commands are promulgated through special revelations only. In that case the commands do generate genuine obligations, but the obligations seem only to bind those who can recognize the revelation as authentic. Alternatively, one can say that God's commands are promulgated in more general ways, but in that case it is not clear how the commands can successfully generate obligations.

I believe the defender of a DCT must grasp the second horn of this dilemma by defending the claim that God's commands can generate obligations even for those who do not recognize those commands as coming from God. To do this two distinctions must be made. First, one must distinguish between the *recognition* of a moral obligation and the recognition of a moral obligation *as* a divine command. This distinction in turn requires that one distinguish a recognition of a moral obligation from an *explanation* of the existence of a moral obligation. The defender of a DCT who wants to affirm that God's commands are promulgated through general revelation must hold that it is possible for a reasonable non-believer to recognize a moral obligation without realizing that the obligation is in fact a divine command. This ignorance on the part of the non-believer may prevent the non-believer from being able to give an adequate explanation of the existence of the moral obligation, but there are many cases in which a person may reasonably accept the existence of something, but lack an adequate explanation of the existence of this something.

So how might God give those who do not believe in him the ability to recognize moral obligations? One way this could happen would be for God to make it possible for an individual directly to perceive moral obligations. A person who cannot perceive a moral obligation as a divine command might still be able to perceive it as an obligation. The reason for this is that, on Adams' account, being a non-believer does not bar an individual from having the *concept* of an obligation. Adams' version of a DCT is built on his social theory of obligations, which holds that there are obligations of many kinds, all of which are constituted by various kinds of relationships. Non-believers in God know what obligations are by virtue of being citizens in a community, parents, and so on. So a person's ignorance of God's existence would not necessarily prevent that person from recognizing that he or she is under an obligation of some kind, by way of a direct perception of the obligation, even if the person fails to perceive the obligation as a divine command.

Here is an analogy that might help illuminate the situation. Suppose I am hiking in a remote region on the border between Iraq and Iran. I become lost and I am not sure exactly what country I am in. I suddenly see a sign, which (translated) reads as follows: "You Must Not Leave This Path." As I walk further, I see loudspeakers, and from them I hear further instructions: "Leaving the path is strictly forbidden." In such a situation it would be reasonable for me to form a belief that I have an obligation to stay on the path, even if I do not know the source of the commands. For all I know the commands may come from the government of Iraq or the government of Iran, or perhaps from some regional arm of government, or even from a private landowner whose property I am on. In such a situation I might reasonably believe *that* the commands communicated to me create obligations for me, even if I do not know for sure who gave the commands. I might of course have doubts about the authority of whoever it is who has issued the commands, but such doubts are always possible in any case where commands are communicated, and in some cases might well be unreasonable. If I violate the commands and stray from the path, it would be reasonable for me to believe that I am risking adverse consequences.

In a similar manner it would seem possible for God to communicate commands that would be perceived as authoritative and binding without necessarily making it obvious to all recipients that he is the source of the commands. For example, God might communicate that an act is forbidden through conscience, which could be understood as a faculty that directly perceives the wrongness of certain acts.[40] Conscience could here be understood in various ways, as operating through the intellect or through emotions, or some combination of the two. God could give humans such a faculty without necessarily making it evident to all that he is the source of conscience.

Why might God do this? There are several possibilities. One lies in the thought that God has good reasons to remain partially "hidden."[41] Many thinkers have believed, with Pascal, that God wants humans to serve him freely and that this requires a certain degree of epistemic ambiguity, for if God's reality were too obvious, it would be difficult or impossible for any human persons to go against his will. Those who think this is the case normally think that God grants humans some evidence of his reality, but that the evidence is not so clear and undeniable that belief is inescapable. If this is the case, we can easily understand why God might communicate his commands to humans in ways that do not make his own existence as the source of the commands undeniable.

Another possible reason is this: If God makes the source of his commands somewhat obscure, this may alleviate the guilt of those who disobey those commands. Think again of my hiking analogy. Suppose I do know that the source of the commands is the Iranian government, and, suppose that I am angry at this government, and because of my attitude I decide to disobey the order by leaving the path. If the government later apprehends me, it would rightly see my behavior as an act of conscious defiance and perhaps judge me more severely. If, however, the government knows that I was somewhat

---

[40] For more on this see the discussion of moral intuitions in Chapter 6, pp. 169–81, and also pp. 41–5 in Chapter 2.

[41] The theme of God's hiddenness has been extensively discussed in contemporary philosophy of religion. For a development of the idea that God may have good reasons to be partially hidden, see my *Natural Signs and Knowledge of God*, pp. 154–69.

unsure of the source of the command, it would be reasonable for it to regard this as a mitigating factor. (Of course, we know that actual human governments are not always reasonable!) Similarly, if I violate what I perceive to be my obligations, I have done wrong. However, if I do so knowing that those obligations are divine commands, I may be guilty in a deeper way for I have failed to show gratitude to the one who created me and gave me every good I have. A God who knows that humans will often disobey might then have reason to hide the source of his commands, and thereby lessen the guilt of those humans.[42]

The fact that God does not makes his reality as the source of his commands undeniable does not mean that those commands could not be a way in which humans come to know him. There are various ways this could happen. I have argued in another work that our experience of moral obligation is a "natural sign" that points to God's reality.[43] Natural signs do not provide irrefutable proof, and they leave open the possibility of doubt. However, when interpreted properly they point to the reality they are a sign of, and can provide reasonable belief and even knowledge in a direct, non-inferential manner. Alternatively, one might recognize the reality of moral obligations and argue inferentially to the existence of God as the best explanation of that reality. In both these cases moral experience could provide knowledge of God, while still allowing for the possibility that non-believers could recognize the reality of moral obligations.

If God does not make the source of his commands completely evident, does this undermine the advantages of a DCT? Perhaps some of the advantages are lost, or at least lessened. For example, one of the pluses for a DCT is that it makes moral obligations something objective, while still providing a powerful motive for being moral, since humans have very good reasons to desire a happy relationship with God. However, if someone does not realize that God is the source of moral obligation, or does not even believe in God, then it looks like this motivation will be lost. However, although some of the advantages of a DCT may be lost or lessened, others remain.

To see this, we must properly understand the function of a DCT. As I see it, a DCT is a philosophical theory, an attempt to explain what a moral obligation is. If a DCT provides the true account

---

[42] I owe this last point to a paper by Travis Dumsday. See his "Divine Hiddenness and the Responsibility Argument," *Philosophia Christi* 12 (2010), pp. 357–71.

[43] See my *Natural Signs and Knowledge of God*, pp. 107–48.

of moral obligations, then it does follow that someone who fails to know that truth misses out on something of importance. I will try to say below just what is lost, but the fact that something is lost does not imply that all is lost from a moral point of view. A person who does not have a good explanation of morality may still recognize the reality of morality, and also have reasons to be moral.

What reasons to be moral might such a person have? One reason might simply be the emotions inspired by conscience itself, understood as a kind of perception of what is morally obligatory and forbidden. Humans are so constituted that when they do what they know is wrong, they have a disposition to feel guilt and shame, and both guilt and shame are emotions that we rightly want to avoid. Another reason might lie in the goodness and badness of the acts commanded and forbidden. Recall that for an Adams-type DCT, God's commands are directed towards the good, and thus we should expect that those acts we are commanded to do will generally be recognizable as good or leading to good and those that are forbidden as bad or leading to what is bad. Thus, even though someone who does not realize that moral obligations are divine commands lacks some reasons to be moral, such a person might still have reasons sufficient to motivate moral behavior.

A DCT as I have described it is an ontological claim about the relationship between God and morality. One might think that a DCT would also support an epistemological dependence between God and moral obligations. Perhaps, someone might think, if it can be shown that God provides an explanation of moral obligations, and no alternative explanation is available, this would provide those who do not believe in God with a reason to doubt the reality of moral obligations. However, this is simply the view that Elizabeth Anscombe seemed to take, a view that I have already considered and rejected, on the grounds that people can reasonably believe in the reality of something that they cannot explain.[44] This is particularly true if moral obligations are something that people can be directly aware of, and I have suggested that this is the case.

One of the reasons it is possible for a person to recognize a moral obligation without realizing that those obligations are divine commands is that we already have the concept of obligation in general because of our participation in such social institutions as the family and

---

[44] See my discussion and critique of Anscombe's claim in Chapter 1, pp. 20–2.

the state. It seems possible then for someone to sense an obligation to act in a certain way, even if that person is somewhat unclear about the source of the obligation and therefore not clear about its exact nature. If moral obligations depend on God ontologically it does not follow that belief in God is necessary to believe in moral obligations.

I conclude that there is no reason why a defender of a DCT cannot hold that moral obligations can be promulgated by God through general as well as special revelation. Such a communication of God's commands to humans could in fact be one of the ways whereby humans can gain what we may call a natural knowledge of God's existence. Someone who experiences themselves as morally obligated might well on reflection come to see these obligations as pointing to a moral law-giver. Alternatively, someone who recognizes the reality of moral obligations might realize that they are best explained as divine commands. In either case, it will be possible for non-believers to recognize moral obligations. Moreover, if those non-believers are not dogmatically committed to metaphysical naturalism, they might well be led by their moral experiences to question naturalism. However, even if they are unable to do this, and can find no good way to explain moral obligations, it may still be reasonable for them to continue to believe in morality. The promulgation objection gives no reason to doubt the viability of a divine command account of moral obligations.

5

Alternatives to a Divine Command Theory

In Chapter 2 I tried to demonstrate the strengths of a divine command theory of moral obligation. A DCT makes sense of many of the features of moral obligations that were described in Chapter 1, such as their objectivity, overriding character, universality, verdict-like character, and motivating power. In Chapter 3 I tried to show that natural law theories of ethics and virtue ethics really do not have to be seen as rivals to a DCT, but as complementary theories. In Chapter 4 I explained and tried to rebut a number of objections to a DCT. I have thus mounted what I believe to a strong case for a DCT. However, philosophical theories are often assessed not in absolute terms, but relative to competitors. In this chapter I want to look at metaethical views that some will see as a rival to a DCT, and see what strengths and weaknesses they have. I shall try to show that some of these metaethical views (discussed near the end of the chapter) are not really competitors to a DCT but are, suitably interpreted, fully consistent with it. With respect to those metaethical views that are genuine competitors for a DCT, I will try to show that these views face serious objections that a DCT does not face.

Of course my discussions of these views can hardly be comprehensive. Each view I shall discuss is complex and comes in many forms. There is a large scholarly literature connected to each one, and I will not be able to do justice to this literature. I shall try to pick examples of each view that are prominent and representative, but I do not claim that these views exhaust the territory, or that the arguments I will provide are decisive. When I argue against a view, I shall try to focus on difficulties that seem to me to be endemic to the position and that are likely to be present in some form in other versions of the view. I do recognize that there may be other forms of the views I consider that will not be vulnerable in the same way to the problems I present, and I recognize that the defenders of these views may have answers to the problems I have not considered. I consider my arguments the beginning of a discussion and not the end. My aim is to show that a DCT is a serious competitor that ought to be part of the conversation.

ERROR THEORY

J. L. Mackie famously defended what he called "moral skepticism" in metaethics, and he termed his view an "error theory," since "a belief in objective values is built into ordinary moral thought and language."[1] Ordinary morality is best thought of as a kind of "folk theory" which turns out to be false. Moral values are not in fact objective, but subjective creations. Though the term "error theory" is usually associated with Mackie, it is important to recognize that the view accurately describes a number of philosophers, such as Nietzsche, who think of morality as a human invention, but who admit that this is not how morality presents itself to most people.

Mackie presents a number of arguments for this view.[2] First, he claims that seeing morality as subjective gives a good explanation of the relativity and variability we see in moral beliefs and practices. Second, he argues that objective moral values would be "queer" in the sense of being peculiar; they have no foundation in the world as described by science, and even if they did have rootage in scientific facts, Mackie claims it is hard to see how such objective truths could be intrinsically motivating. Third, Mackie thinks it is hard to see why moral values should supervene as they do on natural features of the world. Fourth, epistemologically it is hard to see how such objective values could be known even if they were real. Finally, Mackie claims that a reductive explanation of beliefs about values undermines any claim to objectivity; even if there are no objective values we can tell a convincing story about why people might believe that they exist, making it unnecessary to posit any actual objective values to account for such beliefs.

---

[1] Mackie, *Ethics: Inventing Right and Wrong*, pp. 48–9.
[2] For Mackie's arguments, see his Chapter 1, and the summary he provides on p. 49.

How should a defender of a DCT respond to these arguments? I shall postpone my major response to the skepticism about moral objectivity implicit in error theories until the next chapter. For now I note that the DCT defender may well wish to join hands with defenders of other metaethical views, including secular views, in challenging some of Mackie's arguments. For example, it can be argued that relativity does not really undermine the objectivity of the good, both by arguing that the relativity is not complete (there is also a good amount of consensus among diverse human cultures about the value of such things as honesty, friendship, hospitality, etc.), and also by arguing that the remaining variability in moral beliefs is compatible with moral objectivity. One does not have to deny objective moral truth to account for the variability that is present, since some cultures may have a better grasp of moral truth than others, and some humans within particular cultures may be in a superior position than other people in those cultures. Moral insights do not have to be perfectly equally distributed to be genuine. Such arguments for the objectivity of the good contra relativism are common currency among utilitarians (at least among those who reject subjectivist or preference views of the good), "sentimentalists" (who will be discussed later in this chapter), reductive naturalists, Kantians, and natural law theorists, and a DCT advocate may well join in this chorus.

However, rather than simply criticizing Mackie's position, I think it is interesting to see how many of his arguments, recontextualized, can actually be seen as providing support for a divine command theory. The argument from queerness, for example, can be seen as cutting two ways. If one thinks, as Mackie clearly did, that the world should be understood in a naturalistic manner, then values and other moral properties may indeed appear odd or peculiar. To focus on the deontic moral properties that are my major concern, how could one begin to explain the existence of actual moral obligations if the universe consists solely of subatomic particles configured in various ways? In a theistic universe, however, neither values nor obligations seem odd. In such a universe the ground of all concrete reality is a moral being who is completely good, and so it is not surprising that God's creation is one in which moral properties are "deep" and not mere surface phenomena.

Similar remarks can be made about the epistemic argument that Mackie poses. If we think that humans are the product of an un-guided evolutionary process that has no ends in view, then it certainly might seem strange that humans have cognitive capacities that give them knowledge and understanding of the good and the bad, and of right and wrong.[3] However, even when one accepts the scientific account of humans as the product of an evolutionary process, things look different in a theistic world. In such a world it is eminently plausible to suppose that God has created humans and given them a moral task. To be human is to be involved in a journey, and the goal of the journey requires moral transformation. If that is true, then it is hardly surprising that humans have evolved in ways that have given them capacities to discern what is good and what is evil. To conclude, the argument from queerness that Mackie mounts is only effective against naturalistic metaethical views. Both normative properties and human cognitive capacities to grasp such properties are to be expected if God created and sustains the world.

Interestingly, Mackie himself gives a sketch of the role God might play in ethics that closely parallels the account given in this book.[4] After first discussing the standard Euthyphro objection to theories that root ethics in God, Mackie suggests that the dilemma posed by this objection can be dissolved if we "take apart" moral qualities and see them as related to God in different ways. We might, Mackie says, think that God has created humans in such a way that "there is one kind of life which is, in a purely descriptive sense, most appropriate for human beings as they are—that is, that it alone will fully develop rather than stunt their natural capacities and in it, and only in it, can they find the fullest and deepest satisfaction."[5] Such facts about human flourishing would imply that "certain rules of conduct and dispositions" would be best suited to human life. Mackie seems here to have in mind the kind of natural law theory that I discussed in Chapter 3 as providing a foundation for a DCT.

Mackie then goes on to suggest that God's commands might add a significant new dimension to this picture:

God might require men to live in this appropriate way, and might enjoin obedience to the related rules. This would add an objectively prescriptive element to what otherwise were hard, descriptive truths,

---

[3] Sharon Street has given a well-developed argument that an evolutionary account of human development is incompatible with moral realism. See her "A Darwinian Dilemma for Realist Theories of Value." David Enoch has given a response to Street from a naturalistic perspective. I discuss these issues again in Chapter 6, pp. 179–81, chiefly to argue that a theistic context makes Enoch's reply to Street far stronger.

[4] See Mackie, pp. 230–2.   [5] Mackie, p. 230.

but in a quite non-mysterious way: these would be literally commands issued by an identifiable authority.[6]

The theory Mackie sketches here bears a close resemblance to the "no-discretion" version of a DCT I discussed in Chapter 2. In fact, if the sharp dichotomy Mackie holds between the "descriptive" and "prescriptive" were abandoned I think there would be no difference at all between the view he sketches and this type of DCT.

Of course Mackie himself was an atheist and did not believe that this account is true, since for him there was no God to provide the created order that grounds the good or to provide the commands that give preceptorial force to the rules about how to live that are rooted in the good. Nevertheless, it is significant, I think, that he admits that such a view is coherent, and that if it were true the dilemma posed by the Euthyphro objection would "fall apart." One might say that Mackie here provides an argument that *if* there were a God (to be sure, a pretty significant *if*) a DCT would be a powerful and plausible view.

One can also see the way an error theory provides a kind of indirect support for a DCT by looking at the views of Friedrich Nietzsche. Nietzsche famously announced the "death of God," and thus might seem an unlikely ally for a defender of a divine command theory of moral obligation. However, Nietzsche's critique of modern philosophy, and particularly of modern moral philosophy, comes precisely from his conviction that a genuinely objective moral order, particularly one that gives us obligations to show compassion for others, would require a God as its foundation:

> The *lie* of "the moral world order" runs through the entire development of philosophy, even modern philosophy. And what does "moral world order" mean? That there is a will of God—once and for all—relating to what human beings do and do not do; that the value of a people, of an individual, can be measured by how much or how little each one obeys the will of God.[7]

Nietzsche's conviction that God is the basis of morality as it has been conceived in the west gives rise to a scathing critique of secular moralists of his day, who believe that they can hold on to an objective morality without God. The following remark about utilitarianism is typical: "Utilitarianism . . . criticizes the origin of moral evaluations,

---

[6] Mackie, p. 231.

[7] Friedrich Nietzsche, *The Anti-Christ* (published with *Twilight of the Idols*), ed. Michael Tanner (London: Penguin Books, 1990), section 26 (emphasis original).

but it *believes* them just as much as the Christian does. (Naiveté: as if morality could survive when the *God* who sanctions it is missing! The 'beyond' [is] absolutely necessary if faith in morality is to be maintained.)"[8] Nietzsche himself is emphatic about this point: "When you give up Christian faith, you pull the rug out from under your right to Christian morality as well. This is *anything* but obvious: you have to keep driving this point home, English idiots to the contrary."[9] By "Christian morality" Nietzsche does not mean merely the morality defended by Christians. From his perspective the moral views defended by European secular moralists of his day, even including Marxists, are essentially forms of Christian morality.

Obviously Nietzsche, like Mackie, was an atheist and he was anything but a friend of a divine command theory of morality. From his point of view, our beliefs about our moral obligations are rooted in an illusion; they are profoundly false. Nevertheless, as is often said, one person's *modus ponens* is another person's *modus tollens*, and, for those unable or unwilling to give up belief in objective moral obligations and willing to take seriously the possibility of God's existence, Nietzsche offers the testimony of an "unfriendly witness" that objective moral obligations require God and only make sense if God exists. In Chapter 6 I shall try to say why it continues to be reasonable to believe in objective moral obligations; here I only want to point out that Nietzsche seems to affirm the conditional claim that we can only make sense of such obligations if God exists.

EXPRESSIVISM

Expressivism as a metaethical theory comes in a variety of forms, ranging from the emotivism of A. J. Ayer and Charles Stevenson to the sophisticated "quasi-realism" of philosophers such as Simon Blackburn.[10] What is common to all such views is sometimes called

---

[8] Friedrich Nietzsche, *The Will to Power*, trans. Walter Kaufmann and R. J. Hollingdale (New York: Random House, 1968), p. 147. Passage is from Book II, part II, section 253 (emphases original).

[9] *The Anti-Christ*, section 10 (emphasis original).

[10] Blackburn has published prolifically, but perhaps his most important work in ethics is *Ruling Passions: A Theory of Practical Reason* (Oxford: Oxford University Press, 1998).

"non-cognitivism" and sometimes "anti-realism." Blackburn himself likes to refer to such views, particularly his own version, as various types of "projectivism." I take it that the common element is simply a rejection of the idea that moral propositions express objective truths.[11] Instead moral statements express emotions (Ayer), attitudes (Stevenson), prescriptions as to how oneself and others should behave (R. M. Hare), plans to which one is committed (Gibbard), or perhaps a complex mix of such subjective states (Blackburn). As Alan Gibbard explains the view, relying on Stevenson, if Jack says that all pleasures are intrinsically good, but Jill says that guilty pleasures are not intrinsically good, the disagreement between them boils down to the fact that Jack is *for* all pleasures, but Jill is not.[12]

The strength of an expressivist position is that it appears to account for why morality matters, and why moral claims can motivate as they do. If "stealing is wrong" expresses my emotional repugnance to stealing, or if it expresses an attitude that gives me an aversion to stealing and to people who steal, or if it expresses a firmly held life-plan in which stealing plays no role, then we can indeed see why the statement is linked to my actions. While acknowledging that expressivism links morality with behavior, I want to raise a question about whether it links morality to behavior in the right way. The question I want to raise is not whether moral judgments can motivate, but whether on expressivist views, such judgments can have the kind of authority morality ought to have.

Many of the early objections to expressivism were based on the claim that such views do not seem to do justice to moral disagreements and arguments. If I say "stealing is wrong" and my neighbor, who is a professional thief, says "stealing is not wrong," we seem to be contradicting each other, but if all we are doing is expressing attitudes there is no real logical contradiction. I like bananas and my wife does not, but we do not thereby contradict each other. A related objection

---

[11] Mark Van Roojen complicates things by distinguishing "semantic nonfactualism," the claim that moral sentences do not express propositions that have truth conditions, from "psychological non-cognitivism," the denial that the states of mind that moral utterances express are beliefs. I shall ignore this complication because most non-cognitivists accept both of these claims and see them as connected. See Mark Van Roojen, "Moral Cognitivism vs. Non-Cognitivism," in *Stanford Encyclopedia of Philosophy* <http://plato.stanford.edu/entries/moral-cognitivism>.

[12] Alan Gibbard, "The Reasons of a Living Being," *Proceedings of the American Philosophical Association* 62 (2002), pp. 49–60; the relevant passage is on p. 50.

comes from Peter Geach, who argued that moral propositions often figure in logically valid arguments, as in this case: "It is wrong to lie. Telling my boss I am sick when I am not is lying. Therefore it is wrong to tell my boss I am sick when I am not."[13] It would seem that moral propositions cannot be used in logical arguments employing truth-functional logical operators if they lack objective truth values, and yet they do seem to figure in valid arguments, can be negated, etc.

Such objections as these have led expressivists to develop more sophisticated versions of their view, such as Blackburn's "quasi-realism." At the heart of such views lies the idea that even though moral statements do not express propositions with genuinely objective truth values, there is a natural human tendency to "project" our emotions, attitudes, prescriptions, plans, etc. onto the objective world. We talk and perhaps even think *as if* our moral statements referred to some objective reality. This projective theory gives a reductive explanation of why moral language has the features it does that enable moral statements to mimic propositions that have genuine representational content. The features of our moral language that make it appear that it represents something objective are, given the projective theory, just what one would expect to be the case, even if the moral language does not "correspond" to anything. Blackburn and others have in turn developed accounts of the "logic" of moral statements that explain how it can be that these statements mimic the properties of genuinely representational propositions, even though they actually don't refer to anything.[14]

I shall not argue the case against expressivism in its various forms by relying on problems such as the one Geach developed. The debate around these issues involves fairly technical questions in the philosophy of language. More importantly, I think that such issues are not the crux of the matter but are at best a symptom of deeper problems. The real difficulty lies with the way that expressivism, even in its

---

[13] This particular example is mine. For the argument see Peter Geach, "Assertions," *Philosophical Review* 74 (1965), pp. 449–63.

[14] Mark van Roojen's *Stanford Encyclopedia of Philosophy* article on "Moral Cognitivism vs. Non-Cognitivism" (referenced in footnote 11) has a good discussion of these issues and many other technical problems raised by non-cognitivism. Simon Blackburn, in *Spreading the Word* (New York: Oxford University Press, 1984), explains ethical statements in unasserted contexts as expressions of higher-order attitudes, while in *Ruling Passions* he views such statements as ways of tying ourselves to "trees" of commitments. I thank Mark Nelson for helping me see the difference between these views.

projectivist, quasi-realist form, undermines the authority of moral judgments, especially judgments about moral obligations.

To see this think first about one of the simpler, earlier forms of expressivism, such as emotivism. On this type of view, if James says to Mary that "it would be wrong not to report that income on your tax return" he is not stating a proposition that is true or false, but rather expressing an attitude of disapproval towards the proposed action. However, it is simply not clear why this should matter to Mary. Mary may not care whether James approves of her behavior; she may be amused or even pleased by the fact that James disapproves. If the moral judgment simply expresses some emotion or attitude of James, then it lacks the authority that most of us think is possessed by genuine moral judgments, especially judgments about moral obligations.

One might think that the problem is that James does not matter enough to Mary. Would it help if the attitude expressed is not solely that of James but one that "society" or "most people" who judge about the matter have? Anyone who finds it plausible that genuine moral authority can be grounded in the attitudes or emotions of "most people" or "society" should reflect on the kinds of unsavory moral attitudes that human societies through the centuries have embodied. If the authority of morality is to be grounded in the prevalent attitudes of society or the state, it will be impossible to mount a moral critique of society or the state.

Now the more sophisticated quasi-realism of Blackburn may appear to help with this problem, but the help is illusory, at least for those who understand and believe the theory. For in the end moral judgments merely *mimic* statements that can be true or false independently of the stance of the person making the judgment. The whole point of expressivism is that there simply is no stance-independent moral reality. The naïve, philosophically unsophisticated person who does not know this may make moral judgments and believe in their authority, but it is difficult to see how this can be true for the person who has embraced expressivism, even in its quasi-realist form.

Blackburn anticipates the problem here: "There is one last charge of the would-be realist. This claims that projectivism must lead to relativism. 'Truth' must be relative to whatever set of attitudes is grounding our ethical stances; since these may vary from place to place and time to time, truth must be relative."[15] Blackburn admits that

---

[15] Simon Blackburn, "How To Be an Ethical Anti-Realist," in Russ Shafer-Landau and Terence Cuneo (eds), *Foundations of Ethics: An Anthology* (Oxford: Blackwell,

there is a "sideways, theoretical perspective" from which things indeed look this way, but he claims that this is not a problem. Of course when one sees the world "from the viewpoint that sees different and conflicting moral systems" then one will inevitably "see no truth in just one."[16] The solution, as Blackburn sees things, is "stepping back into the boat, putting back the lens of a sensibility."[17] If we do this, "there is nothing relativistic left to say."[18] Presumably, by "stepping back into the boat" Blackburn means that the person in question once again takes a moral stance towards the world. But for the person who has awakened to the truth of projectivism, this will be difficult to do or even impossible for some. To do so will require something like Sartrean "bad faith," in which one "forgets" what one knows. How can I get back into one particular boat and believe that it is the "right" boat, when I know there is no such thing as the *right* boat?

In effect Blackburn claims that the truth of quasi-realism allows him to have his cake and eat it too. He can, to echo Berkeley, speak with the vulgar while thinking with the learned, thus helping himself to moral judgments that appear objectively true even while knowing that they are not objectively true. At times he simply helps himself to traditional moral claims, speaking as if they were made true by the way the world is: "But our actual responses are inappropriate anchors for the wrongness of cruelty. What makes cruelty abhorrent is not that it offends us, but all those hideous things that make it do so."[19] Blackburn here speaks as if it is the badness of cruelty that makes it wrong, but surely it is difficult not to remember that the official view (explained in the same article) is that it is not true that there is anything objectively bad, but that our judgments that some things are bad are merely a projection of our sentiments. If we could segregate our beliefs about normative ethics from our metaethical beliefs, perhaps Blackburn's view would work, but it is not easy to wall off our beliefs *about* morality from our actual moral convictions.

In order to see the problems with quasi-realism more clearly, imagine a form of quasi-realism developed to apply to legal obligations

2007), p. 55. Originally published in Simon Blackburn, *Essays in Quasi-Realism* (Oxford: Oxford University Press, 1993), pp. 166–81.

[16] Blackburn, "How To Be an Ethical Anti-Realist," p. 55.
[17] Blackburn, "How To Be an Ethical Anti-Realist," p. 55.
[18] Blackburn, "How To Be an Ethical Anti-Realist," p. 55.
[19] Blackburn, "How To Be an Ethical Anti-Realist," p. 51.

rather than moral obligations. Suppose there is a region of the world with no actual state. Perhaps the area once had a state, but it is now a "failed state" with no functioning government. This condition has persisted for a long time. Since there is no functioning state, there are no actual legal obligations, and thus no claims that "such and such is a legal obligation" could be true. In an obscure and inaccessible part of the region, some dim memories of the old legal order remain. (Here there is an analogy with Anscombe's claim that modern moral philosophy rests on a vestigial memory of an earlier belief in divine laws.) Let us suppose that in this region people still believe that there are "legal obligations" that are grounded in the state. We can give an evolutionary explanation of the persistence of such beliefs, since it is conceivable that families and tribes that believe in such obligations will cooperate and perhaps do better than families and tribes that lack such beliefs. Perhaps at one time there really were legal obligations, but the belief in such things has survived because the beliefs are useful and convenient. People "project" onto a non-existent state their attitudes and emotions about various ways of acting. In reality, in this region, when people claim that one is "legally obligated" to perform some civic obligation what they are really doing is expressing an attitude of approval for this behavior. The usefulness of the behavior thus motivated explains its survival.

Now what will occur if a person travels to another part of the region, and becomes "enlightened" by realizing that the state does not in fact exist and there are actually no such things as "legal obligations"? In fact, this person acquires an understanding of why his former neighbors believe in such things; he himself becomes a quasi-realist about legal obligations and understands that what explains why some acts are considered "legal obligations" stems entirely from the attitudes and emotions of the society. It is hard not to see that this person will find it hard to take his or her earlier "realistic" attitude as justified. As much as this person might like to return to naiveté, there is no going back once the person realizes that there are actually no genuine legal obligations. One can imagine such a person deciding to keep private the new insight so as not to disturb the social order, but it is hard to imagine that this cannot change his or her own view of legal obligations.

One could of course at this point reply that if projectivism is true, then it is true. We cannot avoid moral skepticism just because we do not want it to be so. I fully agree with this, and I shall try in the last chapter to give some reasons why moral skepticism should be rejected. The point here is that quasi-realism in the end is, like Mackie's error theory, a form of moral skepticism, only Mackie's theory is transparent and honest, while the skepticism on Blackburn's part is disguised by the fact that he continues "voicing some elements" of his own moral stance as if they were objectively true judgments, thereby offering us "ethical truth."[20] But the truth that is on offer seems a pseudo-truth, a "semantic shadow" of the attitudes and stances taken by ordinary people.

CONSTRUCTIVISM

I take constructivism to be a metaethical stance that attempts to steer a middle course between realist, cognitivist accounts of the moral life and expressivist views. Like realists, constructivists want to argue that moral judgments have an objectivity such that they can be judged true or false, but they want to hold that such judgments gain that status because of our activities. They thus share the expressivist view that the moral world is a human creation. I shall discuss three different versions of this project. Two of them see moral obligations as the result of a social contract or agreement, while the third is inspired by the Kantian-type view that morality is something that is created by the autonomous self.

GILBERT HARMAN'S RELATIVISTIC SOCIAL CONTRACT ACCOUNT

One of the simplest and most natural ways of thinking of morality as a human construction is to see it as the result of a social agreement, for such an agreement would obviously be the result of human activity, yet if morality were grounded in such an agreement, it would appear to have a degree of objectivity. A key question that must be faced by social contract theories of morality concerns the nature of the agreement:

---

[20] Blackburn, "How To Be an Ethical Anti-Realist," p. 55.

Is the agreement supposed to be an actual agreement or is it merely a hypothetical ideal, an agreement that people *would* make if certain conditions were fulfilled, even if those conditions never in fact hold? Each option presents problems. The difficulty with a hypothetical agreement is understanding how it can ground obligations that are actual and not just hypothetical. Since an actual agreement does not face this problem, it has one clear advantage.

Both the strengths and weaknesses of the actual agreement model can be seen in the metaethical thought of Gilbert Harman.[21] Since Harman is committed to metaphysical naturalism (a position he describes as a "scientific conception of the world"[22]), he thinks that moral realism could only be true if one could achieve a "naturalistic reduction" of moral terms, which would require definitions of ethical terms solely in terms of non-moral facts.[23] Harman is, however, skeptical that such reductions can be achieved, and so thinks that naturalism leads to ethical skepticism.[24] Seeing morality as the result of a human agreement can perhaps salvage a degree of objectivity for ethics. Harman wants to distinguish his own view, which he calls ethical relativism, from the view he terms ethical nihilism, which simply denies that ethical propositions have any truth at all. Moral nihilism would thus logically lead to the view that morality should be rejected altogether, and Harman does not wish to go that far.[25]

Why does Harman commit to ethical relativism? The answer is that if morality is the result of actual human social agreements, it must be relative, because there are many different social groups, and the agreements that the members of those groups make with each other differ significantly. One might of course propose that there would be no relativity if the agreement is an ideal one, an agreement that all humans would agree to if they were fully rational and had the opportunity to make such an agreement. Harman is skeptical that any

[21] For a more detailed exposition and critique of Harman's views, see Chapter 12 of my *Kierkegaard's Ethic of Love: Divine Commands and Moral Obligations*, pp. 280–98. What follows in this subsection draws on this earlier treatment of Harman.

[22] Gilbert Harman, "Is There a Single True Morality?" in *Explaining Value and Other Essays in Moral Philosophy* (Oxford: Oxford University Press, 2000), p. 78.

[23] Harman, "Is There a Single True Morality?" p. 83.

[24] Harman, "Is There a Single True Morality?" p. 93.

[25] Gilbert Harman and Judith Jarvis Thomson, *Moral Relativism and Moral Objectivity* (Oxford: Blackwell, 1996), p. 3. This book contains essays by both authors with responses. All my references will be to Harman's portion of the book.

agreement could be achieved among all humans, and even if we could determine the content of such an ideal agreement, he does not see how such a hypothetical agreement could obligate actual humans, a skepticism I share.[26] Any moral obligations we have must then be grounded in actual agreements made by concrete social groups. Since there are many such groups, there are many different moral frameworks. "[D]ifferent people are subject to different basic moral demands depending on the social customs, practices, conventions, values and principles they accept."[27]

This means, Harman says, that moral claims will be analogous to claims about motion that are made in the context of Einstein's theory that space and time are relative. There are alternative spatio-temporal frameworks and any claim about whether an object is in motion (as well as how fast it is moving) are always made relative to some particular spatio-temporal framework. When understood as relative to a particular framework, claims about motion can be true or false, but it makes no sense to see such claims as "absolute." In a similar way, just as no spatio-temporal framework can be privileged as the "correct" framework, no one moral framework can be correct in the sense of holding for everyone, even though such claims can be made relative to a particular framework:

> [M]oral right and wrong (good and bad, justice and injustice, virtue and vice, etc.) are always relative to a choice of moral framework. What is morally right in relation to one moral framework can be morally wrong in relation to a different moral framework. And no moral framework is objectively privileged as the one true morality.[28]

The view that there is one correct moral framework Harman terms "absolutism," and he wants to maintain that one can reject absolutism while avoiding nihilism. I shall, however, raise questions about whether Harman's relativism really differs significantly from nihilism.

Ultimately, the problem with Harman's view is similar to the problem that emerged with expressivism: the authority of morality is undermined. In Chapter 1 I argued that the key features of moral obligation include objectivity and universality. Harman is forthright

---

[26] See Harman, "Is There A Single True Morality?" p. 84; and also "Justice and Moral Bargaining," also in *Explaining Value and Other Essays in Moral Philosophy*, pp. 66–8.
[27] Harman, "Is There a Single True Morality?" p. 85.
[28] Harman, "Is There a Single True Morality?" p. 85.

that his view implies that there are no universal moral obligations. He gives as an example a "successful criminal" who works for "Murder, Incorporated," a firm whose employees accept that it is part of their normal duties to murder people they have been hired to kill.[29] On Harman's view such an employee may be fully informed and rational; his commitment to murdering other people may not result from any kind of mistake at all, but stems from the special moral agreement of the group with which he identifies. It is thus not wrong for this person to murder. Of course Harman might say at this point that this is not a problem; it is simply his view. But surely it is his view that is the problem. It contradicts some of the deepest moral intuitions of most people to say, as Harman does, that "it strikes us as a misuse of language to say of the assassin that he ought not to kill. . . . or that it would be wrong of him to do so."[30]

It is hardly a misuse of ordinary moral language to say that this employee of Murder, Incorporated, ought not to kill. "Thou shalt not kill" is one of the oldest and most venerable principles of morality. If Harman's metaethical theory implies that someone can participate in such practices and yet violate no moral duty, then there is surely something wrong with the metaethical theory in question. What is wrong is that morality has been emptied of *authority*. In particular, our conviction that moral obligations are universal and apply to everyone has been undermined. Of course it may be true that the assassin does not *recognize* an obligation not to kill others, and it may be true that such a person will be unmoved if someone else appeals to him to stop his immoral actions. But it is for just such reasons that we must judge this person morally defective in a deep way. It is surely true that this person *ought* not to murder innocent people, whether the person recognizes this or not. To say that morality has authority is in part to say that such claims about what people ought to do can be true regardless of what people believe.

One can also see that Harman's view empties morality of authority by examining his view of the question as to why people should adhere to their moral agreements. There is an obvious reason why people should enter into such agreements; they are grounded in such considerations as "I don't push you around so that you won't push me

---

[29] Gilbert Harman, "Moral Relativism Defended," in *Explaining Value and Other Essays in Moral Philosophy*, p. 5.
[30] Harman, "Moral Relativism Defended," p. 5.

around. You are nice to me so that I will be nice to you."[31] We promise to behave in certain ways towards other people on the condition that they will behave in certain ways towards us in return. However, it is one thing to make an agreement; another thing to keep the agreement. It is an obvious fact of human life that people do not always keep their agreements. If the motivation for the agreement is self-interest, as Harman says it is,[32] it is not clear why it is not sometimes reasonable for a person to fail to keep their moral agreements.

The most obvious reason for adhering to such agreements is of course that it may be costly not to do so. If I fail to behave as I have promised towards others, then they may reciprocate by behaving badly towards me. However, it is certainly the case that there will be times when humans can behave badly without this being detected. Assume for instance that most moral codes include agreements not to cheat or lie. Perhaps people who are flagrant cheaters and liars will gain a bad reputation and lose the trust of others. However, it seems highly plausible that people who are skillful can selectively lie and cheat with little fear of detection. Many university students admit to cheating on exams; many taxpayers admit to cheating on tax returns, and those who are skillful at doing this have little risk of being detected and punished. Why, then, should a person agree to live by a set of moral rules and yet selectively disregard those rules when it is in the person's interest? Why should the rules of morality be seen as possessing genuine authority?

This problem is pressing for any social contract account of morality that roots morality in self-interest, but it is particularly severe for a view such as Harman's, because he asserts that what creates moral obligations is the individual's decision to accept a particular moral agreement as binding.[33] Naturally, since it is my decision that creates the obligation, the obligation can also be undone by my decision: "People can always opt out of the morality they currently accept; and they can always threaten to opt out if their self-interest is not sufficiently taken into account by the current morality."[34] What kind of authority do moral obligations have if individuals can always choose

---

[31] Harman, "Justice and Moral Bargaining," p. 68.

[32] See "Justice and Moral Bargaining," p. 68, where Harman says that "the main reason a person accepts the principles he or she does is that it is in her interest to do so if others do too."

[33] Gilbert Harman, "Relativistic Ethics: Morality as Politics," in *Explaining Value and Other Essays in Moral Philosophy*, p. 56.

[34] Harman, "Justice and Moral Bargaining," p. 68.

to opt out if the obligation appears to threaten their self-interest? The whole idea of a moral obligation is that it tells people what they should do even when they don't want to do it and it does not appear to be in their self-interest.

Harman attempts to avoid the problem posed by individuals keeping their moral agreements by arguing that the relevant agreement is constituted by the individuals' intentions. He responds to the worry that an individual could be a "free-rider" or "parasite" in the moral economy by claiming that the worry rests on a misunderstanding of the relevant agreement: "the apparent force of the objection derives entirely from taking the agreement to be a kind of ritual."[35] Harman says that we should not think of the agreement that established morality as akin to a verbal promise that a person might not live up to. Rather, "[t]o agree in the relevant sense . . . is to intend to do something—namely, to intend to carry out one's part of the agreement on the condition that others do their parts. If one agrees in this sense to do something, one intends to do it, and intending to do it is already to be motivated to do it."[36]

However, this will not do. Even if we admit that a moral agreement can be tacit and grounded in actions and intentions rather than an explicit promise, it still must involve an element of commitment over time. One must agree at time T_1 that one will act in a certain way at some later time T_2. If I agree at time T_1 in a tacit manner to act in a certain way by intending (at T_1) to act in a certain way at T_2, this does not mean that at T_2 I will not change my mind and act differently. If the authority of morality is grounded in human intentions to act in certain ways, it has no real authority at all. Harman sees moral obligations as grounded in relative agreements I can always opt out of, but it is easy to see that a moral skeptic might claim that the view that there are such obligations does not differ significantly from the moral nihilist claim that genuine moral obligations do not exist at all. It hardly seems possible to account for the objectivity of morality if morality rests on actual human agreements.

Harman's account fails in one other significant way. In Chapter 1 I discussed the two-fold way in which moral obligations can be seen as universal. First, all humans are subject to moral obligations, and second, some moral obligations apply to how we treat all other humans. If we see moral obligations as grounded in self-interested

---

[35] Harman, "Moral Relativism Defended," p. 13.
[36] Harman, "Moral Relativism Defended," p. 13.

bargains that various groups of humans make, it is easy to see that morality will not be universal in either of these senses. Since individuals can opt out of morality altogether, there is no reason to believe that all are subject to moral obligations. Nor is there any reason to think that any of us have moral obligations that extend to all human persons. Rather, my moral obligations will hold for those who belong to the group with which I identify. Since the motivation for the agreement is self-interest, and the obligation created is contingent on the willingness of others in the group to act in ways that are to my benefit, I have no obligations that extend to people in other parts of the world whom I do not know or interact with. Nor does it seem I have any obligations to people in my own neighborhood I may come in contact with, if these are people who cannot benefit me or harm me. However, it seems arguable that some of our deepest and most serious moral obligations are precisely obligations towards people who may be in such categories; for example, those who may be senile or handicapped or unable to act towards me in ways that my self-interest should take into account.

MORALITY AS AN IDEAL SOCIAL AGREEMENT

Perhaps, one might think, the objectionable features of Harman's view come from his decision to treat moral obligations as the outcome of relativistic social bargains that individuals freely enter into. It is therefore worth investigating whether moral obligations can be understood as the result of a social agreement that is ideal and perhaps for that reason universal. Ronald Milo, for example, has proposed a view he calls "contractarian constructivism," which holds "that moral truths are most plausibly construed as truths about an ideal social order."[37] According to this view, "a certain kind of act is wrong, for example, just in case a social order prohibiting such acts would be chosen by rational contractors under suitably idealized conditions."[38]

---

[37] Ronald Milo, "Contractarian Constructivism," in Shafer-Landau and Cuneo (eds), *Foundations of Ethics*, p. 121. Originally published in *Journal of Philosophy* 92 (1995), pp. 181–204.
[38] Milo, "Contractarian Constructivism," p. 121.

There are many difficulties involved in such a proposal. For example, how should we think of the contractors making their decisions? If we think of them as choosing to require or forbid actions so as to make possible some good, then it looks as if constructivism has been abandoned, at least with respect to the good, since it will be facts about the good that guide the contractors' decisions.[39] Milo attempts to avoid this problem by suggesting that the practical reasoning of the contractors will be shaped by "means–end" reasoning as to how best to satisfy our desires: "Practical reasoning is primarily controlled by the constraint of coherence with our intrinsic (that is, unmotivated) desires, because our aim here is to improve the satisfactoriness of our lives."[40] However, this stance still involves a theory of the good, namely a desire-fulfillment theory, and such an account of the good is as realistic as any other, since it seems committed to the claim that it is objectively good for humans to satisfy as many of their desires as possible. It is also controversial; desire-fulfillment theories come in many forms, and none of them are without difficulties.[41] There are many similar problems that emerge as a theorist such as Milo tries to develop the account, arising from how one understands the "ideal conditions" the contractors are supposed to be in, what it might mean for them to be rational, etc. I shall not, however, explore these kinds of difficulties any further, because there is a more fundamental problem with the whole project.

That problem is this: What authority do the decisions of these hypothetical contractors have over actual individuals? It is admittedly difficult to determine whether there are any facts about what such contractors might decide, and, if there are such facts, determine what they are. However, even if these problems could be resolved, and we decided that there are true counter-factuals of this type and that we could know what they are, why should the decisions of these

---

[39] One might worry here that my criticism is dialectically misplaced, since I am defending a realist theory about obligations. Presumably Milo might accept a realist account of the good and propose a constructivist account that applies only to obligations. This is correct, but Milo's motivation for avoiding realism seems to apply both to the good and to duties. If we have to accept realism about the good, it is not clear why one needs to avoid realism about duty. In any case, my more fundamental objection to Milo's view is given below.

[40] Milo, "Contractarian Constructivism," p. 123.

[41] For an excellent account of various versions of desire-fulfillment theories, and a strong argument that none of them are satisfactory, see Murphy, *Natural Law and Practical Rationality*, pp. 50–90.

non-actual people be binding on actual people? Suppose, for example, that these people accept a certain account of the good life for humans and that this view of the good shapes their decisions about what is right and wrong. If I do not accept this view of the good myself, then there is no reason to think I would agree with the views about right and wrong that they base on their theory of the good.[42] Yet it is certainly possible that I might hold a different account of the good.

One might try to avoid this problem by specifying that the contractors will hold no theory of the good at all. However, this just creates more difficulties. First, it is not clear that they can make any progress towards deciding what is right and wrong with no knowledge of the good. At the very least they will need beliefs about the good. Moreover, the problem of lack of authority is not thereby solved but just compounded. Why should I defer to the decisions about right and wrong of people who have no understanding of the good, or who have different beliefs about the good than I do? I would in fact have excellent reasons for being suspicious of the decisions of such people.

The best attempt I know to resolve this problem of authority is provided by David Gauthier in his *Morals by Agreement*.[43] In this work Gauthier tries to motivate a social contract approach to moral theory by seeing such an agreement as a way of trying to resolve "prisoner's dilemma" situations. In the classic "prisoner's dilemma" situation, a prosecutor holds two individuals, Ed and Fred, who have committed a serious crime, but the prosecutor does not have enough evidence to convict them of that crime, though she does have evidence to convict them on a less serious charge. The prosecutor makes the following offer to both Ed and Fred: "Confess to the serious crime, and if your partner does not confess, you will get one year while your partner will get ten. However, if your partner confesses and you do not, you will get the ten years, while he gets only one year. If neither of you confesses you will each get two years for the less serious crime. If both of you confess to the serious crime, you will each get five years."

---

[42] It is likely for this reason that John Rawls specifies that the people who are in the "original position" and thus agree on the rules of justice are behind a "veil of ignorance" which precludes knowledge about what substantive view of the good they will hold as actual humans. For the initial statement of the "veil of ignorance" idea, see John Rawls, "Distributive Justice," in Peter Laslett and Walter Runciman (eds), *Philosophy, Politics, and Society*, 3rd. series (New York: Barnes and Noble, 1967), p. 60.

[43] David Gauthier, *Morals by Agreement* (Oxford: Oxford University Press, 1986).

What should Ed and Fred do? It might appear that the rational strategy is to confess. Let's look at matters from Ed's point of view. Ed knows that either Fred will confess or he will not. Suppose Fred does not confess. In that case if Ed confesses then Ed gets only one year. Suppose Fred does confess. In that case if Ed does not confess, he will get ten years. So it appears that whatever Fred does, Ed will be better off confessing. However, if Ed and Fred could somehow count on each other not to confess, then each would only get two years. It looks like the best strategy for both of them would be to reach an agreement not to confess, but there is little reason for them to behave in this way without some assurance that the other will keep the agreement.

Gauthier believes that such prisoner's dilemma situations are not simply unusual possibilities, but capture many features of actual human social interaction. There are many situations in which, if every individual in a group pursues his or her self-interest, the outcome for everyone in the group will be much worse than would be the case if the individuals accept some restraints on their self-interest. Without an agreement regulating our behavior, in the actual world we are doomed to "non-optimal outcomes that, in 'Prisoner's Dilemma-type' situations, may be little better than disastrous."[44] The solution is an agreement that creates duties that limit our quest for self-interest, though in the long run the agreement actually furthers our self-interest. "Duty overrides advantage, but the acceptance of duty is truly advantageous."[45] The authority of the agreement lies in the advantages the agreement makes possible, along with the fact that those who are party to the agreement will withdraw their cooperation towards those who fail to comply.

Is this agreement actual or hypothetical? I believe that Gauthier thinks that both can be true. The agreements "may of course be implicit rather than explicit," but they are not a "mere fiction" since they give rise to "new modes of interaction."[46] Such actual agreements may appear to be like Harman's relativistic ones, but Gauthier thinks that the authority of these agreements depends upon the degree to which they resemble an ideal agreement:

> Actual moral principles are not in general those to which we should have agreed in a fully rational bargain, but it is reasonable to adhere to them in so far as they offer a reasonable approximation to ideal principles. We may defend actual moral principles by reference to ideal

---

[44] Gauthier, p. 82.   [45] Gauthier, p. 2.   [46] Gauthier, p. 117.

co-operative arrangements, and the closer the principles fit, the stronger the defence.[47]

Gauthier gives an impressive explanation of the ideal agreement as one that adheres to the "principle of minimax relative concession," in which the maximum that each party is asked to concede is as small as possible, thus giving everyone reason to commit to the agreement.[48]

Gauthier's attempt to see morality as a solution to the disasters that stem from unfettered pursuit of self-interest is powerful. In particular, his view that our social agreements are binding only to the degree they approximate an ideal one is a creative attempt to get beyond Harman's relativism. Nevertheless, in the end I think many of the problems that beset Harman's view are still present, as well as the problems inherent in Milo's ideal contractarian constructivism. To begin with the latter, it is still not clear why an agreement that *would be made* by ideally rational agents under certain conditions (which in fact do not hold) is binding on actual individuals.

Consider the original prisoner's dilemma situation again. Perhaps it would be rational for Ed to agree not to confess if Fred also agrees, and if Ed can be assured that Fred will keep the agreement. In the real world, however, what assurance can Ed have about such things? It seems very likely that Fred will double-cross him, and so what it would be rational for Ed to do *if* Fred could be counted on is quite different from what it is rational for Ed to do, given what Ed knows is actually true about Fred. In a similar manner, it seems unlikely that the agreement that it would be reasonable for an individual to keep *if* other people could be counted on to behave morally is binding on actual individuals, who know that in the real world people frequently lie and cheat.

Nor does it seem true that Gauthier has a convincing answer to the question as to why individuals should keep their agreement to behave morally. It is true that those who are known to violate the agreement can be penalized by others who keep the rules, but this only gives a reason to keep the agreement when breaking it is likely to be detected and the offender is likely to face some serious sanction if it is detected. Gauthier responds to this problem in a number of ways, but none of them seems successful. One response is simply to

[47] Gauthier, p. 168.
[48] Gauthier, p. 137. For a more developed exposition of this idea, and Gauthier's view as a whole, see Chapter 11 of my *Kierkegaard's Ethic of Love*, pp. 250–79.

concede that morality is not always the reasonable path to take: "[W]e do not claim that it is never rational for one person to take advantage of another, . . . never rational to comply with unfair practices. Such a claim would be false."[49] This, however, is simply to abandon key elements of the Anscombe intuition, since on such a view moral obligations are not always overriding and do not apply with equal force to everyone.

Perhaps because of this problem, Gauthier suggests another response to the problem of why individuals should keep their agreement to behave morally. Morality cannot really survive if we are purely self-interested individuals who behave like "economic man." What must happen is that we must strive to be like the "just man," whose feelings are engaged by morality and adheres not because of self-interest but because he simply loves the ideals he is committed to.[50] In a later section of this chapter, I shall consider whether human emotions provide an adequate basis for morality, but I think it is obvious that if the authority of morality is grounded in such feelings, then that authority will be limited in its application to those with the relevant feelings.

The final difficulty I want to raise with Gauthier's theory concerns the scope of the moral obligations as these are understood. In Chapter 2, I argued that we understand moral obligations as universal in scope. Not only do they apply to all humans, but we have at least some obligations that extend to all humans. However, it is very difficult to see how an agreement that is grounded in self-interest could be the basis for obligations of this type. Indeed, Gauthier concedes the fact: "Animals, the unborn, the congenitally handicapped and defectives fall beyond the pale of morality tied to mutuality."[51]

Nor is it easy to see why people in one human society should have obligations towards people in some distant land, particularly if the people in the distant land are too poor and weak to threaten or benefit the people in the first society. Gauthier himself gives a hypothetical example of cultural contact, in which the peoples (called the "purples" and the "greens") from two hitherto isolated islands become aware of each other.[52] The purples have a very prosperous society based on cooperative principles, but the greens "live in totally chaotic squalor." What should the purples do if they come into contact with the greens?

[49] Gauthier, p. 232.   [50] Gauthier, p. 328.
[51] Gauthier, p. 268.   [52] Gauthier, pp. 282–8.

Gauthier gives three reasons why the purples might decide to treat the greens in a moral way. The first is that doing so may in the long run be in the purples' self-interest.[53] Perhaps that is possible but it seems equally possible that it is in the self-interest of the purples to treat the greens in ways analogous to the ways in which European settlers to North America treated the indigenous peoples.

The second reason Gauthier gives is that the purples may have become the kind of people who are so disposed to kind and compassionate treatment that they literally have no choice but to treat the greens well.[54] The purples are psychologically incapable of any other kind of behavior. This seems far-fetched if the purples are actual human beings. It may be *possible* for humans to be generous and fair in their dealings with other cultural and racial groups, but human history suggests that it is not easy for humans to take such a stance. The claim that it is not even possible for humans to mistreat those who are "other" would only be plausible if human nature were completely transformed.

The third possible reason Gauthier gives for the purples treating the greens well is that "the purple people may possess a certain measure of sympathy for all whom they consider human."[55] Of course actual humans have throughout human history not usually displayed such sympathy for all humans; indeed they have often displayed a regrettable tendency to view strange peoples as less than fully human. So it seems, on empirical grounds, highly unlikely that this would be the case for any recognizable human group. But even if the purples do recognize the humanity of the greens, it seems far from inevitable that any feelings of sympathy they have will overpower other emotions they have, not to mention naked calculations of self-interest. Such feelings of sympathy might provide motivational power for the purples if the purples recognized a moral obligation towards the greens, and cared enough about those obligations. However, it is hard to see how such feelings of sympathy by themselves could be the *basis* of real moral obligations. All of the considerations to which Gauthier appeals manifestly fail to provide a foundation for genuine moral obligations that are overriding, binary in character, motivating, and universal. The contrast between such a view and a divine command account of moral obligations is clear.

---

[53] Gauthier, p. 286.   [54] Gauthier, p. 286.   [55] Gauthier, p. 286.

CONTEMPORARY KANTIANISM: KORSGAARDIAN CONSTRUCTIVISM

The final version of constructivism I shall consider is the contemporary Kantianism of Christine Korsgaard. I want to distinguish this contemporary Kantianism clearly from the historical Kant. Although in textbook treatments of Kant, his moral philosophy is often presented as a rival to a divine command theory, I believe these textbook characterizations provide a truncated and distorted understanding of Kant's views. I see no need to argue against the views of the historical Kant, for I do not believe that Kant himself provides an alternative to a divine command theory. Rather, I believe that Kant actually held a minimal, "no discretion" version of a DCT. It is true that Kant holds that people can recognize and follow their moral obligations without realizing that such obligations are divine commands, but that is a view I have already endorsed and is fully compatible with a DCT. Kant just as clearly holds that it is correct to understand moral obligations as divine commands, and also that God plays a significant role as the "Head" of the Kingdom of Ends of which moral agents are citizens.[56]

Christine Korsgaard is strongly influenced by Kant's attempt to find the source of normativity in the law-like universal "form" that she sees as present when we "reflectively endorse" some possible way of acting.[57] In her contemporary theory, Korsgaard attempts to deal with a criticism frequently made of Kant, which is that his categorical imperative is too formal and abstract to give fully determinate content to the moral law.[58] Her solution is to introduce a distinction between the categorical imperative and the moral law itself. The categorical imperative provides a necessary condition for morality, since it rules out some principles of actions because they cannot be rationally willed as universal. However, for Korsgaard the particular "maxims" that have moral authority for an individual in the end are grounded in a person's identity, since "a view of what you ought to do is ultimately

---

[56] For an exposition of Kantian ethics that is historically faithful and pays full attention to the role God plays in Kant's ethic, see Chapter 3 of Hare, *God and Morality*, pp. 122–83.

[57] See Christine Korsgaard (with G. A. Cohen et al.), *The Sources of Normativity* (Cambridge and New York: Cambridge University Press, 1996), pp. 92–8.

[58] This section draws on a brief discussion of Korsgaard found in my *Natural Signs and Knowledge of God*, pp. 129–31.

a view of who you are."[59] The problem with this idea is that people conceive of their identity quite differently, and so it looks like the universality and objectivity of morality will be lost.

Korsgaard attempts to prevent her view from turning into sheer relativism by claiming that, even though people have different ideas about their identity, all of these conceptions of the self ought rationally to include a recognition of the person's value simply as a human being. Thus, she claims that "our identity as moral beings—as people who value themselves as human beings—stands behind our more particular practical identities."[60] This allows her to endorse the "end in itself" version of Kant's categorical imperative as expressing the heart of moral obligation: rational beings must be viewed as ends in themselves, and never as a mere means.

I agree with Korsgaard that this version of Kant's principle has great force, and I also agree with her implicit view that the "end in itself" formula is not, as Kant himself thought, equivalent to the form of the categorical imperative that stresses universality. I think that the "end in itself" formula captures a central element of morality, and so with respect to normative ethics my own view is actually in significant ways close to Korsgaard's.[61] Let me try to explain the similarities.

In developing a DCT in Chapter 2, I stressed the idea that some of what God commands he commands necessarily. The reason this is so is that God's commands are necessarily directed towards the good and for some types of acts, the goodness of the acts means that there are no alternatives that God could command. I think the most plausible candidates for divine commands that have this character of necessity are the command to love God and the command to love our neighbors as ourselves, with the "neighbor" understood as including all human beings. The former command certainly seems necessary, as God is supremely good and there could be no alternative to God that is worthy of our supreme devotion. However, if God created humans in his image, as Christians and Jews affirm, then it would seem that humans must also possess an intrinsic value that God's commands would recognize. If it is necessarily good to love God, then it also seems plausible that it will be necessarily good to love humans who are created in the image of God. The command to love the

---

[59] Korsgaard, p. 117.   [60] Korsgaard, p. 121.
[61] For an attempt to show how powerful this Kantian principle is, see Alan Donagan, *The Theory of Morality* (Chicago: University of Chicago Press, 1977).

neighbor as oneself is, I believe, equivalent to the Kantian principle that all human persons have an intrinsic dignity that ought to be acknowledged. One might say that it is a necessary truth that human beings have a value that ought to be acknowledged. This does not mean that God's command does no work, of course, since God's command to love they neighbor as oneself adds a new moral quality to this way of acting, giving it the status of a duty we owe to God, even though that way of acting would be intrinsically good even apart from the command.

Despite my sympathy with Korsgaard's view, I still find it problematic in two ways. The first is that I do not believe that the view she develops is really a form of constructivism, but rather that it is a form of moral realism. Recall that the project of the constructivist is to find a middle ground between moral realism and expressivism, a position that give morality the objectivity of moral realism without introducing moral facts into our ontology. Now it is obviously true that not all humans view all other humans as ends in themselves; nor do they love their neighbors as themselves. Perhaps it is true that none of us do this perfectly, but some people fail because they do not even try. They don't recognize their identity as human beings as fundamental to how they should treat others and themselves. Instead they center their identity on some particular feature that is supposed to give them value; their sense of themselves is grounded in such things as gender or race or nation-state or being rich, or any of a myriad such things.

Korsgaard and I would agree that such people are making a mistake, but what kind of mistake are they making? In my view they are failing to recognize the value they have as responsible human beings, moral agents made in the image of God. This intrinsic worth (or dignity, to use Kantian language) is a quality that humans *possess*. It is not the result of a decision on the part of any humans and not the product of human activity. Kantian-type views such as Korsgaard's capture an important element in the truth about the *good*, namely that human persons have an intrinsic value that is not grounded in what they achieve or produce but simply in the kinds of beings they are. But this is not constructivism, but a view that fits well with a natural law account of the good.[62]

---

[62] See the use made of a similar Kantian-type principle in Murphy's *Natural Law and Practical Rationality*, pp. 187–9. As Murphy claims (on p. 189), a similar use of

This leads to my second criticism. Even if a Korsgaardian account gives the right view of the good (or a substantial portion of the right view), it does not follow that it has captured all that is important in our concept of moral obligation. Just as I argued in connection with natural law theory (in Chapter 3), an account of the good does not automatically give us an account of moral obligations. Korsgaard's attempt to ground obligations in our sense of identity places too much of a burden on this psychological concept. As she admits herself, people understand themselves very differently. In some way, of course, moral obligations must make contact with who we are. A divine command theory does this by explaining moral obligations in terms of our relation to God, who is our Creator and who has rightful authority over us. That is our true identity, and this gives a basis for making claims about how people *should* conceive of themselves. Without this kind of objective basis, it is hard to see what is wrong with the person whose identity is suffused with racist or nationalist or sexist notions that distort how the person relates to other persons. Such a person has an identity to be sure, but a mistaken one. The mistake is not merely a "procedural" one but concerns the substantive truth about what a human being is. There may be a sense in which it is correct to say that moral obligations must be understood as connected to a person's identity, but I would argue that the best account of that identity sees humans as God's creatures, subject to divine authority.

SENSIBILITY THEORIES

I shall discuss three more metaethical positions in this chapter, but in a briefer fashion, since the crucial issues can be straightforwardly addressed. I can be brief because I shall argue that the three metaethical views I shall discuss do not have to be seen as rivals of a DCT. Hence it is not necessary for me to argue against them. Their truth would not undermine a DCT.

The first view I want to consider is often termed "sensibility theory," which I shall characterize as an attempt to ground morality

this Kantian-style principle can be found in other natural law thinkers, including Germain Grisez, Joseph Boyle, John Finnis, and Robert George.

in our human affective responses to certain properties which thereby become designated as "moral." Sensibility theory, thus characterized, is ambiguous and can be developed in a number of distinct ways. One can, for example, develop a sensibility account of moral *concepts*, which views such concepts as "response-dependent" in the sense that we can grasp the extension of the concept only by including a reference to the kinds of responses (especially emotional responses) that are evoked by the things the concept refers to.[63] On this view, a moral concept can be understood as referring to something that has a tendency or disposition to evoke a certain response on our part. Alternatively, one might characterize a sensibility theory as an account of the moral properties themselves, understanding moral properties as analogous to such "secondary properties" as color, which ontologically consist in a power to produce certain sensations in us.[64] Sensibility theories are appealing in that they seem to provide a certain measure of objectivity to ethics while nevertheless doing justice to the link between morality and motivation.

Taken as an account of moral *concepts*, a proponent of a DCT has no reason to object to a sensibility theory. As Russ Shafer-Landau and Terence Cuneo affirm, such a position about moral concepts "has no ontological ramifications."[65] It seems entirely consistent with the claim that moral obligations are divine commands to hold that those commands can be sensed or perceived (perhaps through the emotions).[66] I have already argued that this is one of the ways that

---

[63] See the helpful discussion of this distinction by Russ Shafer-Landau and Terence Cuneo in the "Introduction" to the section on "Sensibility Theories" in their *Foundations of Ethics*, pp. 132–5.

[64] For good examples of sensibility theories that develop this analogy between moral properties and such secondary properties as color, see John McDowell, "Values and Secondary Qualities," in Ted Honderich (ed.), *Morality and Objectivity* (Oxford: Routledge, 1985), pp. 110–29; and David Wiggins, "A Sensible Subjectivism," in his *Needs, Values, Truth*, 2nd edn (Oxford: Blackwell, 1991), pp. 185–211.

[65] Shafer-Landau and Cuneo, *Foundations of Ethics*, p. 133.

[66] For a defense of the claim that emotions can be a means of perceiving moral properties, see Robert Roberts, *Emotions in the Moral Life* (forthcoming from Cambridge University Press), particularly Chapters 3–5, and also Adam Pelser's Baylor University doctoral dissertation, "Emotion, Evaluative Perception, and Epistemic Goods," Chapters 1 and 2, available online <http://hdl.handle.net/2104/8237>. Roderick Chisholm also provides support for the idea that emotions can be a means of perceiving moral properties in his *Theory of Knowledge*, 2nd edn (Englewood Cliffs, NJ: Prentice-Hall, 1977), p. 126.

God's commands might be communicated to humans.[67] If this were the case then it seems very plausible that our concepts of moral properties make at least some implicit reference to the means whereby we become aware of those properties.

Suppose we take a sensibility theory in a more ambitious sense, as providing an account of moral properties themselves? David Wiggins, for example, says that we must not think of value properties merely as projections; they have a kind of reality, insofar as value properties and our human sensibilities by which we perceive them are "made for each other" and are "equal and reciprocal partners."[68] So far as I can see, if this were true, it would not be a problem for a DCT. On the contrary, such a view would make more sense if we presuppose a theistic framework in which moral development is part of the *telos* of human existence. For in that case it is not surprising that there are moral properties in the natural world and that we humans have the capacity to recognize them. However, if we understand such a view as part of a reductive program in which morality is given a natural explanation (and it is only when understood in this way that a sensibility theory is a rival to a DCT), then it is puzzling that such properties should be part of nature.

Simon Blackburn makes the case for this very powerfully.[69] He claims that a projectivist view such as his own makes more sense from a naturalistic viewpoint than does a sensibility theory that is a realist account. The idea that the "properties are made for the sensibilities" is better understood as the claim that the properties are the projections or reflections of human attitudes, according to Blackburn.[70] What really makes no sense to Blackburn is the claim that our human sensibilities have as their function the perception of moral properties. On his view the evolutionary history of the development of our faculties has no room for such a claim: "But it is the other half, that sensibilities are 'made for' the properties, that really startles. Who or what makes them like that? (God? As we have seen, no natural story explains how the ethical sensibilities of human beings were made for the ethical properties of things, so perhaps it is a supernatural

---

[67] See pp. 41–5, 113–17.
[68] David Wiggins, *Truth, Invention and the Meaning of Life* (Proceedings of the British Academy 62, 1976), p. 348.
[69] Blackburn, "How To Be an Ethical Anti-Realist," pp. 47–57.
[70] Blackburn, "How To Be an Ethical Anti-Realist," p. 51.

story.)"[71] The idea that humans have natural capacities to grasp moral properties, understood as real features of the world, makes perfect sense in a theistic framework, but it makes much less sense if naturalism is true. I do not claim that naturalism makes this impossible. In Chapter 6 I shall discuss an attempt to show that even a metaphysical naturalist can make some sense of the claim that humans can know objective moral values even though our cognitive capacities are the result of evolution, so Blackburn's incredulity here may be somewhat exaggerated. However, it is surely the case that the view that we have such cognitive capacities makes much more sense if the evolutionary story about how we acquired them is put into a theistic context.

Absent the metaphysical underpinning that a theistic worldview can provide, sensibility theories also threaten to undermine the objectivity of morality, and particularly to undermine the authority of moral obligations. The psychological or sociological fact that human beings tend to respond to some particular act with such emotions as shame or guilt is hardly an adequate basis for giving that act the moral property of being wrong. Our emotions may be a means whereby we discover or recognize such properties, but they are hardly infallible, and one should certainly not say that the truth-maker for the claim that "x is morally wrong" is something like "humans who do x feel guilt and/or shame." There are certainly people who do what is wrong without feeling much in the way of guilt or shame, and there are people who do nothing wrong who feel these emotions. If we understand moral properties simply as ones that have a causal link to particular human emotions, we will lose the normativity of morality. The causal links may suggest something about morality, just as facts about what we desire give us plausible candidates for what is desirable. However, in the end we must make normative judgments about such matters. If an act is morally wrong, this implies that it is *appropriate* or *fitting* for an individual who has performed that act to feel guilt or shame, regardless of what emotion the individual actually feels.

I conclude that a sensibility theory by itself is compatible with a DCT. A sensibility theory is only inconsistent with a DCT when it is interpreted naturalistically. But when so interpreted, a sensibility theory itself seems less plausible than it would if theism were true.

---

[71] Blackburn, "How To Be an Ethical Anti-Realist," p. 51.

ETHICAL NATURALISM

I shall understand "ethical naturalism" as the claim that ethical statements are objectively true or false, and that we can come to know them by coming to know ordinary natural facts about the world.[72] One could understand such a view as a version of a traditional natural law account of values, minus the commitment to theism that has generally been part of such an account. It does not seem at all surprising that a natural law theory might be detached from theism in this way, since it is part of a natural law theory itself that values are in some way grounded in observable features of the natural world. Thus, one can recognize a good, healthy plant as different from a diseased plant without any reference to God, and one can similarly perhaps understand a well-functioning human as different from a person who is crippled by emotional distress without bringing God into the story. Of course if theism is true, and humans are made in God's image and intended for a relation with God, there will be some limits on this. Perhaps without God humans cannot function fully as they were intended to function and cannot reach their full potential. But this is compatible with saying that there are obvious forms of pathology which can be recognized as such by theists and non-theists alike. At least some of the elements of a flourishing life can be agreed on whether one is a theist or not.

This means that ethical naturalism has at least some degree of plausibility, and would have this plausibility whether theism is true or not. It seems good for a human person to live a long and healthy life, to have friends and family, to have enough to eat and drink, and to have meaningful work to do, and these are facts that seem to be evident to anyone. Some value properties then are grounded in observable facts. Richard Boyd, for example, believes that moral properties are natural properties of a particular kind: moral terms refer to "homeostatic property-clusters," groups of properties that co-occur in nature not simply as a statistical oddity but because they serve some natural function, such as "homeostasis" in understanding

---

[72] For a good statement of what ethical naturalism is and a defense of the view, see Richard N. Boyd, "How to Be a Moral Realist," in Geoffrey Sayre-McCord (ed.), *Essays on Moral Realism* (Ithaca, NY: Cornell University Press, 1988), pp. 182–217.

the way the human body maintains itself.[73] This seems recognizably similar to the idea, common in natural law theory, that the good of some biological organism (or some biological organ) must be understood in relation to how that organism (or organ) functions.

I shall not argue for or against such a view as Boyd's, because I have already defended at length the claim that a natural law ethic, understood as a theory of the good, is fully compatible with a DCT. It is true that a defender of a DCT must argue that a knowledge of the good by itself does not give us an adequate account of moral obligations, and I believe the argument given in Chapter 3 for this claim in relation to natural law theory holds equally well for a naturalistic account of the good such as the one Boyd gives. There may well be problems with Boyd's account of the good, but even if it were fully successful as an account of the good, it still leaves room for an account of moral obligations as grounded in God's commands. (For a sketch of a theory that combines such a naturalistic account of the good with a DCT, see the discussion of Mackie in the beginning section of this chapter.) The defender of a DCT may want to argue that Boyd's own account of the good is incomplete in various ways, since it makes no reference to the value of spiritual life or a relation to God. However, Boyd himself claims that it is an empirical question, open to discovery, exactly what the good for humans will turn out to be, so there is no reason for the defender of a DCT to argue that ethical naturalism must be false in principle. One might interpret Aristotle's ethics as providing a kind of ethical naturalism (though very different from Boyd's), and the fact that Aristotle's thought was so easily incorporated into a framework of divine law by Aquinas shows that there is no inherent tension between such a view and a DCT.

This does not mean, of course, that a defender of a DCT must be an ethical naturalist. As argued in the early chapters of this book, a defender of a DCT needs some account of the good, and there is good reason to think that a natural law account, if successful, will suffice for a DCT as well, though a defender of a DCT might well accept some alternative theory of the good. Similar considerations apply to ethical naturalism. A defender of a DCT might well find ethical naturalism useful in giving an account of the good. However, since a DCT does not have to commit to this particular view of the good, it follows that a DCT could be true even if ethical naturalism is false.

---

[73] See Boyd, pp. 196–7.

ETHICAL NON-NATURALISM

In the last section of this chapter, I want to look briefly at a realistic version of ethical non-naturalism. According to this view, moral judgments are, or contain, beliefs, and some of these beliefs are true. However, they do not refer to natural properties, or clusters of such properties (as Boyd thinks), but rather to real properties that are not part of the natural, physical world studied by the sciences. Russ Shafer-Landau has been an eloquent defender of such a view.[74] As he explains the position, at least the basic elements of ethics are similar to other parts of philosophy, which Shafer-Landau sees as an a priori discipline. The propositions that are the subject of moral philosophy are then propositions that are conceptually or metaphysically necessary if they are true. I can again be brief in treating such a view, because there is no essential conflict between such a position and a divine command account of moral obligations. It is not a rival view that must be refuted. First of all, as I have repeatedly stressed, a DCT presupposes a framework of moral truths as part of its foundation. For example, it presupposes that humans ought (in some sense of "ought") to obey any commands a good God might give. There is no reason for the defender a DCT to deny that some or all of these moral truths might be necessary truths.

Even statements about moral obligations might be necessary truths. I have repeatedly appealed to the fact that a DCT which understands moral obligations as divine commands can view some—or even all—of these commands as necessary. For example, God necessarily commands humans to worship no one but God, and I have argued that it is plausible that the command to humans to love other humans as their neighbors is also necessary. Even a view that holds that all God's commands are necessary, what I have called a no-discretion version of a DCT, is still a DCT. The defender of a DCT can then agree with Shafer-Landau that at least some of our moral principles are necessary and perhaps can be known a priori. A defender of a no-discretion DCT can hold that all of our moral principles are of this sort.

---

[74] See Russ Shafer-Landau, *Moral Realism: A Defence* (Oxford: Clarendon Press, 2003). For a shorter account, see his "Ethics as Philosophy: A Defence of Ethical Non-Naturalism," in *Foundations of Ethics*, pp. 210–21. Originally published in Terence Horgan and Mark Timmons (eds), *Metaethics after Moore* (Oxford: Oxford University Press, 2006), pp. 209–32.

However, one might think that there is a conflict between ethical non-naturalism and a DCT because the necessary status of ethical truths implies that they need no explanation. The person who makes such an objection to a DCT might see moral facts as simply brute facts. Moral facts neither need not have any explanation, so there is no need to explain them as divine commands. Erik Wielenberg appears to hold such a view, giving arguments recently that it is just a brute fact about the universe that some actions are morally right and others are morally wrong.[75]

However, it should be evident that the conflict here is not between a DCT and ethical non-naturalism per se, but rather between a DCT and the claim that all non-natural ethical facts are brute in character. The latter thesis is far from obviously true. Certainly, it seems to be the case that some necessary truths can be explained by other necessary truths.[76] Take for example the proposition that "It is false that every prime is odd." This proposition is necessarily true, but its truth is explained by the truth of "2 is both even and prime." There are also obvious examples from ethics. Perhaps, for example, "It is bad to torture innocents for fun" is necessarily true because it is also necessarily true that "Torturing humans for fun is not respecting them as ends in themselves" and "It is bad not to respect humans as ends in themselves." So the fact that a proposition is necessarily true does not by itself imply that it cannot be explained or that it does not require explanation.

What about truths about moral obligations? Do we have good reasons to think that such propositions are brute? Let us assume, as I argued in Chapter 1, that humans have moral obligations, and that some of their obligations extend towards all other humans, including people they do not even know and who cannot benefit or harm them. This fact, even if it is true and even if it is necessarily true, seems surprising. Many people doubt it or even flat-out deny it. If it is true, then it seems to be the kind of truth that cries out for an explanation. The fact that so many naturalists, including philosophers such as Mackie and Nietzsche, find the idea of non-natural moral facts odd or queer, shows that they are indeed the kind of thing one would like to have an explanation for.

---

[75] See Erik Wielenberg, "In Defense of Non-Natural, Non-Theistic Moral Realism," *Faith and Philosophy* 26:1 (2009), pp. 23–41.

[76] I thank Alexander Pruss for the examples given below.

The oddness or queerness of morality in a world without God is the basis of a provocative argument by George Mavrodes that morality makes more sense in a theistic world than it does in a non-theistic world.[77] Mavrodes begins the essay by discussing Bertrand Russell's view that "man is the product of causes that had no prevision of the end they were achieving; that his origin, his growth, his hopes and fears, his loves and his beliefs are but the outcome of accidental collocations of atoms."[78] Mavrodes goes on to argue that moral obligations do not really make sense in such a "Russellian world," and that various attempts to explain them naturalistically fail.

However, Mavrodes also considers a position similar to Wielenberg's, in which it is just "an ultimate fact about the universe that kindness is good and cruelty is bad."[79] If the claim that such moral facts are brute in nature is simply put forward as a bald assertion, then there is no argument given that one could refute. However, Mavrodes makes an astute observation with which I concur: a world with brute moral facts does not seem very much like a Russellian world. One would think that in a Russellian world the "deep" facts about the world would be facts about the basic particles of physics. A world in which there are deep moral truths, especially truths that hold necessarily and are known a priori, seems more like Plato's world than Russell's.

As Mavrodes admits, Platonism is a view that can be, and has been, held by non-theists. However, Platonism as a worldview has usually seemed to be "congenial (especially congenial when compared to some other philosophical views) to a religious understanding of the world."[80] It is no accident that there is a long tradition of theistic (and even Christian) Platonism, running from Augustine to Robert Adams. It seems almost irresistible for a Platonist to ask what the fact that moral truths are deep truths about the universe says about the nature of ultimate reality. Platonism itself in some ways makes the world mysterious and posits features of the world that cry out for

---

[77] George I. Mavrodes, "Religion and the Queerness of Morality," in Robert Audi and William J. Wainwright (eds), *Rationality, Religious Belief, and Moral Commitment: New Essays in the Philosophy of Religion* (Ithaca, NY: Cornell University Press, 1986), pp. 213–26. I also discuss this essay in *Natural Signs and Knowledge of God*, pp. 114–16, and the following paragraphs draw on this discussion.

[78] The passage from Russell is from "A Free Man's Worship," in *Mysticism and Logic: And Other Essays* (New York: Barnes and Noble, 1917), pp. 47–8. Quotation in Mavrodes, "Religion and the Queerness of Morality," p. 215.

[79] Mavrodes, p. 224.   [80] Mavrodes, p. 224.

explanation. Many theists in fact have thought that Platonism itself makes far more sense in a theistic universe than it does otherwise, since in a theistic world the Forms do not have to be seen as independent realities but can be understood as Ideas in the divine mind. In any case the fact that Robert Adams successfully combines Platonism with a divine command theory of moral obligation shows again that there is no inherent conflict between ethical non-naturalism and a DCT.[81]

[81] I here refer of course to Adams' *Finite and Infinite Goods.*

6

Conclusions: The Inescapability of Moral Obligations

This book began with an exploration of the distinctive features of moral obligations as most people experience them, seeing them as objective, verdict-like, overriding, motivating, and universal (in two senses). I then argued in Chapter 2 that seeing moral obligations as divine commands makes it possible to give a powerful explanation of all those features. Chapter 3 attempted to show that a DCT is not a rival to a natural law ethic or virtue theory, but that all three theories can be seen as complementary. In Chapter 4 I presented the most powerful objections to a DCT that have been presented and argued that none of them provide strong reasons to reject a divine command account. In Chapter 5 I attempted to show that if one examines other leading metaethical theories, one finds that some of those theories are not really rivals of a DCT, while those that are genuine rivals face significant difficulties that a DCT does not face. I have thus tried to build a strong case that those who believe in the reality of moral obligations and recognize them as having the features I claim they have should find it attractive to see moral obligations as divine commands.

Of course not everyone will find the argument convincing. Some will doubtless find problems with various elements in the case. There will likely also be readers who find the inferences plausible enough, but who balk at the conclusion, and it is these readers I want to engage in this final chapter. Such readers might agree that those who believe in the reality of moral obligations and accept that they have the features I have described as characteristic of moral obligations should find a divine command account of moral obligations to be plausible. Such readers could reasonably view moral obligations as divine commands, *if belief in God were plausible.* That is, however, a very big "if" in the

contemporary intellectual situation. A reader who finds God's existence enormously implausible might well see the whole argument of
the book as a long *reductio ad absurdum* argument. They might agree,
if they have found my arguments to be powerful, that the following
argument is logically valid, and that the first premise is true:

(1) If moral obligations exist, then God exists.
(2) Moral obligations exist.
(3) Therefore God exists.

However, the critic may reason that since (3) is false, and (1) is true,
premise (2) must be false, given the validity of the argument.

In the end, therefore, the specter of "error theory" must still be
confronted. One might grant that morality, as it is understood by most
people, has features that point to God's reality, but conclude that this
gives us a powerful reason to doubt the reality of morality understood
in this way. An error theorist, such as J. L. Mackie, might very well
grant that many of my inferences are persuasive, but hold that what
I have really done is given very good reasons for thinking that morality
as it is understood by most people is a kind of illusion. I should like in
this concluding chapter to confront this moral skepticism head-on.[1]
Why should a person believe in the reality of moral obligations?

One way of rebutting such a view is to attack the claim that God
does not exist. If it is possible to know that God exists, or even
reasonable to believe that God exists, then the fact that moral obligations depend on God for their reality will not provide any reason to
doubt the reality of moral obligations. There has been a major out-
pouring of work in the philosophy of religion in the last half-century
devoted to the goal of showing that belief in God is reasonable, and
I have myself recently attempted to make such a case.[2] However,
building such a case for the existence of God or the reasonableness

---

[1] I am using the term "moral skeptic" here in a broad sense, to cover both those
who doubt the reality of morality and those who think that even if there are moral
truths they are not knowable.

[2] For my attempt to argue for the reasonableness of belief in God, see my *Natural
Signs and Knowledge of God*. The recent literature on belief in God is massive, but the
works of Alvin Plantinga and Richard Swinburne provide two influential and impressive attempts, albeit rooted in two quite different epistemological perspectives, to
support the reasonableness of theistic faith. See Alvin Plantinga, *Warranted Christian
Belief* (New York: Oxford University Press, 2000), and Richard Swinburne, *The
Existence of God*, 2nd ed. (Oxford: Clarendon Press, 2004).

of belief in God is a major project in itself, one that certainly lies outside the scope of this book. In any case, if a direct argument for the reality of moral obligations can be given, and moral obligations require God's existence as part of their explanation, that will itself provide part of the case for belief in God. What then can be said on behalf of taking moral obligations as real?[3]

The first thing to be said is that it is unrealistic and unreasonable to expect a "proof" about such a question, if one means by a proof something like a logical argument that will necessarily convince any reasonable person who considers the argument carefully. Such proofs are hard to come by in philosophy; it is difficult to come up with an example of any interesting and substantive philosophical claim that has been proven. No philosopher has given a proof in this sense that humans possess or do not possess free will, that human consciousness is or is not reducible to brain activity, or that mathematical objects (such as numbers) are or are not timeless objective realities. This is not just true for controversial claims, since it seems extremely difficult (if not impossible) to prove propositions that almost no one seriously doubts are true, such as the belief that there are external physical objects, or the belief that the universe was not created one hour ago, complete with apparent memories and other evidences of apparent age. Hence the fact that no ironclad proof of the objectivity of moral obligations is possible does not mean that good reasons to believe in such obligations cannot be given.

There are in fact special reasons why a proof of the existence of moral obligations is not to be expected, if a divine command account of such obligations is true. I have already argued in Chapter 4 that God has good reasons not to make his reality so obvious that it cannot

---

[3] A note on terminology here: I understand a DCT to be a species of moral realism, since it holds a realistic view of the good, and sees statements about human moral obligations as ones that have an objective truth value. The reason I do this is that I understand moral realism as the view that moral propositions have a truth value that is independent of human beliefs and desires. But obviously, on a DCT, propositions about moral obligations are not independent of God's preferences and commands. Thomas Carson, in "Divine Will/Divine Command Moral Theories and the Problem of Arbitrariness," (*Religious Studies* 2012, doi:10.1017/S00344125100031X) does not describe a DCT as a realist theory, since he thinks of realism as the view that moral facts hold independently of the preferences of any being, including God. So far as I can see, this disagreement between Carson and myself is purely semantic. Carson makes a case for a type of divine preference theory (at least a cousin of a DCT) and says that his case depends on moral realism being false. However, moral realism can be false in his sense and true in mine.

be denied, and that this means that in communicating his requirements to humans, he can do so without always making it obvious that
he is in fact the source of those requirements.[4] It seems plausible that
a God who wants human persons to serve him freely, motivated by
love and devotion, would be partly "hidden," and this requires that
the evidence for God's reality be of a special character. I have argued
in another work that the evidence for God, though widely accessible,
should also be easily resistible.[5] However, I think it is not only
reasonable to think that God might make his own reality as the source
of moral obligations less than fully obvious; he might also have good
reasons for making the reality of moral obligations themselves less
than totally undeniable. I do not mean to suggest that the existence of
morality is something "hidden." Moral obligations seem to be something that the great majority of human beings experience at some
points in their lives. However, the experience is not such as to make it
simply impossible to deny the reality of these obligations.

Why should this be so? The answer is that, just as God wants
humans freely to love and obey him, he desires that their commitment
to morality be something that is not coerced or grudging. After all, if
the kind of DCT I have described is true, then moral obligations come
from God and provide a way of coming to know God's reality. As
I argue in Chapter 3, a plausible DCT will see moral obligation as
something that has as its *telos* the transformation of humans. The
point of morality is to help humans acquire the virtues or excellences
that will make it possible for them to become friends of God. It seems
fitting for God to make humans aware of their moral obligations, but
not to do so in such a way that those who have no desire to follow the
path they direct us towards would be forced to recognize their reality.
Perhaps those who are completely unwilling to acknowledge God's
authority and who have no willingness to embark on such a process of
personal transformation are able to doubt the reality of the requirements themselves. William James wrote in his Journal that "my first
act of free will shall be to believe in free will."[6] Perhaps what James
thought was that it was somehow fitting or appropriate that free will be

---

[4] See pp. 110–17.

[5] For my discussion of the "Wide Accessibility Principle" and the "Easy Resistibil-
ity Principle," see *Natural Signs and Knowledge of God*, pp. 12–17 and 154–69.

[6] This quotation can be found in the selections from James's Journal found in *The
Writings of William James*, ed. John J. McDermott (New York: Modern Library,
1968), p. 7.

something that one must believe in freely. It seems even more fitting that belief in the reality of the moral life be a conviction that a person is not coerced into holding. I shall therefore seek to build the kind of case for the reality of moral obligations that would be sufficient to convince someone who is disposed to take the moral path seriously.

MORAL EXPERIENCE AND THE PRINCIPLE OF CREDULITY

One way of making a case for realism about moral obligations is to argue that we should take seriously our moral experience. Most people have experienced situations in which they are tempted to do what they believe they ought not to do. Imagine that a young man (call him Sam) has played his trumpet for a wedding and been given an honorarium of $300 in cash. When it comes time for Sam to report his income for tax purposes, the government will have no way of knowing about this income. Sam is tempted to "forget" the payment when filling out his tax return, but he also knows he will feel guilty if he does so, because he believes he ought honestly to report his income and thereby pay his fair share of taxes.

We can see right away from this example that Sam may have some motivation to doubt the reality of moral obligations, for it is precisely such obligations that constrain our behavior. If he decides morality is an illusion, perhaps he will feel less guilty if he does not report the income. The situations in which we are most clearly aware of our moral obligations are precisely ones in which we strongly desire to do what is not morally permissible. However, if Sam becomes skeptical about moral obligations so that he can pay less taxes, he has not come to believe that morality is illusory because of evidence. Rather, his reasons seem practical and self-interested. He experiences his duty to be honest as a genuine obligation, but he is tempted to deny this duty is real partly because he wants to be free of such obligations.

To see this is so, notice that Sam is much less likely to experience this temptation to doubt the reality of moral obligations if someone *else* is violating a moral duty, particularly if this violation of duty is at Sam's expense. Suppose, for example, that Sam was promised that he would be paid $300 for playing at the wedding, but that he has never been paid. It seems highly likely that he will believe that he *ought* to have been paid, and that it was *wrong* of the person who made the promise to fail to fulfill the promise. He is much less likely to be tempted to think that such obligations are an illusion. To the contrary, he is likely to feel moral outrage that he has been cheated in this way. When Sam is the one under obligation, the duty is perceived as an uncomfortable fact (though a fact nonetheless), but when Sam is the one who has been wronged, the duty seems even more evident.

Sam's kind of experience is by no means uncommon. Almost everyone, with the exception of sociopaths, knows what it feels like to be tempted to do what one nonetheless believes to be wrong. Sadly, most of us, perhaps nearly all of us, know what it feels like to give in to such temptations and to feel guilt as a result of doing so. And almost everyone knows what it feels like to have been wronged, to perceive another person as having treated oneself (and others) in a way that is not morally permissible. Hence a good case can be made that moral obligations are experienced as objective; they seem to have the kind of objectivity we associate with "facts." In the moral case these are facts that we sometimes feel very certain about, and at some times wish were not facts, but they still (often enough) feel like facts. We find it hard (though not impossible) to wish them away when we want to, and we are usually quite confident of their reality when we see ourselves as having been wronged.

If moral obligations are experienced as something objective, this provides at least prima facie evidence that they are objective. Or so it seems to many philosophers, who are attracted to what is often called the "principle of credulity." Richard Swinburne, a defender of this principle, states it as follows: "it is a principle of rationality that (in the absence of special considerations) if it seems (epistemically) to a subject that x is present (and has some characteristic), then probably x is present (and has that characteristic); what one seems to perceive is probably so."[7] Swinburne employs this principle in the context of religious experience as part of an argument for belief in the existence of God, but it should be evident that if it is a general principle of rationality then it will apply equally to moral experience.

The proviso ("in the absence of special considerations") is important, because Swinburne does not want to defend an unqualified version

---

[7] Swinburne, *The Existence of God*, p. 303.

of the principle of credulity. Don Loeb, for example, has criticized this kind of argument from moral experience to moral realism, on the grounds that the principle of credulity gives wrong results in some cases and so must not be a basic principle of rationality.[8] Loeb argues, for example, that if I am watching a Lotto drawing on television, and have a strong sense that the next number drawn will be even, this does not provide warrant for my believing that the next number drawn will be even. I am only justified in believing that the probability of the next number being even is 0.5, despite the fact that it "seems" to me that the next number will be even.

The defender of the principle of credulity will not be troubled by such cases, for in this situation there are "special considerations" that apply.[9] The special consideration is simply that I have a defeater for the belief that the next number drawn will be even, namely my knowledge that the odds of this happening are 50/50. It would be unreasonable to claim that moral experience, in conjunction with the principle of credulity, *proves* the reality of objective moral obligations, but that concession is fully consistent with the view that such experience does provide prima facie evidence for objective moral obligations.

Some philosophers might object to this by claiming that moral experience would only provide evidence for the reality of moral obligations if the existence of such obligations were necessary to explain the occurrence of moral experience, or at least were necessitated by the explanation of such experience. Some philosophers maintain that one can give an evolutionary explanation of such experiences that does not require the reality of moral obligations.[10] The flaw in this objection is that it seems to treat experience only as something to be given a causal explanation. However, it is easy to see that this is not how we normally treat experience, and equally easy to see that such a view of experience leads straight to skepticism. As Berkeley showed, if we treat our perceptual experience of the external world simply as data to be causally explained by the hypothesis that there is an external

---

[8] Don Loeb, "The Argument from Moral Experience," in R. Joyce and S. Kitchin (eds), *A World Without Values* (Heidelberg: Springer, 2007), pp. 101–18. Terence Cuneo has a clear discussion of Loeb's article in his twin articles, "Reidian Metaethics" I and II, in *Philosophy Compass* 6/5 (2011), pp. 333–40, and 341–9.

[9] Swinburne gives a detailed account of what kinds of special considerations there might be in *The Existence of God*, pp. 310–22.

[10] For a well-known example, see Street, "A Darwinian Dilemma for Realist Theories of Value."

world, the causal explanation immediately runs into trouble. If we have no direct awareness of the external world, how could we possibly know anything about its causal powers? If, however, we follow the principle of credulity, skepticism about the external world can be avoided. Our experience of the external world as an objective reality gives us reason to believe it is an objective reality. The proponent of moral realism holds that we have no reason to treat our moral experience differently than we treat perceptual experience of the physical world. We experience moral obligations as real and objective; that experience provides us with at least some reason to believe moral obligations are real and objective. Moral experiences should not be viewed simply as odd sensations that need somehow to be causally explained.

Of course there might be defeaters for the claim that morality should be understood as realists do; prima facie justification can be overridden. However, in the absence of such defeaters, a belief in morality seems justified.

THOMAS REID'S DEFENSE OF MORAL REALISM

The principle of credulity seems generally to fit well with at least the spirit of Thomas Reid's epistemology, which is known for its vigorous defense of trust in our human faculties. Hence it makes sense to take a closer look at Reid's philosophy to see what he has to say about these issues in ethics. Terence Cuneo has recently given a powerful interpretation of Thomas Reid's writings on ethics that shows how a case for moral realism can be made that goes well beyond any simple appeal to the principle of credulity.[11] Cuneo does not claim that this case is air-tight, but only that it may suffice to make moral realism the "default position" in metaethics, but this would itself be a significant achievement. As I understand it, there are two elements in Reid's strategy. The first element (logically, not necessarily temporally in Reid's exposition) is an attempt to show that human experience, action, and social interaction all presuppose the reality of morality. This goes beyond a simple appeal to moral experience by trying to

---

[11] Cuneo, "Reidian Metaethics" I and II.

show that moral realism provides the best explanation for evident features of human life. The second element is an attempt to show that we ought to accept the evidence provided by these first elements, on pain of inconsistency or some other rational failure. I shall give a brief discussion of each element in this strategy.

As Cuneo tells the story, Reid points to a number of distinct points to show how a belief in moral objectivity is embedded in our ordinary lives. First, Reid highlights the way in which we perceive other persons as manifesting moral qualities; we see other people as kind or cruel, as compassionate or merciless, as generous or selfish, and in countless other morally qualified ways.[12] How do we do this? Reid claims that we do so in the same way that we perceive complex, high-order, non-moral traits that other people display, such as shrewdness or eloquence. All of these qualities are recognized from the "signs" that others display in their conduct, and there is no more reason to be skeptical about the moral qualities than the non-moral ones.[13] The moral judgments seem to be as reliable as the non-moral ones, and we seem to have about the same degree of confidence in both.

Second, Reid points out that when we make promises, and perform other speech acts and other actions of various kinds, we believe that we thereby place ourselves under moral obligations.[14] To make a promise just is to put oneself under a moral obligation. That is how we understand the act of making a promise, and so if we did not believe that there were real moral obligations, then making a promise would be unintelligible. For how could we intend to perform an act that placed us in a state that we did not believe could really exist?

Finally, Reid points out the strong disanalogy between moral properties and the properties we attribute to others because of our affective attitudes.[15] We understand that "being esteemed" is a property that someone has by virtue of the attitudes taken towards that person by others; if we no longer admire a person, then that person ceases to be esteemed. No one would think, however, that if we ceased to disapprove

---

[12] Cuneo, "Reidian Metaethics" I and II, p. 336.

[13] See Thomas Reid, *Essays on the Intellectual Powers of Man*, ed. Derek R. Brookes (Edinburgh: Edinburgh University Press, 1785/1969), VI.vi: 503.

[14] Cuneo, "Reidean Metaethics" I and II, p. 336. For Thomas Reid's discussion of promises and contracts see his *Essays on the Active Powers of Man* (Edinburgh: Edinburgh University Press, 2010), pp. 327–44.

[15] Cuneo, "Reidean Metaethics" I and II, p. 337. For Thomas Reid's discussion of this point see *Essays on the Active Powers of Man*, pp. 344–63.

of killing other humans for pleasure, this would somehow change the moral status of such killing from being unacceptable to being acceptable. In the first case, what is true is decided by our human attitudes but we don't think that is the case with moral properties.

So it looks like moral realism is firmly embedded in our moral experiences and practices, or perhaps provides a framework which best explains those features. But why should we think this common perspective is correct? Here is where the second element of Reid's strategy is relevant. Reid appeals to the analogies between our ability to discern moral truths and our abilities to discern other types of truths. One might say that our ordinary moral practices depend upon our ability to discern moral truths, just as our actions depend on our ability to discern truths by the use of perception. "As we rely upon the clear and distinct testimony of our eyes, concerning the colours and figures of the bodies about us, we have the same reason to rely with security upon the clear and unbiassed [*sic*] testimony of our conscience, with regard to what we ought and ought not to do."[16] We have an ability to grasp basic moral truths that seems just as "original" as our ability to grasp truths about the external world through sense perception or our ability to understand logical connections through reason. Reid says that it is clearly reasonable to trust our human faculties in general and we have no special reason to doubt our ability to grasp moral truths, that ability he describes as conscience:

> Every man in his senses believes his eyes, his ears, and his other senses. He believes his consciousness with respect to his own thoughts and purposes, his memory, with regard to what is past, his understanding, with regard to abstract relations of things, . . . And he has the same reason, and indeed, is under the same necessity of believing the clear unbiassed [*sic*] dictates of his conscience, with regard to what is honorable and base.[17]

Perhaps Reid goes too far in claiming that we are under a "necessity" to believe the dictates of conscience. After all, there are plenty of moral skeptics, and plenty of philosophers who accept non-cognitivist metaethical theories, such as expressivism, and such people seem to be able to go about their lives normally in a way that would be impossible for someone who did not trust sense perception. So there are

---

[16] Reid, *Essays on the Active Powers of Man*, p. 179.
[17] Reid, *Essays on the Active Powers of Man*, p. 180.

some differences between what we might call our moral epistemic practices and our perceptual epistemic practices. But those disanalogies are not complete and do not undermine the similarities. We should remember that there are also those who claim to be skeptics about our non-moral faculties. For example, there are idealists who deny that we can achieve knowledge of physical objects through sense perception. Perhaps when Reid says that we find it necessary to rely on our senses, he means that it is practically necessary, and that this practical necessity provides evidence that such reliance is reasonable, for he is certainly well aware of Berkeley's philosophy. The same kind of practical necessity may attach to our moral epistemic practices.

Reid is well known for his argument that certain types of philosophical skepticism are in some sense not completely genuine; the philosopher who claims we have no good reason to believe in the external world nevertheless seems to live as if he did believe in it. It may not be quite so hard to be a moral skeptic as a skeptic about the physical world, but it is still hard, especially when we are the victim of others' wrongdoing. Just as is the case with other types of skepticism, it is easier to be a moral skeptic in the study than it is when one comes out of the study to live a full human life. It seems plausible to say we have a strong inclination to accept the deliverances of conscience, and that this inclination parallels our inclination to accept the outputs of other human cognitive faculties.

One objection that will surely occur to many contemporary readers stems from doubt about what Reid calls conscience. Do humans really have a faculty called conscience, a moral sense that is in some ways analogous to other human cognitive faculties? And if they do have such a faculty, is it really as reliable as Reid claims? If we reflect on the widespread moral disagreements we find among humans, both between and within cultures, one may wonder if we humans really have a reliable cognitive faculty that allows them to grasp moral truths. I have already discussed these questions and will turn to them again later in this chapter.[18] However, before doing so, I want first to consider two recent arguments of David Enoch that, taken together, provide further support for the reality of moral obligations.[19]

---

[18] See pp. 41–5 and 171–81.
[19] In addition to the articles on Reidean metaethics discussed above, I would also like to recommend the following defense of moral realism from Terence Cuneo:

ENOCH'S CASE FOR MORAL REALISM

David Enoch's *Taking Morality Seriously: A Defense of Robust Realism* offers the most comprehensive and sophisticated case for moral realism to be found in the literature. As Enoch himself admits, convictions about such matters in most cases stem partly from deep intuitions and not solely from arguments. For example, Enoch affirms a suspicion that the arguments against expressivism rooted in the Frege–Geach problem (dealing with the role normative propositions play in truth-functional arguments, an issue I briefly discuss in Chapter 5), are not decisive. "Expressivists putting forward a solution to the Frege–Geach problem will—if God whispers in their ears that their solution fails—proceed to look for another one, rather than convert to cognitivism (or some such)," and he affirms that those who worry about expressivism as an adequate metaethical theory will not be convinced if a successful solution to the Frege–Geach problem is found.[20] The real source of the disagreements lies deeper than such arguments.

Nevertheless, philosophical arguments can be helpful and powerful in helping us see the power of our intuitions and making it clear what the costs and benefits of adopting a particular view are. Enoch thus offers two original arguments that bear on the issues. One, directly concerned with metaethics, tries to show that some of the most popular types of anti-realist theories have unacceptable first-order moral consequences. The second, dealing not just with morality but more general metanormative propositions, tries to show that a realist stance towards normative truths is presupposed by the deliberations we unavoidably engage in as practical beings. While original, both arguments can, I believe, be viewed as being at least in the spirit of the Reidean arguments discussed above.

The first argument takes a notion of impartiality as its starting point.[21] Imagine two people who are having a disagreement that is understandable as a conflict in preferences or attitudes. For example, suppose two friends want to spend the afternoon together, but one wants to go bike-riding while the second person wants to go to the zoo.

"Moral Realism," in Christian Miller (ed.), *The Continuum Companion to Ethics* (London: Continuum Press, 2011), pp. 3–28.

[20] Enoch, *Taking Morality Seriously*, p. 9.

[21] See Enoch, pp. 16–49. Enoch's argument is obviously more complicated and nuanced than the brief summary I here provide; here I simply convey the central idea.

How should they resolve the disagreement? If we assume the only relevant issues are their desires or other subjective attitudes (i.e. it is not the case that the zoo is closed that day), it seems that the right thing to do is to take both views into account and look for some resolution that takes account of both preferences in an impartial way. Perhaps they should agree to follow the first person's preference on this occasion and then the second person's preference on their next occasion together. Or maybe they should simply flip a coin. It would seem high-handed and unjustified for one person simply to insist that his or her desires be satisfied while the other's preferences are ignored.

There is a dramatic difference if we compare this disagreement to one where a significant moral principle is in play. Imagine that the first person wants to catch and torture a cat, while the second believes this is wrong and should not be done. In this situation the second person would by no means be high-handed or unfair to stand his or her ground, and refuse to consider being a party to torturing an animal. Flipping a coin or agreeing to the other's plan as a compromise ("We will follow my preferences next time") are things the person should not even consider in this case. If we thought that this disagreement was, like the first one, simply a matter of different preferences, why should there be this difference? If we believe that the disagreement in the second situation is a disagreement about the moral facts, then it is easy to see why the second person may be justified in standing his or her ground. For, in general, when we are dealing with a question of objective fact, there is no requirement that parties to a disagreement "split the difference" or come to some impartial compromise, as is the case when one has a clash of desires. Enoch makes the case for this first by considering a very simple anti-realist view that he calls "Caricatured Subjectivism," but he then goes on to argue that the argument generalizes and applies to many prominent forms of anti-realism, including such forms of expressivism as Blackburn's quasi-realism.[22] The argument by itself does not suffice to establish moral realism, since it does not apply to such non-realist positions as Korsgaard's constructivism, but those who find the argument plausible will certainly find it more plausible to "take morality seriously."

The second argument Enoch offers he terms the "argument from deliberative indispensability."[23] Enoch argues, and here he is surely

---

[22] See Enoch, pp. 27–38.
[23] See Enoch, pp. 70–84, for the heart of the argument.

right, that human life is inconceivable without practical deliberation. Virtually every day every person is faced with decisions, and sometimes it is not clear what option should be chosen. In some of these cases the choices are trivial, and it is reasonable to choose randomly, as when one picks one box of Cheerios at the grocery store out of the twenty identical boxes on the shelf. But many decisions are significant: Should I apply for a new job or keep my old job? Should I quit philosophy and go to law school? We believe very firmly that in many cases some choices will be better than others, and so we deliberate about what we should do; we try to decide which option is better. Deliberation of this sort would make no sense if we did not believe that in some cases some options *are* really better. If deliberation is something that is "rationally inescapable" (essential to human life), and if deliberation requires us to believe in the truth of certain normative propositions such as "my life will be better if I continue to do philosophy" or "my life will be better if I quit philosophy and go to law school," then it seems we are committed to the view that some normative propositions have a truth value.

Enoch carefully concedes that this argument gets us only to meta-normative realism in general and not necessarily all the way to metaethical realism, since it is conceivable that a person could deliberate while only believing in the truth of normative propositions that are non-moral in character.[24] However, it is difficult to see why someone should admit normative facts into one's ontology and then balk at moral facts. And it seems plausible that Enoch's argument could be extended in the following way so that it applies to moral obligations: imagine that the deliberation that is in view is specifically moral deliberation, deliberation that presupposes some option is morally better than another. Perhaps, for example, a person is under conflicting obligations and must deliberate about which obligation takes preference. (The following might be an example: I have a duty to meet you for lunch because I promised to do so, but on the way there I see a terrible accident and recognize a duty to stop and render aid, thus requiring me to miss lunch.) A person might object that moral deliberation is not truly "indispensable" for human life, as is deliberation in general, so that this extended version of the argument is less powerful than Enoch's. Even if this is so, the argument

---

[24] Enoch, p. 50.

may well have considerable force for morally sincere persons. Indeed, it seems plausible that a person who never considers moral issues in making decisions about life is living a sub-human life.

Someone may object that arguments such as this one, as well as Enoch's first argument, presuppose that one is already committed to some first-order moral views. It is only if one believes firmly that it would be morally wrong to torture a cat that Enoch's argument that this case differs strongly from a case where the differences are merely preferences has bite. And it is only a person who deliberates some-times about what is morally permissible and what is not who will feel the force of my more specific version of Enoch's argument. A person who lacks moral character may not care about morality and such a person may fail to feel the force of the argument, since the person has no concern for doing what is morally right and does not deliberate about such issues. However, I do not think that it is at all plausible to think that one's ability to grasp moral truth is completely independ-ent of one's moral character. No less an ethical authority than Aris-totle famously said that a person is unlikely to make much progress in learning about what is "noble and just" unless the person has had a good upbringing and has thus acquired the right kind of character.[25] This does not mean that arguments such as Enoch's (or my exten-sion) will necessarily be question-begging and/or ineffective. For many people who may claim theoretically to be moral skeptics none-theless may have moral character; their lives may be better than their theories and thus they may feel the force of arguments that appeal to normative commitments.

CONSCIENCE AS A MORAL FACULTY AND MORAL INTUITIONS

In several sections of this work I have appealed to the idea that God's requirements are communicated to humans not merely through special revelations but through natural means. For example, in Chapter 2 I discussed how traditional African religious beliefs that moral obligations are rooted in God or gods fit well with traditional

---

[25] Aristotle, *Nichomachean Ethics* 1095b, trans. W. D. Ross, p. 937.

African beliefs about conscience as a faculty by which we can come to know our moral obligations.[26] In Chapter 4 I argued that God can communicate his requirements through conscience, and thus that it is possible for people who do not believe in God to be aware of what are in reality his commands.[27] In this concluding chapter I have discussed Reid's argument against moral skepticism, which partly depends on his claim that we have conscience, a cognitive faculty that is a source of moral knowledge, and that we have reasons to trust this faculty that are on a par with our reasons to trust our other human epistemic faculties.

However, is it really plausible that we have such a cognitive moral faculty? Do we really have a special "moral sense"? Even if we have such a faculty, should we rely on it? If it is a reliable faculty, how can there be so much moral disagreement? If moral realism is true, and people generally disagree about what the moral facts are, then it would seem any such faculty does not work very well, since if people hold competing beliefs, some or all of these beliefs must be wrong. A critic may urge that the tremendous differences in moral beliefs we see between different cultures and different historical eras surely suggests that our moral beliefs are not the product of some "moral sense" that is comparable to sense perception or memory in its reliability.

The first question I want to raise concerns the basic nature of conscience: What does it mean to claim that human persons have a "moral sense," or that we have "moral intuitions" that can provide moral knowledge or justified moral beliefs? The first thing to be said is that the language of a "moral sense" is misleading in that it seems to imply that humans have some special cognitive faculty that is analogous to sense perception or reason, but this is not necessary to affirm that humans have reliable moral intuitions. A belief that humans have an intuitive capacity to recognize moral truths does not commit its holder to a claim that humans have a special "part" of the mind that gives them the ability to know moral truth (though of course it is compatible with such a claim).

For example, W. D. Ross, one of the well-known defenders of "moral intuitionism," rejects the view that humans have such a dedicated, special moral faculty. Ross held that humans can indeed "apprehend" or recognize moral truths intuitively, but he thought

---

[26] See pp. 40–5.   [27] See pp. 110–17.

that such truths are recognized in the same way that mathematical and logical truths are known.[28] He is committed to the claim that humans have a capacity to recognize certain truths that are a priori in character, but he does not think that such a capacity is distinctively "moral." It is simply that human capacity that many philosophers call "reason," where reason is taken as a special capacity to recognize a distinctive kind of truth, namely the kind of truth especially linked to the relation certain qualities (or concepts on some versions) have to other qualities (or concepts).

Actually, it is not altogether clear what it might mean to affirm the existence of a particular faculty or "part" of the mind. Contemporary evolutionary psychologists, for example, seem increasingly drawn to seeing the mind as "modular," and there are plausible theories that view beliefs about both God and morality as the products of specific "modules" selected for by evolution.[29] However, it is not clear to me that the "separateness" of the module is more than a functional separateness; that is, there is an identifiable set of activities that serve certain purposes within the mental life of the organism. Obviously, any functional capacity must be realized in some way, and presumably in bodily creatures such as humans, there must be some physical configuration that makes possible the relevant processing of information. However, so far as I can see, this does not mean that if the human mind contains a "moral module," then the relevant information processing must be done by some discrete region of the brain. It seems sufficient to say that there is some process by which this occurs that has a distinctive character, regardless of how that process is physically realized. The defender of moral intuitions can then be neutral on the question as to whether humans have a distinct faculty or part of the mind. The moral intuitionist may hold that there is a distinctive functional "moral module," that operates in the same way

---

[28] For W. D. Ross's views on moral intuitions see his *Foundations of Ethics* (Oxford: Clarendon Press, 1939), pp. 79–89, and especially 168–91.

[29] Many thinkers see morality and religion as connected and similar in the evolutionary story they tell. See, for example, Scott Atran, *In Gods We Trust: The Evolutionary Landscape of Religion*; Pascal Boyer, *The Naturalness of Religious Ideas: A Cognitive Theory of Religion* (Berkeley: University of California Press, 1994). For an example of recent work devoted solely to morality see William D. Casebeer, *Natural Ethical Facts: Evolution, Connectionism, and Moral Cognition* (Boston: Bradford Books, 2003).

as other modules postulated by cognitive psychology, or hold that the relevant truths are known by some more general capacity.

Let us say then that the claim that humans have an ability to intuitively know some moral principles is simply the claim that some moral principles can be known (or rationally believed) non-inferentially, and that the justification for these non-inferential beliefs derives from the way these beliefs seem (epistemically) to be true when considered in the right way by competent people. For many people (perhaps even the great majority of people) the following claim seems intuitively correct: "It is morally wrong to inflict pain on an innocent human person simply because the person inflicting the pain enjoys watching other people suffer." It is not hard to come up with a list of moral principles that have similar intuitive appeal, at least when stated in terms of moral features that prima facie make for moral wrongness or moral rightness. Most people agree that, other things being equal, people should keep their promises, tell the truth, and be grateful to benefactors. The claim that humans have a "moral sense" is simply a somewhat metaphorical way of saying that humans have a capacity to know such things non-inferentially, and that this capacity is in some way grounded in our nature.

The claim that humans have such an intuitive capacity should be distinguished from several other claims with which it is sometimes combined.[30] Ethical intuitionism is often thought to include claims that moral truths can be known infallibly or incorrigibly, or that moral truths can be known to be self-evident, or that they can be known to be necessary truths. However, the core intuitionist claim is that people have the capacity to recognize the *truth* of such propositions as "people ought to keep their promises." It is clear that someone can recognize the truth of such a moral proposition without knowing that the proposition is self-evident (even if it is) and without knowing that the proposition is necessarily true (even if it is). Nor does it seem necessary to understand the intuitionist as claiming that when a person grasps a moral truth, the person does so infallibly or incorrigibly. It may well be true that some moral truths seem highly certain to many people, but it seems quite consistent with this to

---

[30] Many of the points that follow are taken from Robert Audi, *Moral Knowledge and Ethical Character*, especially pp. 32–58. Audi provides a strong defense of a moderate intuitionism in this volume, and also in "Intuition, Inference, and Rational Disagreement in Ethics."

admit the general possibility of a mistake. After all, people are often quite confident about some particular judgment, without making any kind of claim to infallibility. I can be very certain that I am looking at a computer screen at the moment without claiming that my perceptual abilities are infallible. In any case, the intuitionist will certainly not want to claim that our moral intuitions are always correct; the fact that some moral decisions are difficult supports that, as does the fact that some of our moral intuitions change over time. Most of us can recall having moral intuitions at one time that we no longer think are correct. But the fact that some of our moral intuitions are mistaken does not show that such intuitions are generally unreliable. Moral intuitions can have genuine epistemic weight without being infallible, just as apparent memories, which are obviously sometimes mistaken, have genuine epistemic weight.

How should our moral intuitions be understood? Moderate rationalists think that our fundamental or basic moral intuitions are known in an a priori manner. Although this is a plausible view, the intuitionist does not have to commit to such a rationalist view. As Robert Audi maintains, it is also possible for the intuitionist view to be developed in an empiricist manner.[31] One might hold, for example, that our moral emotions are experiences by which we come to know moral truths, in a manner that fits the "sentimentalist" view of morality discussed in Chapter 5.[32] My own view is that the most plausible view of moral intuitions is a mixed rationalist-empiricist account, in which we come to recognize particular claims through experience (most likely ones that involve emotions), but we recognize in an a priori way the relations of moral qualities to others. Perhaps, for example, we can recognize a priori that cruelty is morally bad, but recognize through concrete experience that some particular act is an act of cruelty. I shall assume in what follows that at least some of our moral intuitions are a priori in character. However, if this assumption turns out to be incorrect, I suspect that many of the important points I make could be reformulated in a more empiricist manner.

The claim that our moral intuitions have this kind of epistemic value should really not be controversial, in my view, since practically all moral philosophers, even those who officially cast aspersions on our moral intuitions, appeal to those very intuitions at certain key

---

[31] See Audi, *The Good in the Right*, pp. 55–8.
[32] See pp. 145–8. Also see Audi, *The Good in the Right*, pp. 56–7.

points. Take, for example, Peter Singer's utilitarian views.[33] Singer argues that we have moral obligations that most of us do not recognize. Singer thinks, for example, that it is very plausible that I have an obligation not to spend money on such optional pleasures as attending the cinema this weekend, since I could give that money to an aid agency that could use it to save someone's life in a developing country. One might think that if Singer is right then our moral intuitions are unreliable, since most people would not intuitively perceive going to the cinema as immoral. However, a closer look shows that it cannot be Singer's view that our moral intuitions are generally or completely unreliable. Singer's argument appeals to our intuitions concerning some clear moral cases: For example, it would be morally wrong for me to walk by a shallow pond in which a child is drowning, and do nothing, if I could easily stop and save the child without unduly risking death or significant harm to myself. From that intuition Singer draws the conclusion that it is morally wrong not to save the lives of others when we can do so without risking any significant harm or loss to ourselves. Far from dispensing with moral intuitions, the argument depends on the reliability of such basic intuitions, and uses those intuitions to critique the moral *beliefs* of most people.

It is not hard to show that other prominent moral philosophers are similarly committed to the epistemic value of moral intuitions. John Rawls' method of "reflective equilibrium," for example, in which we test moral principles by appeal to moral intuitions and also refine and correct moral intuitions by considering moral principles, clearly requires that moral intuitions (perhaps including intuitions about principles) have some independent epistemic weight.[34] One might think that Rawls' method implies that intuitions cannot be relied upon, since they are open to being corrected in light of further reflection. However, this is fully compatible with the view that moral intuitions do have epistemic weight, so long as we recognize, as Robert Audi does in his defense of intuitionism, that our moral intuitions are fallible.[35] In fact, it is more than compatible with such a

---

[33] See Peter Singer, "Rich and Poor," in *Practical Ethics*, 3rd edn. (New York: Cambridge University Press, 2011), pp. 191–215.

[34] See John Rawls, *A Theory of Justice*, rev. edn. (Cambridge, MA: Harvard University Press, 1999), pp. 18–19, 40–6.

[35] See Robert Audi's nuanced and complex account of what a "moderate intuitionism" might be like in *The Good in the Right*, especially Chapter 2, pp. 40–79.

view; it requires it, since without some independent epistemic weight we could not use these intuitions in formulating moral principles.

HOW RELIABLE ARE MORAL INTUITIONS?

To say that we have a power to grasp the truth of moral principles is not to say that this power can be exercised independently of human nurture and human culture. Consider, for example, how mathematical knowledge is acquired, another form of a priori knowledge in which some basic principles seem to be known non-inferentially on the basis of epistemic seemings. It seems plausible that a capacity to recognize mathematical truth is a native capacity, since mathematical discoveries have been made independently in different cultures at different times. However, a person certainly must receive a proper education in order for these capacities to be actualized, and there are doubtless cultural conditions that must be in place for this to happen.

Thomas Reid, who defends the claim that the basic principles of morality are self-evident and can be known by virtually all humans, still recognizes both the importance of education and the possibility of error:

> In like manner, our moral judgment, or conscience, grows to maturity from an imperceptible seed, ... These sentiments are at first feeble, easily warped by passions and prejudices, and apt to yield to authority. By use and time, the judgment, in morals and other matters, gathers strength, and feels more vigour. We begin to distinguish the dictates of passion from those of cool reason, and to perceive, that it is not always safe to rely upon the judgment of others. ... There is a strong analogy between the progress of the body from infancy to maturity, and the progress of the powers of the mind. This progression in both is the work of nature, and in both may be greatly aided or hurt by proper education. It is natural to a man to be able to walk or run or leap; but if his limbs had been kept in fetters from his birth, he would have none of those powers. It is no less natural to a man trained in society, and accustomed to judge of his own actions and those of other men, to perceive a right and a wrong, an honourable and a base, in human conduct; and to such a man, I think, the principles of morals I have above mentioned will appear self-evident. Yet there may be individuals of the human species

so little accustomed to think or judge of anything, but of gratifying their animal appetites, as to have hardly any conception of right or wrong in conduct, or any moral judgment; as there certainly are some who have not the conceptions and the judgment necessary to understand the axioms of geometry.[36]

The intuitionist view I am defending is then far from committed to any claim to infallibility in our moral judgments. It can recognize the strong role that culture, nurture, and education plays in developing our moral judgments. Thus, it can make sense of the fact that fallible humans, often shaped by vastly different cultural and educational experiences, can and do disagree in their moral judgments.

But do the many moral disagreements present in human experience undermine the claim that our moral intuitions are reliable? Clearly, when two people make contradictory moral judgments, both cannot be right. The first question to ask in this connection is how reliable our moral intuitions need to be for moral realism to be viable. Strictly speaking, one could be a moral realist and be a complete skeptic about moral knowledge, since logically there could be objective moral truths we cannot know. However, it would seem pointless (perhaps even paradoxical) to defend the existence of objective moral truths if we had no access to such truths. So any interesting version of moral realism must hold that we have some access to moral truths.

However, it does not seem that our knowledge of morality must be infallible or exhaustive, even under the kind of favorable circumstances Reid mentions above (including proper education and nurture). Reid himself, while admitting fallibility, may have been overly optimistic in his account of the amount of moral knowledge (and agreement) that is possible. At the very least it does not seem *necessary* to claim that our moral knowledge is as extensive or firm as Reid seems to think. For if some human persons can gain some knowledge (or justified true beliefs) about just some moral truths, such knowledge (or true belief) could still have immense value to those people in helping them to live their lives well.

This seems especially true in the case of a moral realist who holds a divine command theory of moral obligations. For in that case our knowledge of moral obligations is a way of coming to know God's

---

[36] Reid, *Essays on the Active Powers of Man*, V, I, p. 277.

requirements for us humans. If the identity version of a DCT is correct, one might go so far as to say that an awareness of a moral obligation is a direct *de re* awareness of God. Even if people only know a few of their moral obligations, and even if this knowledge were mixed with error, what remains would have enormous value. For morality on this view is a pathway towards a proper relation with God, a relation that has as its end the transformation of humans so as to make it possible for them to become friends of God in a rich and full sense.[37] Even a scanty and faulty knowledge of this sort could have enormous value if it is sufficient to enable people to begin the journey that leads to communion with God. In this case if our moral knowledge is mixed with error, and if at least some of those errors are ones that humans are not culpable for (perhaps being the result of nurture and education), then God, being omniscient, will know this, and will presumably make allowances when he holds humans morally accountable. Some of the significant purposes of moral obligations can still be fulfilled even if our knowledge of such obligations is not highly reliable.

Within the Christian tradition, there is something else of great value that even scanty moral knowledge might make possible, and this is awareness of our own moral shortcomings. Christianity teaches that humans all fall short of God's requirements and are in need of God's grace and forgiveness. Presumably, if a person had a proper understanding of just *one* moral requirement that the person has failed to live up to, this would be sufficient to make possible a recognition of moral guilt and the need for grace and forgiveness. Even a moral outlook that is riddled with errors and uncertainty could be adequate to give a person an understanding that they are morally responsible and accountable. Even if I only have accurate knowledge of a few moral obligations, that might be sufficient for me to realize I have not lived my life as I should have.

In any case, the fact that there are significant moral disagreements does not undermine moral realism, even if we agree that such disagreements imply that our moral knowledge is fallible. Fallible moral knowledge can still be knowledge and can be of great value. As is often noted, it is not clear how much moral disagreement there actually is, since much of what may appear to be moral disagreement

---

[37] See the discussion of virtue as the end of morality in Chapter 3, pp. 83–7.

is likely disagreement over facts. A disagreement over whether abortion is morally permissible, for example, may really be a disagreement over whether a fetus is a human person. Both parties to the disagreement may agree on the underlying moral principle that human persons have a right to life; they just disagree over what makes someone a human person. Also, it is important, in recognizing the moral disagreements that are present, not to lose sight of the tremendous amount of moral agreement that is present.[38] Human cultures that are vastly different in many ways and separated from each other historically and geographically have nonetheless generally recognized such principles as the following:[39] (1) A general duty not to harm others and a general duty to benefit others; (2) Special duties to those with whom one has special relations: friends, parents, children, family members, fellow-citizens; (3) Duties to be truthful; (4) Duties to keep one's commitments and promises; (5) Duties to deal fairly and justly with others.

The fact that our moral intuitions are neither exhaustive nor infallible does little to undermine the view that they do provide us with some genuine moral insight. The moral disagreements that are present are at most evidence for the fallibility and finitude of our moral judgments. Many moral disagreements may stem from the kind of bias that Reid mentions above, since we clearly have plenty of motivation to misunderstand or deny our moral obligations when they constrain us. But even unresolvable moral disagreements where both parties are rational and unbiased would not be evidence for moral anti-realism, unless we adopt some kind of verificationist view of truth. It would at most be evidence that our cognitive moral powers, like our other cognitive powers, are finite and fallible. It is true that the moral realist needs to avoid moral skepticism. However, to do this, it seems to me that all that is necessary is that our moral abilities be such that, with respect to some important moral issues, it is possible for those who use those abilities well to gain moral truth. It seems very plausible that our moral abilities do rise to this level at least.

---

[38] James Rachels has a good discussion of this agreement in *The Elements of Moral Philosophy*, pp. 25–6.

[39] C. S. Lewis, in an Appendix to *The Abolition of Man* assembles a very interesting collection of moral proverbs and teachings in each of these areas from cultures as diverse as ancient China, India, Old Norse, Australian aborigine, and ancient Egypt, as well as classical Greece and Rome. See pp. 95–121.

CAN THE RELIABILITY OF MORAL INTUITIONS
BE EXPLAINED?

Let us suppose then that our moral faculties are reliable enough to provide us with some moral knowledge. There is at least one other epistemological challenge that the realist needs to face. If basic moral truths are a priori in character, as seems most likely the case, then it is puzzling as to *how* humans could have reliable intuitions about them. Surely, it cannot just be a coincidence or a fluke that we have a set of moral intuitions that reliably track such truths. In the case of perception, it is not hard to explain how it is that our perceptual seemings can correspond to the way the world is, since there is a causal connection between the world and our perception of the world. But most philosophers agree that timeless a priori truths are causally inert. How then is it that our moral intuitions can correspond to them?

David Enoch raises this question and argues it is the most pressing epistemological challenge to moral realism.[40] Enoch himself tries to meet the challenge by hypothesizing that there is a kind of "pre-established harmony" between our moral intuitions about what is morally good and what is morally bad.[41] The correlation between the two is not explained by any kind of causal connection between our moral intuitions and the moral facts, but by a link between both of them and a third thing, the process of natural selection. If we assume that survival is itself a good (i.e. that this is one of the normative truths that hold), then it does not seem too surprising that an evolutionary process, which is shaped by survival and reproduction, should select for moral beliefs that are often correct. "[O]ur normative beliefs have been shaped by selective pressures towards ends that are in fact—and quite independently—of value. The connection between evolutionary forces and value—the fact that survival is good—is what explains the correlation between the response-independent normative truths and our selected-for normative beliefs."[42]

Enoch's "pre-established harmony" is an explicitly "godless" version of such a view, because he does not want to burden moral realism with any unnecessary ontological commitments. However, moral realism in the context of a divine command theory of moral obligations is in quite a different situation. Such a view is already committed

---

[40] Enoch, pp. 151–63.   [41] Enoch, pp. 163–77.   [42] Enoch, p. 168.

to the existence of God; there is no ontological parsimony gained by ignoring God's reality. In this context, a view such as Enoch's can be enriched and made far more plausible. Suppose that it is true that humans have the moral intuitions (and faculties) they have, along with their other cognitive faculties, because of an evolutionary process. Of course, if God exists, he is the creator of everything, including both the natural world that has evolved and human beings with their various cognitive faculties. Since God is a moral being, essentially good and loving, then it is hardly surprising that he has designed the natural world so that humans have acquired capacities to grasp moral truths. If God has created humans through an evolutionary process, then that process would surely be one that allows them to develop abilities to grasp some of the moral truths they need to know so as to understand their lives rightly and live wisely. Since God is already part of the picture if a DCT is true, then there is no additional "ontological cost" in making God part of the explanation for the fact that our moral intuitions are at least somewhat reliable.

Something like this point can be put in a more general form as a response to what is often called the objection to moral realism from the "queerness" of objective moral truths. J. L. Mackie coined this phrase to describe the idea that in a naturalistic universe, the place of such objective moral truths would be mysterious and inexplicable, both ontologically and epistemically.[43] It should be clear, I think, that Mackie's objection only has force against forms of moral realism that are also committed to metaphysical naturalism. If the universe includes God, and it must if moral obligations are divine commands, and God is a moral being, then it hardly seems odd that moral qualities should appear to be "deep" ones, and it will be unsurprising that humans have capacities to grasp such qualities.[44]

To see how plausible it is that humans have an ability to grasp moral truths once God is part of the story, I call once more as an "unfriendly witness" Simon Blackburn. Blackburn's "quasi-realism," which is a form of projectivism or expressivism, was considered in Chapter 5, and I also looked briefly there at his critique of a "sensibility theory," such as that of David Wiggins, who maintains that moral properties are in some way objective though they are grasped through

---

[43] See Mackie, *Ethics: Inventing Right and Wrong*, pp. 38–42.
[44] See George Mavrodes, "Religion and the Queerness of Morality," especially the discussion on pp. 223–4.

our emotional responses to them. Blackburn accepts the idea that in some sense the "properties" that we call moral are reflections of our emotional responses; that is in fact the heart of his own view. But he strongly objects to the idea that our "sensibilities" (emotional responses) are in some way attuned to recognize moral properties:

> But it is the other half, that the sensibilities are 'made for' the properties, that really startles. Who or what makes them like that? (God? As we have seen, no natural story explains how the ethical sensibilities of human beings were made for the ethical properties of things, so perhaps it is a supernatural story.)[45]

There is little doubt that Blackburn is being sarcastic here, and thinks that the fact that a theory needs God to make sense is a *reductio* of the theory. Nevertheless, it is significant that even an atheist such as Blackburn can easily see that if God were real, a plausible story could be told about how to explain the fact that human emotions correspond to the way things are, normatively speaking.

CONCLUSION: THEOLOGICAL ADVANTAGES OF A DIVINE COMMAND THEORY

This book has been an exercise in moral philosophy, and has attempted to show that a divine command account of moral obligations has many philosophical virtues. In Chapters 1 and 2, I tried to describe many striking features of moral obligations, such as the fact that such obligations are objective, motivating, binary in nature, universal, overriding, and allow us to bring deliberation to closure. In Chapter 2 I then go on to argue that a DCT provides a natural explanation of all these features. A DCT is consistent with the claim that moral truths can be known by general revelation rather than simply through special revelation, and it fits well with the idea that God has endowed humans with conscience, an ability to grasp moral truths, either through emotional perceptions or a priori intuitions (or both). Thus a DCT is not saddled with the implausible implication that religious unbelievers cannot recognize and believe in moral truths.

---

[45] Blackburn, "How to Be an Ethical Anti-Realist," p. 51.

In Chapter 3 I show that a DCT is not a rival to a natural law theory of the good or a theory of human virtue, but rather complements such theories well. Once we distinguish between the divine discretion thesis and the modal status thesis, and see that only the latter is essential to a DCT, then those who think God's commands are settled by what is necessarily true and/or the created natures God has given natural things are free to endorse a minimal version of a DCT. (Although the divine discretion thesis is plausible as well.) In Chapter 4 I argue that many alleged objections raised against a DCT are either rooted in misunderstandings or else simply turn out not to be very powerful. In Chapter 5 I argue that other metaethical views that conflict with a DCT face severe problems of their own. There are then strong philosophical reasons for those who are moral realists (defended in this chapter) to take a DCT seriously.

Since this has been a work in moral philosophy, I have not attempted to argue that a divine command account of moral obligations can be defended theologically. For example, a Christian theologian might do this by trying to show that such an account is taught in Scripture or by showing that it is implied by or fits best with other theological doctrines. However, I am convinced that a DCT is theologically attractive, and in conclusion I should like to offer some suggestions as to how such a case could be made.

To begin with what is obvious, a DCT provides a way of taking full account of the central role played in the Christian and Jewish Scriptures of the related concepts of divine law and divine commands. It is arguable that the notion of Torah or divine law is central to the Hebrew Bible, and is taken over as central by early Christians when they accepted those writings as part of their own sacred canon. Nor, as is sometimes facilely said, is it the case that the New Testament somehow abandons the notion of commands in favor of "love." To the contrary, the New Testament is full of commands given by Jesus and his apostolic followers, many of them commands to love, and these commands have a central importance. Obedience to God's commands is not opposed to love; rather, Jesus says that those who love him will keep his commandments.[46] This fact alone does not establish a DCT as the best theological option. However, it is striking to consider how central and powerful these themes are in Scripture,

---

[46] John 14:15.

and see how little a role they play in some contemporary religious ethical accounts. I suspect that part of the reason for this is that the contemporary world has lost the sense the biblical writers had that God's commands are to be loved and cherished, since they are given for our good. God's commands are not arbitrary restrictions on our freedom, but principles that make it possible for humans to live meaningfully and purposefully.

A second set of theological advantages a DCT offers is that it provides a convincing account of how knowledge of God is possible. Since the Enlightenment many apologists have been unsure as to how to make the case that belief in God is not contrary to reason, and the popularity of "new atheists" such as Christopher Hitchens, Sam Harris, and Daniel Dennett makes this problem obvious. If moral obligations are God's requirements for humans, and these obligations are knowable by humans, then it seems possible to give a straightforward answer to the new atheists. Perhaps a moral argument can be given that God is required to explain moral obligations.[47] Or perhaps no argument is needed, because moral obligations are one of the "grounds" of a reasonable belief in God that is "properly basic."[48] It can be argued that even atheists have a kind of *de re* knowledge of God, if they are aware of their moral obligations. They are aware of God's claim on their lives, even if they are not aware of that claim *as* God's claim on their lives. Such a view might even allow us to make sense of a strange claim of Kierkegaard's, that there "has never been an atheist, even though there certainly have been many who have been unwilling to let what they know (that the God exists) get control over their minds."[49]

---

[47] I show how such an argument could be developed in *Natural Signs and Knowledge of God*, pp. 132–9.

[48] For the idea that a properly basic belief still requires a ground, see Alvin Plantinga, "Reason and Belief in God," in *Faith and Rationality: Reason and Belief in God* (Notre Dame, IN: University of Notre Dame Press, 1983), pp. 16–93. The discussion of "grounds" can be found chiefly on pp. 78–82.

[49] This is a passage from Søren Kierkegaard's *Philosophical Fragments* that Kierkegaard deleted from the final manuscript when he removed his own name as author and attributed the book to a pseudonym. It presumably represents Kierkegaard's own view, but one he found inappropriate to attribute to the non-Christian pseudonym, Johannes Climacus. The passage can be found in the "Supplement" to *Philosophical Fragments*, ed. and trans. Howard V. Hong and Edna H. Hong (Princeton, NJ: Princeton University Press, 1985), pp. 191–2. I have here slightly modified the Hong translation of the passage.

Finally, a DCT, even in the weak form that affirms only the modal status thesis, vindicates and explains an important claim made by many theologians: that all sin is sin against God.[50] If we understand moral wrongdoing as sin, and understand our moral obligations as divine commands, then all moral wrongdoing is objectively an offense against God, a violation of God's law. Of course most moral wrongdoing harms someone other than God as well, and thus forgiveness from those humans who are harmed is often called for. However, if all sin is sin against God, then God's forgiveness is always needed and always appropriate as well.

It thus seems that a divine command theory of moral obligations is one that is not only philosophically defensible, but has significant theological advantages. Those theological strengths can be clearly seen both when we focus on the role of God's law in Scripture, and the important role played by divine law in traditional theology.

I am well aware that some will argue that the notions of law and command are too unpopular to be given a central role in ethics, even Christian ethics, just as some will argue that belief in God is too far out of the philosophical mainstream to play a role in moral philosophy. However, neither philosophers nor theologians should confuse their task with that of an advertising agency. Both the person who defends a philosophical theory and the person who tries to give an account of genuine Christianity (or some other religion) must not succumb to the temptation to disguise the nature of how things are so as to gain adherents. The task is to discover the truth and defend what seems true to the best of one's ability. My aim in this work has been to encourage contemporary thinkers to take seriously the role that divine authority might play in morality, and thereby perhaps to think seriously about the reality of God.

I hope that my arguments will encourage those who believe in God to think again about the role God plays in morality, and that the arguments will encourage non-believers who are open to reconsidering the issues to take a fresh look at the issues as well. To accomplish the second goal we may need more than philosophy by itself can

---

[50] See, for example, Thomas Aquinas, *Summa Theologica*, Part I of 2nd part, Q. 72, A. 4. Aquinas here says that although there are indeed sins that are especially against God, it is equally true that all sins are sins against God. Kierkegaard also stresses the importance of the fact that all sins are sins against God. For Kierkegaard's view see his *Concluding Unscientific Postscript*, ed. and trans. Howard V. Hong and Edna H. Hong (Princeton, NJ: Princeton University Press, 1992), Vol. I, p. 530.

provide; we need religious people who live with moral integrity and show the power of their ideas in practice. Philosophical arguments are valuable, but perhaps we need the testimony of such living witnesses to the truth if the imaginations and hearts of contemporary people are to be open to understanding the link between God and moral obligation.

Bibliography

Adams, Marilyn, "Ockham on Will, Nature, and Morality," in Paul Spade (ed.), *The Cambridge Companion to Ockham* (Cambridge: Cambridge University Press, 1999), 245–71.

Adams, Robert, *Finite and Infinite Goods* (New York: Oxford University Press, 1999).

Almeida, Michael, "Supervenience and Property-identical Divine Command Theory," *Religious Studies* 40 (2004), 323–33.

Anscombe, G. E. M., "Modern Moral Philosophy," reprinted in *The Collected Philosophical Papers of G. E. M. Anscombe, Volume 3: Ethics, Religion, and Politics* (Oxford: Basil Blackwell, 1981), 26–42.

Antony, Louise, "Atheism as Perfect Piety," in Robert K. Garcia and Nathan L. King (eds), *Is Goodness without God Good Enough?* (Lanham, MD: Rowman & Littlefield, 2009), 67–84.

Aquinas, Thomas, *Summa Theologica*, trans. Fathers of the English Dominican Province (New York: Benzinger Bros., 1947–8; repr. Allen, TX: Thomas More, 1981).

Aristotle, *Nichomachean Ethics*, trans. W. D. Ross, in Richard McKeon (ed.), *The Basic Works of Aristotle* (New York: Random House, 1941), 935–1112.

Atran, Scott, *In Gods We Trust: The Evolutionary Landscape of Religion* (Evolution and Cognition) (Oxford: Oxford University Press, 2002).

Audi, Robert, *Moral Knowledge and Ethical Character* (Oxford: Oxford University Press, 1997).

——*The Good in the Right: A Theory of Intuition and Intrinsic Value* (Princeton, NJ: Princeton University Press, 2005).

——"Intuition, Inference, and Rational Disagreement in Ethics," *Ethical Theory and Moral Practice* 11 (2008), 475–92.

Baggett, David, and Walls, Jerry L., *Good God: The Theistic Foundations of Morality* (New York: Oxford University Press, 2011).

Blackburn, Simon, *Spreading the Word* (New York: Oxford University Press, 1984).

——*Ruling Passions: A Theory of Practical Reason* (Oxford: Oxford University Press, 1998).

——"How To Be an Ethical Anti-Realist," in Russ Shafer-Landau and Terence Cuneo (eds), *Foundations of Ethics: An Anthology* (Oxford: Blackwell, 2007), 47–57. Originally appeared in *Essays in Quasi-Realism* (Oxford: Oxford University Press, 1993), 166–81.

Boyd, Richard, "How to Be a Moral Realist," in Geoffrey Sayre-McCord (ed.), *Essays on Moral Realism* (Ithaca, NY: Cornell University Press, 1988), 181–228.

Boyer, Pascal, *The Naturalness of Religious Ideas: A Cognitive Theory of Religion* (Berkeley: University of California Press, 1994).

Brandom, Robert, *Making It Explicit: Reasoning, Representing, and Discursive Commitment* (Cambridge, MA: Harvard University Press, 1994).

Carson, Thomas, "Divine Will/Divine Command Moral Theories and the Problem of Arbitrariness," *Religious Studies* (2012), 1–24; doi: 10.1017/S00344125100031X.

Casebeer, William D., *Natural Ethical Facts: Evolution, Connectionism, and Moral Cognition* (Boston: Bradford Books, 2003).

Chisholm, Roderick, *Theory of Knowledge*, 2nd edn. (Englewood Cliffs, NJ: Prentice-Hall, 1977).

Cosmides, Leda, and Tooby, John, "Can a General Deontic Logic Capture the Facts of Human Moral Reasoning? How the Mind Interprets Social Exchange Rules and Detects Cheaters," in Walter Sinnott-Armstrong (ed.), *Moral Psychology Volume 1: The Evolution of Morality—Adaptations and Innateness* (Cambridge, MA: MIT Press, 2008), 53–119.

Cudworth, Ralph, *A Treatise Concerning True and Immutable Morality* (London: J. and J. Knapton, 1731); reprint edition (New York: Garland, 1976).

Cuneo, Terence, "Moral Realism," in Christian Miller (ed.), *The Continuum Companion to Ethics* (London: Continuum Press, 2011), 3–28.

——"Reidian Metaethics, Part I," *Philosophy Compass* 6:5 (2011), 333–40.

——"Reidian Metaethics, Part II," *Philosophy Compass* 6:5 (2011), 341–9.

——"Reid's Ethics," *The Stanford Encyclopedia of Philosophy* (Spring 2011 Edition), ed. Edward N. Zalta <http://plato.stanford.edu/archives/spr2011/entries/reid-ethics/>.

Donagan, Alan, *The Theory of Morality* (Chicago: University of Chicago Press, 1977).

Doris, John M., *Lack of Character: Personality and Moral Behavior* (Cambridge: Cambridge University Press, 2002).

Dumsday, Travis, "Divine Hiddenness and the Responsibility Argument," *Philosophia Christi* 12 (2010), 357–71.

Duns Scotus, John, "The Decalogue and the Law of Nature," in *Duns Scotus on the Will and Morality*, selected and translated with an introduction by Allan B. Wolter, OFM (Washington: Catholic University of American Press, 1986), 268–87.

——*Duns Scotus on the Will and Morality*, selected and translated with an introduction by Allan B. Wolter, OFM (Washington: Catholic University of American Press, 1986).

Dworkin, Ronald, *Justice for Hedgehogs* (Cambridge, MA: Harvard University Press, 2011).

Dworkin, Ronald, "What Is a Good Life?" *New York Review of Books* (LVIII, 2; February 10, 2011), 41–3.

Enoch, David, *Taking Morality Seriously: A Defense of Robust Realism* (Oxford: Oxford University Press, 2011).

Evans, C. Stephen, *Kierkegaard's Ethic of Love: Divine Commands and Moral Obligations* (Oxford: Oxford University Press, 2004).

——*Natural Signs and Knowledge of God: A New Look at Theistic Arguments* (Oxford: Oxford University Press, 2010).

——"Moral Arguments for Theism and Divine Command Theories of Moral Obligation," in Colin Ruloff (ed.), *Reason and Christian Belief: New Essays in Philosophical Theology* (Notre Dame, IN: University of Notre Dame Press, forthcoming).

——and Roberts, Robert C., " Ethics," in *The Oxford Companion of Kierkegaard*, ed. George Pattison and John Lippitt (Oxford: Oxford University Press, 2012), 203–21.

Finnis, John, *Natural Law and Natural Rights* (Oxford: Oxford University Press, 1980).

Foot, Philippa, *Natural Goodness* (Oxford: Oxford University Press, 2001).

Garcia, Robert K., and King, Nathan L. (eds), *Is Goodness without God Good Enough?* (Lanham, MD: Rowman & Littlefield, 2009).

Gauthier, David, *Morals by Agreement* (Oxford: Oxford University Press, 1986).

Geach, Peter, "Assertions," *Philosophical Review* 74 (1965), 449–63.

Gibbard, Alan, "The Reasons of a Living Being," *Proceedings of the American Philosophical Association* 62 (2002), 49–60.

Grotius, Hugo, *De jure belli et pacis*, Prolegomena, §§ 6, 9, 11, trans. Francis W. Kelsey et al., 2 vols (Oxford: Oxford University Press, 1925), 2:11, 13.

Gyekye, Kwame, "African Ethics," *The Stanford Encyclopedia of Philosophy* (Summer 2011 Edition), ed. Edward N. Zalta, <http://plato.stanford.edu/archives/sum2011/entries/african-ethics>.

Hare, John, *God's Call: Moral Realism, God's Commands, and Human Autonomy* (Grand Rapids, MI: Wm. B. Eerdmans, 2001).

——*Why Bother Being Good? The Place of God in the Moral Life* (Downers Grove, IL: InterVarsity Press, 2002).

——*God and Morality: A Philosophical History* (Malden, MA: Wiley-Blackwell, 2009).

Harman, Gilbert, *Explaining Value and Other Essays in Moral Philosophy* (Oxford: Oxford University Press, 2000),

——"Moral Relativism Defended," in *Explaining Value and Other Essays in Moral Philosophy* (Oxford: Oxford University Press, 2000), 3–19.

——and Thomson, Judith Jarvis, *Moral Relativism and Moral Objectivity* (Oxford: Blackwell, 1996).

Hauerwas, Stanley, "Obligation and Virtue Once More," in *Truthfulness and Tragedy*, with Richard Bondi and David Burrell (Notre Dame, IN: University of Notre Dame Press, 1977), 40–56.

——*A Community of Character: Towards a Constructive Christian Social Ethics* (Notre Dame, IN: University of Notre Dame Press, 1991).

——*The Peaceable Kingdom: A Primer in Christian Ethics* (Notre Dame, IN: University of Notre Dame Press, 1991).

Hegel, G. W. F., *Hegel's Philosophy of Right*, trans. T. M. Knox (Oxford: Oxford University Press, 1967).

Henry, Douglas, "Does Reasonable Nonbelief Exist?" *Faith and Philosophy* 18 (2001), 75–92.

——"Reasonable Doubts about Reasonable Nonbelief," *Faith and Philosophy* 25 (2008), 276–89.

Hobbes, Thomas, *Hobbes's Leviathan*, reprinted from the edition of 1651 (Oxford: Oxford University Press, 1909).

Horgan, Terry, and Timmons, Mark, "Nondescriptivist Cognitivism: Framework for a New Metaethic," *Philosophical Papers* 29 (2000), 121–53.

Howard-Snyder, Daniel, and Moser, Paul K. (eds), *Divine Hiddenness: New Essays* (Cambridge: Cambridge University Press, 2002).

Hursthouse, Rosalind, *On Virtue Ethics* (Oxford: Oxford University Press, 1999).

——"Virtue Ethics," *Stanford Encyclopedia of Philosophy (Summer 2012 Edition)* Edward N. Zalta (ed.) <http://plato.stanford.edu/archives/sum2012/entries/ethics-virtue>.

James, William, *The Writings of William James*, ed. John J. McDermott (New York: Modern Library, 1968).

Kant, Immanuel, *Critique of Pure Reason*, trans. Norman Kemp Smith (New York: St. Martin's Press, 1965).

——*Grounding for the Metaphysic of Morals*, trans. James W. Ellington, 3rd edn of translation (Indianapolis, IN: Hackett Publishing Co., 1993).

Kierkegaard, Søren, *Philosophical Fragments*, ed. and trans. Howard V. Hong and Edna H. Hong (Princeton, NJ: Princeton University Press, 1985).

——*Concluding Unscientific Postscript*, ed. and trans. Howard V. Hong and Edna H. Hong (Princeton, NJ: Princeton University Press, 1992).

——*Works of Love*, ed. and trans. Howard V. Hong and Edna H. Hong (Princeton, NJ: Princeton University Press, 1995).

Korsgaard, Christine (with G. A. Cohen et al.), *The Sources of Normativity* (Cambridge and New York: Cambridge University Press, 1996).

Lewis, C. S., *The Abolition of Man* (New York: MacMillan Publishing Co., 1947).

Locke, John, *Of Civil Government Second Treatise* (South Bend, IN: Gateway Editions, 1955).

Loeb, Don, "The Argument from Moral Experience," in Richard Joyce and Simon Kitchin (eds), *A World Without Values* (Heidelberg: Springer, 2007), 101–18.

Louden, Robert B., "Kant's Virtue Ethics," *Philosophy* 61:238 (October 1986), 473–89.

McDowell, John, "Values and Secondary Qualities," in Ted Honderich (ed.), *Morality and Objectivity* (Oxford: Routledge, 1985), 110–29.

Mackie, J. L., *Ethics: Inventing Right and Wrong* (London: Penguin Books, 1977).

Macquet, J. J., "The Kingdom in Ruanda," in Daryll Forde (ed.), *African Worlds: Studies in the Cosmological Ideas and Social Values of African Peoples* (Oxford: Oxford University Press, 1954), 164–89.

Manis, R. Zachary, "Virtues, Divine Commands, and the Debt of Creation: Towards a Kierkegaardian Christian Ethic," Ph.D. Dissertation, Baylor University, 2006.

Mavrodes, George I., "Religion and the Queerness of Morality," in Robert Audi and William J. Wainwright (eds), *Rationality, Religious Belief, and Moral Commitment: New Essays in the Philosophy of Religion* (Ithaca, NY: Cornell University Press, 1986), 213–26.

Mellema, Gregory, *The Expectations of Morality* (Amsterdam: Rodopi, 2004).

Milliken, John, "*Euthyphro*, the Good, and the Right," *Philosophia Christi* 11:1 (2009), 145–55.

Milo, Ronald, "Contractarian Constructivism," in Russ Shafer-Landau and Terence Cuneo (eds), *Foundations of Ethics: An Anthology* (Oxford: Blackwell, 2007), 120–31. Originally in *Journal of Philosophy* 92 (1995), 181–204.

Morriston, Wes, "The Moral Obligations of Reasonable Non-Believers," *International Journal for Philosophy of Religion* 65:1 (2009), 1–10.

Mouw, Richard, *The God Who Commands* (Notre Dame, IN: University of Notre Dame Press, 1990).

Murphy, Mark, *Natural Law and Practical Rationality* (Cambridge: Cambridge University Press, 2001).

——*An Essay on Divine Authority* (Ithaca, NY: Cornell University Press, 2002).

——"Reply to Almeida," *Religious Studies* 40 (2004), 335–9.

——*God and Moral Law: On the Theistic Explanation of Morality* (Oxford: Oxford University Press, 2011).

——"The Natural Law Tradition in Ethics," *The Stanford Encyclopedia of Philosophy* (*Spring 2011 Edition*), Edward N. Zalta (ed.) <http://plato.stanford.edu/archives/spr2011/entries/natural-law-ethics>.

Nietzsche, Friedrich, *The Will to Power*, trans. Walter Kaufmann and R. J. Hollingdale (New York Random House, 1968).

——*The Anti-Christ* (published with *Twilight of the Idols*), ed. Michael Tanner (London: Penguin Books, 1990).

Nowell-Smith, Patrick, "Morality: Religious and Secular," in Baruch Brody (ed.), *Readings in the Philosophy of Religion* (Englewood Cliffs, NJ: Prentice-Hall, 1974), 581–9.

Oakley, Francis, *Natural Law, Laws of Nature, Natural Rights: Continuity and Discontinuity in the History of Ideas* (New York: Continuum, 2005).

Pelser, Adam, "Emotion, Evaluative Perception, and Epistemic Goods," Ph.D. Dissertation, Baylor University, 2011 <http://hdl.handle.net/2104/8237>.

Plantinga, Alvin, "Reason and Belief in God," in *Faith and Rationality: Reason and Belief in God* (Notre Dame, IN: University of Notre Dame Press, 1983), 16–93.

——*Warranted Christian Belief* (New York: Oxford University Press, 2000).

Plato, *Euthyphro*, trans. Lane Cooper, in Edith Hamilton and Huntington Cairns (eds), *Plato: The Collected Dialogues* (Princeton: Princeton University Press, 1961).

——*Socrates' Defense (Apology)*, in Edith Hamilton and Huntington Cairns (eds), *Plato: The Collected Dialogues,* (Princeton, NJ: Princeton University Press, 1961).

Porter, Jean, *Nature as Reason: A Thomistic Theory of the Natural Law* (Grand Rapids, MI: Eerdmans, 2005).

Pruss, Alexander, "Another Step in Divine Command Dialectics," *Faith and Philosophy* 26:4 (October 2009), 432–9.

Quinn, Philip, *Divine Commands and Moral Requirements* (Oxford: Oxford University Press, 1978).

Rachels, James, "The Challenge of Cultural Relativism," in *The Elements of Moral Philosophy*, 2nd edn (New York: McGraw-Hill, 1993).

Rawls, John, "Distributive Justice," in Peter Laslett and Walter Runciman (eds), *Philosophy, Politics, and Society*, 3rd series (New York: Barnes and Noble, 1967).

——*Political Liberalism* (New York: Columbia University Press, 1993).

——*A Theory of Justice*, rev. edn (Cambridge, MA: Harvard University Press, 1999).

Reid, Thomas, *Essays on the Intellectual Powers of Man*, ed. Derek R. Brookes (Edinburgh: Edinburgh University Press, 1785/1969).

——*Essays on the Active Powers of Man* (Edinburgh: Edinburgh University Press, 2010).

Roberts, Robert C., *Emotions in the Moral Life* (Cambridge: Cambridge University Press, forthcoming).

Rorty, Richard, *Philosophy and Social Hope* (New York: Penguin, 1999).

——"Religion in the Public Square: A Reconsideration," *The Journal of Religious Ethics* 31:1 (2003), 141–9.

Ross, W. D., *Foundations of Ethics* (Oxford: Clarendon Press, 1939).

Ruloff, Colin (ed.), *Reason and Christian Belief: New Essays in Philosophical Theology* (Notre Dame, IN: University of Notre Dame Press, forthcoming).

Russell, Bertrand, "A Free Man's Worship," in *Mysticism and Logic and Other Essays* (London: Allen and Unwin, 1917).

Shafer-Landau, Russ, *Moral Realism: A Defence* (Oxford: Clarendon Press, 2003).

——"Ethics as Philosophy: A Defence of Ethical Non-Naturalism," in Russ Shafer-Landau and Terence Cuneo (eds), *Foundations of Ethics: An Anthology* (Oxford: Blackwell, 2007), 210–21. Originally published in Terence Horgan and Mark Timmons (eds), *Metaethics after Moore* (Oxford: Oxford University Press, 2006), 209–32.

——and Cuneo, Terence, *Foundations of Ethics: An Anthology* (Oxford: Blackwell Publishing, 2007).

————"Introduction" to the section on "Sensibility Theories," in *Foundations of Ethics: An Anthology* (Oxford: Blackwell Publishing, 2007), 132–5.

Singer, Peter, "Rich and Poor," in *Practical Ethics*, 3rd edn (New York: Cambridge University Press, 2011), 191–215.

Sinnott-Armstrong, Walter, *Morality ~~Without God?~~* (New York: Oxford University Press, 2009).

——"Why Traditional Theism Cannot Provide an Adequate Foundation for Morality," in Robert K. Garcia and Nathan L. King (eds), *Is Goodness without God Good Enough?* (Lanham, MD: Rowman & Littlefield, 2009), 101–16.

Slote, Michael, *Morals from Motives* (Oxford: Oxford University Press, 2001).

Stout, Jeffrey, *Democracy and Tradition* (Princeton, NJ: Princeton University Press, 2004).

Street, Sharon, "A Darwinian Dilemma for Realist Theories of Value," *Philosophical Studies* 127 (2006), 109–66.

Swinburne, Richard, *The Existence of God*, 2nd edn (Oxford: Clarendon Press, 2004).

Van Hooft, Stan, *Understanding Virtue Ethics* (Chesham, UK: Acumen Press, 2006).

Van Roojen, Mark, "Moral Cognitivism vs. Non-Cognitivism, in *Stanford Encyclopedia of Philosophy* <http://plato.stanford.edu/entries/moral-cognitivism>.

Wainwright, William, *Religion and Morality* (Aldershot, UK: Ashgate Publishing, 2005).

Wielenberg, Erik, *Value and Virtue in a Godless Universe* (Cambridge: Cambridge University Press, 2005).

——"In Defense of Non-Natural, Non-Theistic Moral Realism," *Faith and Philosophy* 26:1 (2009), 23–41.

Wiggins, David, *Truth, Invention and the Meaning of Life* (Proceedings of the British Academy 62, 1976).

——"A Sensible Subjectivism," in *Needs, Values, Truth*, 2nd edn (Oxford: Blackwell, 1991), 185–211.

Wolterstorff, Nicholas, "Why We Should Reject What Liberalism Tells Us about Speaking and Acting for Religious Reasons," in Paul J. Weithman (ed.), *Religion and Contemporary Liberalism* (Notre Dame, IN: University of Notre Dame Press, 1997), 162–81.

——"Jeffrey Stout on Democracy and its Contemporary Christian Critics," *Journal of Religious Ethics* 33:4 (2005), 633–47.

——*Justice: Rights and Wrongs* (Princeton, NJ: Princeton University Press, 2008).

Zagzebski, Linda, *Divine Motivation Theory* (Cambridge: Cambridge University Press, 2004).

Index

Printed in Great Britain
by Amazon